# PSYCHOLOGY OF A SUPERPOWER

# PSYCHOLOGY OF A SUPERPOWER

## SECURITY AND DOMINANCE

*in*

## U.S. FOREIGN POLICY

CHRISTOPHER J. FETTWEIS

Columbia University Press

*New York*

Columbia University Press
*Publishers Since 1893*
New York    Chichester, West Sussex
cup.columbia.edu

Library of Congress Cataloging-in-Publication Data
Names: Fettweis, Christopher J.
Title: Psychology of a superpower : security and dominance in U.S. foreign
policy / Christopher J. Fettweis.
Description: New York : Columbia University Press, 2018. |
Includes bibliographical references and index.
Identifiers: LCCN 2017048101 (print) | LCCN 2018000747 (ebook) |
ISBN 9780231547413 (e-book) | ISBN 9780231187701 (cloth : alk. paper) |
ISBN 9780231187718 (pbk. : alk. paper)
Subjects: LCSH: United States—Foreign relations. | United States—Foreign
relations—Psychological aspects. | United States—Foreign relations—Decision
making. | Unipolarity (International relations)
Classification: LCC JZ1480 (ebook) | LCC JZ1480 .F52 2018 (print) |
DDC 327.73—dc23
LC record available at https://lccn.loc.gov/2017048101

COVER DESIGN: : NOAH ARLOW

# CONTENTS

# PREFACE

I n 2016, Donald Trump accomplished what many would have previously thought impossible: He united the disparate, ever-quarrelsome foreign-policy community. From hawkish neoconservatives to the most ardent of isolationists and everyone in between, elite opinion was aghast at the prospect of such an inexperienced, temperamental, controversial commander in chief. The number of Trump supporters among the national-security elite could be counted on one hand, even by a shop teacher. But the masses did not agree, or at least enough did not in key states, and the unthinkable followed. For the first time in anyone's memory, the rational-actor assumption is about to be put to a severe test.

However, despite the apparent global chaos and geopolitical uncertainty, the structural forces of international relations are fairly stable and will not be much affected by the new president's choices. Most of all, the relative power of the United States during the Trump years will not change drastically from what he inherited. The steady stream of analyses lamenting the coming loss of U.S. leadership largely mistakes emotion for fact and pessimism for empiricism. The United States is going to remain the strongest country in the world for some time to come. What it chooses to do with that power is, of course, hardly predetermined, and that is the subject of this book.

Trump's America will test many theories of political science, and those in this book are no exception. If his policies do not inspire balancing behavior, for example, what will? If the world remains relatively peaceful—which it is, by nearly any measure—when he leaves office, what would cause war to return? We will know more about the fundamental nature of the twenty-first-century system when the Trump clouds clear, for better or worse.

This work draws heavily upon insights from psychology, and I have benefited enormously from the generous assistance of a number of scholars in that field. Those who helped me understand the findings of their profession, pointed me toward the best sources, and corrected my misunderstandings include Art Markman, Michael Kraus, and Carrie Wyland. Anything in these pages that stands uncorrected is obviously my fault alone.

Inchoate versions of some of the arguments to come have appeared in *Security Studies*, *Comparative Strategy*, and *Survival*. What is included here is much updated and, one hopes, improved.

# PSYCHOLOGY OF A SUPERPOWER

# INTRODUCTION

In late 1987, as the Soviet Union was beginning its long, slow circle around the drain, Georgi Arbatov issued a dire warning to the United States. In a letter to the *New York Times*, Arbatov, one of the Kremlin's leading "Amerikanists," wrote that the Soviets were unleashing a "secret weapon," one "that will work almost regardless of the American response." It was not the stuff of Cold War nightmares, a last-minute technological deus ex machina from the Academy of Sciences, that would rescue the USSR from oblivion. No, in this instance the weapon was psychological and unequivocal: the Kremlin was going to deprive America of The Enemy.[1] The event for which generations of U.S. policy makers had worked, prayed, and bled—the implosion of the Soviet Union—was about to occur, and it was going to create unforeseen problems for the United States.

By the end of 1991, even those skeptical of Gorbachev and suspicious of Soviet intentions had to admit that the world was entering an entirely new phase. When the coup by hardliners not only failed but led to the dissolution of the empire, the greatest enemy in the history of the United States—and the raison d'etre of its security community—vanished without a fight. The West's bloodless victory appeared to be the best of all possible outcomes, especially when compared to the rather grim list of alternatives. But it did not come without cost, and forging a new order has not proven easy.

The world left in the wake of that collapse had precedent in neither modern nor ancient history. Regional hegemons had existed many times before, but never had one country been able to exert such drastic dominance over any potential competitor in all traditional measures of power. For the first time, the international system contained one member that, while hardly omnipotent, had precious few constraints on its ability to act. The world had become *unipolar.*

A great deal has been written on the meaning of unipolarity as scholars and policy makers alike struggled to understand the implications of the new, confusing, confounding phase they had entered. Indeed, one might be forgiven for wondering why the world needs yet another work on the subject. Fortunately, such concerns have never stopped anyone before; academic markets rarely reach saturation points. And there are many important questions that remain essentially unanswered, even twenty-five years after the Soviet collapse, while others are still controversial or underexplored.

This is a book about the current world order. It examines a series of structural, strategic, and psychological aspects of unipolarity and speculates not just about the center's effect on the system but also about the other way around: What has the rather sudden realization that it stands alone atop the international hierarchy done to the United States? How has unipolarity affected the way U.S. leaders conceive of their role, make strategy, or perceive others? No one would expect an individual to become the richest, most powerful person in the world without experiencing profound psychological and behavioral consequences. Power corrupts, as everyone knows. The effects of unbalanced, unchecked capabilities on the individual are familiar and relatively uncontroversial; what are its effects on states?

## UNIPOLARITY: WHAT WE KNOW, WHAT WE DON'T

System structure is a concept close to the heart of those who study international relations. Scholars have spent more than fifty years debating the relative merits of various power configurations, particularly those of multipolar and bipolar systems, since for quite some time unipolarity appeared profoundly unlikely.[2] That impression changed in 1991. The vast corpus of work on unipolarity that has emerged since tends to focus on a few core issues: classification, stability, and durability have been discussed many times, and as a result we know some things about how the current system operates. We also have a good sense about what is as yet undetermined. Progress can be a bit difficult in a literature that does not even agree on the meaning of its most basic concepts, however. After a brief review of how this study will employ a series of oft-conflated terms, its attention will turn to an explanation of the "unipolar moment."[3]

## CLARIFYING SOME CONCEPTS

Few things are as tiresome as extended academic discussions of definitions. Clarity matters, however, so in the interest of minimizing confusion in the pages to come, the reader's indulgence is requested for a brief attempt at disentangling a set of related concepts that are conflated almost as often as they are used. The terms *unipolarity*, *hegemony*, *empire*, and *primacy* are sometimes employed interchangeably, as if their differences are too slight to warrant discussion, which wallpapers over their considerable nuance and causes analysts to talk past one another.[4] For these purposes, *polarity* is a description of the distribution of power across the international system, measured by material capabilities. It is not necessarily dependent upon national choices regarding how power is used or grand strategy. Polarity is empirical to the extent power can be measured. Systems in which power is disproportionately concentrated in two countries, such as the Cold War or Greece of the fifth century BC, are bipolar; when power is spread among a few states, as it was before World War I, a multipolar system results. *Unipolarity* obtains when one member of a system towers above the rest, irrespective of how that power is used.

*Hegemony*, on the other hand, is the result of a choice. It is the outcome of a successful, active attempt to dominate, create, and sustain a set of rules.[5] The United States could choose not to exercise hegemony and follow a restrained grand strategy that does not seek to dominate the rest of the world without affecting the polarity of the system.[6] Unipolarity can exist without hegemony, in other words, even if the reverse is much more difficult.[7]

Hegemony falls short of *imperialism* because it seeks neither direct nor indirect rule over other territories but rather the imposition of order. Secondary states under another's hegemony maintain their sovereignty but are aware of the rules limiting their freedom of action. The extent to which the United States plays the role of hegemon is debatable, but it is certainly not an empire, at least in the traditional sense.[8] Finally, *primacy* is a specific grand strategy that seeks to establish hegemony and maintain the top status in the international hierarchy. It is a means to the end of hegemony and a path U.S. presidents have occasionally chosen.

To summarize pithily, advocates of *primacy* recommend the construction of U.S. *hegemony* in order to prolong *unipolarity*. These terms will not be used interchangeably as this work goes on, which should help make their meanings clear for even the most casual reader.

## CLASSIFICATION

By keeping these definitions in mind, the first great debate about the post–Cold War system can be settled, to the extent that such a thing is possible in academia. The dispute in question is one of classification: Is the world unipolar or multipolar, or does it have unique characteristics that demand an entirely new intellectual construction? Although not everyone agrees, for reasons that will be discussed below, in terms of raw, measurable power, there is little doubt that one state towers over all others. "The question [of polarity] is an empirical one," wrote Kenneth Waltz, "and common sense can answer it."[9] Despite skepticism or pessimism in some quarters, common sense—as well as the overwhelming preponderance of the evidence—suggests that the world is unambiguously unipolar.

The statistics are quite familiar but perhaps worthy of brief review. Not only does the United States dominate all potential competitors in every traditional measure of power, but its influence also extends to many nontraditional ones. The United States spends as much on its military as the next eight or ten countries combined, depending on one's method of calculation, and accounts for some 70 percent of global spending on defense research and development.[10] This asymmetry in spending has been continuing for some time, creating a military advantage for the United States without historical parallel. In March 2017, the Trump administration announced its intention to increase that advantage further by raising the Pentagon's budget by nearly 10 percent. That same week, *Jane's Defence Weekly* reported that Moscow was cutting its real defense spending by nearly a quarter.[11] If both proposals are enacted, the increase in the 2018 U.S. budget will be larger than the sum Russia devotes to its entire military.

While China has experienced larger growth rates, in many other ways the dominance of the U.S. economy has grown since the financial crisis of 2008. Confidence in the dollar is high, and the potential for the euro or renminbi to take its place as the primary reserve currency is low.[12] Treasury bills remain the most trusted global financial instrument. As Fareed Zakaria has pointed out, nearly all cutting-edge industries are dominated by U.S. companies, from social networks to mobile telephony to nano- and biotechnology.[13] The last few years have witnessed America's reemergence as an energy superpower, becoming the world's leader in the production of both fossil fuels and green energy. All this is also coming at a time when, while the United States continues to grow, the rest of the world is slowing down not just economically but demographically.

As some of the columns in table I.1 are meant to indicate, the dominance of the United States extends past hard-power indicators into soft. Overall, twenty-five years after the collapse of its only superpower competitor, the United States remains far more powerful in a comparative sense than any country has ever been. China is gaining ground in some ways but remains a far second, Vladimir Putin has a great deal of work to do before Russia returns to peer-competitor status, and a challenge from a united Europe seems farther off than ever. This observation

TABLE 1.1 Unipolarity at a Glance

| | Military spending (2016, billions of dollars) | Aircraft carriers | GDP (2016, trillions of dollars) | Per capita GDP (2016, thousands of dollars, PPP) | Forbes 500 corporations (2016) | Allies | Per capita electricity consumption (2014, kWh) | Top 100 grossing films worldwide (2016) | Nobel Prize winners since 2000 | Top 50 global universities | Top 100 most famous athletes (2016) |
|---|---|---|---|---|---|---|---|---|---|---|---|
| United States | 604.5 | 19 | 18.6 | 57.4 | 132 | 55 | 12,987 | 81 | 103 | 35 | 56 |
| China | 145.0 | 1 | 11.2 | 15.4 | 109 | 1 | 3,927 | 12.5 | 6 | 1 | 0 |
| Russia | 58.9 | 1 | 1.3 | 26.5 | 4 | 1 | 6,603 | 0 | 6 | 0 | 3 |
| Japan | 47.3 | 3 | 4.9 | 41.3 | 51 | 1 | 7,820 | 1 | 17 | 1 | 2 |
| United Kingdom | 52.5 | 1 | 2.6 | 42.5 | 23 | 31 | 5,130 | 0.5 | 25 | 5 | 4 |
| France | 47.2 | 4 | 2.5 | 42.3 | 29 | 31 | 6,938 | 0 | 10 | 1 | 0 |
| Germany | 38.3 | 0 | 3.5 | 48.1 | 29 | 27 | 7,035 | 0 | 9 | 1 | 1 |
| India | 51.1 | 2 | 2.3 | 16.6 | 7 | 0 | 806 | 1 | 2 | 0 | 3 |

*Sources:* Military spending: International Institute of Strategic Studies, *The Military Balance 2017* (London: IISS, February 2017). The Stockholm International Peace Research Institute also keeps track; its numbers are similar, except for China, which it estimates spent $215 billion in 2015. GDP and GDP per capita: International Monetary Fund, "World Economic Outlook Database, April 2017," https://www.imf.org/external/pubs/ft/weo/2017/01/weodata/index.aspx. Films: "Top 2016 Movies at Worldwide Box Office," http://www.the-numbers.com/box-office-records/worldwide/all-movies/cumulative/released-in-2016. The aircraft-carrier total is somewhat misleading, since ten of those from the U.S. Navy are "supercarriers" with a displacement of over 55,000 tons, of which the rest of the world combined has zero. Allies: Compiled by the author and a bit subjective, since some alliances are treaty based and others are not. There is no China-DPRK treaty, for instance, but that is included. The OAS charter theoretically obliges the United States to defend every country in the Western Hemisphere. The list does not include major non-NATO allies of the United States. Corporations: http://fortune.com/global500/. Electricity: "Electric Power Consumption," World Bank, http://data.worldbank.org/indicator/EG.USE.ELEC.KH.PC. Athletes list was compiled according to "a formula that combines salary and endorsements with social media following and Google search popularity": "World Fame 100," *ESPN,* May 31, 2016, http://espn.go.com/espn/feature/story/_/id/15685581/espn-world-fame-100. Universities: "Best Global Universities," *US News and World Report,* http://www.usnews.com/education/best-global-universities/rankings?int=a27a09.

of Robert Jervis is just as relevant today as it was a decade ago: "To say that the world is now unipolar is to state a fact."[14]

The United States does not dominate all measures of power, which leads some to doubt the suggestion that the system is unipolar. Two main objections have arisen. First, the Russians are roughly the equal of the United States when it comes to nuclear weapons, which may allow them to counter U.S. influence and decrease its dominance.[15] Second, Ian Bremmer spoke for many when he argued that the influence wielded by the United States is limited and not indicative of a true unipolar structure.[16] Others have noted that its considerable hard-power assets do not always allow the United States to achieve its preferred outcomes.[17] The influence of the United States might actually be declining, especially in the Trump era. Fortunately for the central premise of this book, none of these objections is terribly convincing.

Rough nuclear parity is, indeed, a continuing feature of the new order. Even though a credible case could be made that U.S. nuclear weapons are substantially more reliable and accurate than those of Russia, quantity has a quality all its own; when it comes to nuclear weapons, the world is bipolar. Unipolarity is a measure of power in the aggregate, however, and does not depend on asymmetry in every single category. Nuclear weapons are an important measure, obviously, but not the most important one, in large part because their political utility is not necessarily obvious.[18] Nuclear arsenals have not mattered much during the various crises of the twenty-first century, from Iraq to the Congo to the South China Sea. Furthermore, according to all nonnuclear measures, the U.S. military has essentially achieved the long-standing dream of its leaders, "full-spectrum dominance." Its range of hard-power capabilities is without peer.[19]

The other objection conflates power with influence and unipolarity with hegemony. Unipolarity does not imply omnipotence; the relative advantages of the United States do not allow it to achieve all its goals. The utility of power without influence has been the subject of long-standing debate in the literature.[20] It may be true that the nature of power is evolving, and some forms long prized by leaders have declining utility in the new system. But such conclusions are hard to prove and certainly controversial. Power does not always confer influence, especially in situations when the reasonable threat of violent coercion is absent. Dominance in measurable categories does not mean that the United States can consistently impose its will on others, especially on low-priority issues. This is especially clear in economic terms, where the United States is not the behemoth it once was, relatively speaking. The fact that the United States cannot, at least in times of peace, use its economic power to achieve its goals as it once could does not mean that the system is less unipolar. To repeat from the unavoidably dull section above, *unipolarity* is a reflection of capability, of measurable power, while choices regarding the *use* of that power are political and strategic. Power, whether potential or kinetic, creates structure; grand strategy creates (or does not create) hegemony. The world is unipolar based on what the United States is, not what it does. Reich and Lebow are correct, in other words, when they say that the United States is not a hegemonic power.[21] But the world remains unipolar and will until another pole rises to challenge the United States.

Scholars can debate the importance of the various measures of power and how they relate to influence, and President Trump can complain to his base about U.S. weakness and vulnerability. He can stumble both verbally and diplomatically, alienating allies and neutrals alike, while the commentariat warns of ending American eras. Systemic polarity will remain unaffected because it is a measure of power, independent of perception. And one nation stands alone above the rest.

What does unipolarity thus defined or any gross imbalance of power do to the state atop the pyramid? How has the United States handled its unipolar moment, and how has the structure of the system affected it in return? How have its perceptions, beliefs, and behavior been shaped by systemic structure, for better and for worse? Political science alone cannot answer such questions. Fortunately, a field exists that can help. Mixing academic fields, like crossing the streams of a proton pack, can create dangers if not done carefully, with a bit of forethought.

## PSYCHOLOGY AND INTERNATIONAL POLITICS

This is not a traditional work of international relations. No sweeping new theories are proposed, no hypotheses are tested, and case studies are not explored. Instead the book examines the effect of one independent variable—unipolarity—on a number of different aspects of international politics, including peace, stability, perception/misperception, and strategy. It engages with a diverse set of literatures and, in particular, introduces a set of interesting findings from psychology to a new audience. Applying lessons from political-science experiments to the real world is difficult enough, as scholars have discussed for decades.[22] Crossing fields raises even more problems, a few of which are worth considering up front.

The first concerns external validity. Since modern psychology draws most of its insights from the controlled setting of the laboratory, it is not immediately clear that its results are relevant to interstate politics. National leaders tend to be exceptional people who may well react differently than the average undergraduate to various stimuli. As Jonathan Mercer once observed, "Bismarck was not an American college sophomore."[23]

However, experimental models need not "look like" the real world to be useful, as Sydney Verba argued a half-century ago: "What is important," he explained, "is the question of whether it operates like the real world in the respects that are relevant to the study at hand."[24] The robustness of the variables under consideration, as well as how well the experiment isolates the effects of those variables, matters far more.

Potentially confounding influences can be filtered out in a well-designed laboratory setting, allowing researchers to zero in on the factors of interest in ways that real-world settings can never do. There are no "control groups" in the real world of international politics. We might not know precisely why Bismarck acted as he did—perhaps even he did not know—but we can be much more confident about what motivates the sophomore, which can at times suggest insight into the nature of human behavior. While national leaders obviously face significantly different tasks than do subjects in the lab or other controlled settings, they are also human beings subject to the same conscious and unconscious processes as everyone else. To the extent that internal factors decide their behavior, they may well do so in manners observed in the lab. Experiments are far from perfect, but they do offer the potential to reach conclusions, and understand processes, that might not be possible with other methods.[25]

Applying insights from the psych lab to the international system involves a leap across levels of analysis, which creates a second potential problem. The studies reviewed in the pages to come typically examine individual behavior in various circumstances, not that of states in the international system. Generalizing their findings therefore runs the risk of repeating the common and problematic tendency among scholars of international politics to anthropomorphize the state, to attribute human characteristics to an essentially imaginary construct.[26] Since states do not have psyches, one must treat attempts to apply psychological theories to them with healthy skepticism. Although states are not individuals, those leading them are. Power hierarchies artificially created in the laboratory are not necessarily dissimilar to those experienced by leaders. One might just as well ask why the effects observed by social psychologists across many different settings should *not* be observed among political elites. Findings from laboratory research into human behavior have direct relevance for the practical arenas humans find themselves in, such as boardrooms and statehouses.

The final hurdle is field specific. Potential red flags always arise when knowledge from one discipline is applied to another, since such transference inevitably draws scholars outside their areas of expertise. While political psychology may be a thriving subfield, few psychological experiments are done primarily to shine light on political issues. Those points that are true across fields, however, should also generate evidence visible to scholars of international politics. As a general rule, those doing cross-disciplinary research should be careful to seek corroboration in both areas of study and be modest in their claims.

These objections will be kept in mind as this book moves forward. I will try to determine which insights do not appear positioned to survive the leap across levels of analysis or fields of study and note their weaknesses or caveats. Only those findings and implications that have substantial, oft-corroborated supporting evidence will be emphasized. Fortunately, psychology—unlike political science—rewards efforts to replicate findings. The various phenomena under consideration in these pages typically have stood multiple tests in a variety of circumstances. The book will search for evidence of their effects in real-world situations as well as in the lab, hoping to separate the important from the peripheral and the real from the illusory. The reader can judge the results.

## OUTLINE OF THE BOOK

While this is a book about international politics, its subject is primarily the United States, specifically its security, character, identity, and strategy. It asks questions about the role Americans play in the world and what that role should be moving forward. And throughout it keeps in mind the peaceful trends in international politics that have been unfolding, quietly, since the collapse of the Soviet Union.

Each of the chapters to come examines one aspect of the unipolar order. The first covers ground most familiar to those who study international relations, the effect of unipolarity on state behavior. Its focus is on the "New Peace," the worldwide, underreported, and underappreciated relative decline in armed conflict. How much has systemic structure affected those pacific trends? In particular, has unipolarity contributed to the current stability, or are the two essentially epiphenomenal? As it turns out, the evidence connecting structure to state behavior is rather thin. Perceptions of hegemonic stability, which are particularly widespread in policy circles, are based on belief rather than fact. The chapter then discusses the psychological foundations of that belief and the roots of misperceived benevolent hegemony. It ends with a grand counterfactual, a scenario in which the United States is quite suddenly removed from international politics, and imagines what the effects would be. And they are different from what some may at first think.

The next chapter maintains a system-level focus, examining the effects of unipolarity on nuclear weapons. The world has entered a "second nuclear age," we are told, which by most accounts is likely to be substantially worse than the first. Chapter 2 reviews the logic and evidence for these claims and finds that the second nuclear age, to the extent it exists, has been a marked improvement over the first in almost every measurable way. The belief that the bipolar nuclear era was somehow more stable and predictable is directly related to puzzlingly high levels of nostalgia for the Cold War that persist in some circles. Once again, perception does not seem to match reality. It is toward those perceptions that the book then turns.

The next two chapters discuss the effect of unipolarity on psychology. How does systemic structure shape perception and the formation of images? Chapter 3 makes a number of different observations and arguments, all grounded in the literature of political and social psychology and all along the same basic theme: The vast power asymmetries that accompany unipolarity provide fertile ground for the growth of misperceptions and misunderstandings. Great power does not necessarily make for great wisdom. One pathological form of misperception is particularly exacerbated by imbalanced power and is therefore likely to grow in importance throughout the unipolar era: the so-called enemy image. Chapter 4 examines that image in more depth and moves in a practical direction, offering a list of possible indicators to help actors recognize when misperception is warping their view of rivals. By recognizing what those indicators are, policy makers in the United States and elsewhere can go a long way toward improving both their perceptions and the behavior that results from them.

The book then turns to strategy. Chapter 5 analyzes the effect of Arbatov's secret weapon: How has the collapse of the Soviet Union and its accompanying threatlessness shaped strategic thought in the United States? The reduction of danger in the unipolar world has been met with denial in Washington, where new threats, either minor or wholly imagined, have risen to take the place of the USSR. Strategy has been redefined and force-planning constructs altered in the post–Cold War United States. A variety of concepts that once were considered important primarily as means to other ends—influence, access, commitments, and credibility, to name a few—have been elevated to become ends in themselves. In the absence of national-security imperatives, domestic and fiscal factors have come to dominate decision making. Chapter 6 then examines grand strategy of both the United States and its allies. It offers thoughts on how post–Cold War policy making can be improved, with a discussion of the underappreciated opportunities that unipolarity affords the lone remaining superpower.

The concluding chapter speculates about conclusions. The end of unipolarity, while not imminent, will almost certainly arrive at some point. What does the preceding analysis suggest will be the effect of declining relative power on systemic stability, psychology, image formation, and strategy? The decline of U.S. power has been steadily predicted for more than six decades, always with ominous implications. With how much determination should the United States, through its grand strategic choices, endeavor to preserve its status? Will we miss the unipolar moment when it's gone? Is it worth trying to save?

Barring unforeseen natural or unnatural disasters, the United States will be by far the most significant international actor throughout the twenty-first century. Helping its leaders understand the role they play in the world and how best to approach the challenges they face is one of the highest callings of the modern academy. This book hopes to take one small step in that direction.

# 1

# UNIPOLARITY AND THE SYSTEM

**L**ost amid the Sturm und Drang of 2016, with Brexit, ISIS, and Donald Trump dominating the headlines, was a much more positive geopolitical event. Its underappreciation was to be expected, since peace generates fewer headlines than war. On June 22, Colombian President Juan Manuel Santos shook hands with the FARC rebel commander Rodrigo Londoño-Echeverri, ending the longest-running civil war in the world and with it the last active armed conflict in the Western Hemisphere.[1] Only deep unfamiliarity with Colombia could produce full confidence in the peace; civil war has been an omnipresent fact of life for most of the country's history, and earlier episodes of optimism have proven short-lived. But the agreement has already survived its first roadblock—a substantial roadblock, rejection by Colombian voters—and entered into force after passing through the Congress in late November. At least for now, in the middle of 2017, the guns are silent in Colombia. And with that, for the first time since at least the 1600s, and possibly for the first time ever, an entire hemisphere is at peace.[2]

The remarkably undercelebrated end to the Colombian civil war is just the latest data point for what the Harvard psychologist Steven Pinker has called the "New Peace," the current era of unprecedented inter- and intranational stability.[3] Although war is hardly gone from the globe, and although a number of high-profile conflicts still rage across the Middle East, there is more peace in 2017 than at any other time in history. Why has conflict declined to historically low levels? What accounts for the post–Cold War peace, and how long is it likely to last? Surely no questions are more important for either the theory or practice of international relations, and few are harder to answer. However, only by understanding the causes of the New Peace can we extrapolate its likely future and plan accordingly.

Of the many possible explanatory variables, none is more controversial than the suggestion that hegemonic stability is at work. The possibility that the United States—wittingly or not—has essentially established a global Pax Americana is generally overlooked by the major scholarly works on the subject. This stands in stark contrast to the policy world, where the many positive aspects of unipolarity and/or U.S. hegemony are articles of faith rarely discussed and never seriously questioned. The scholar and public intellectual Michael Lind spoke for many when he wrote that "in my experience, most members of the U.S. foreign policy elite sincerely believe that the alternative to perpetual U.S. world domination is chaos and war."[4] One of those is certainly Robert Kagan, who noted that "Pinker traces the beginning of a long-term decline in deaths from war to 1945, which just happens to be the birthdate of the American world order. The coincidence eludes him, but it need not elude us."[5] A virtually unanimous foreign-policy community views U.S. power as an obvious force for good in the world, a sine qua non of peace and stability. Rarely are the theoretical, empirical, and psychological foundations of that widespread belief explored.

This chapter examines the relationship between unipolarity and armed conflict. It reviews the evidence commonly used by hegemonic-stability enthusiasts to connect U.S. actions with systemic peace and questions its foundation. The United States was very active in the waning years of the Colombian civil war, after all, and all sides seem to agree that Washington's "Plan Colombia" played an important role in bringing the conflict to an end.[6] Is that just one example of the role the United States plays in the system as a whole? Can we thank Uncle Sam for the New Peace?

## THE NEW PEACE

The suggestion that the world is more peaceful than ever would surprise those who get their conflict information from the media or their leaders. After all, not many predicted it would happen. As the Cold War drew to a close, it was far more common to run across arguments about how the removal of bipolar balance would lead to an increase in violence. The Cold War rivalry at times was a force for stability, according to this school of thought, since the superpowers balanced each other and controlled their allies. Expectations of systemic instability led John Mearsheimer to argue that the West would "soon miss the Cold War."[7] Since a unipolar order would be accompanied by a marked increase in conflict, the West had "an interest in maintaining the Cold War order, and hence has an interest in the continuation of the Cold War confrontation," Mearsheimer wrote. "Developments that threaten to end it are dangerous."[8] If the bipolar order wound down, he predicted, subsequent decades would "probably be substantially more prone to violence than the past 45 years. Many observers now suggest that a new age of peace is dawning; in fact the opposite is true."[9] Christopher Layne concurred, concluding that "the coming years will be ones of turmoil in international politics."[10] Nuno Monteiro updated these arguments two decades later, suggesting that the unipolar world is not peaceful and unlikely ever to be so.[11] As evidence, he pointed to the repeated U.S. misadventures in Iraq, Afghanistan, Libya, and elsewhere.

This is a curious conclusion to have reached in 2014, for surely Monteiro must have been familiar with the mountains of empirical evidence suggesting the opposite was true. The facts were, and remain, unequivocal on this point: Mearsheimer and Layne were (and Monteiro is) not just wrong but spectacularly wrong. The last twenty-five years have seen a steady decline in all kinds of armed conflict.[12] Great-power war has been absent for more than a half-century, and now all interstate warfare is at historic low levels, as are intrastate wars such as civil and ethnic conflicts.[13] By almost any measure the world has become significantly more peaceful, with measurable declines in coups, repression, the chances of dying in battle, border alterations, conquest, genocide, and other forms of violence against civilians.[14] Peace settlements have proven to be more durable over time, and fewer new conflicts are breaking out than ever before.[15] Whether these trends represent a fundamental change in the rules that govern state behavior or a temporary respite between cataclysms remains to be seen, but there is no doubt that—thus far at least— the post–Cold War era has been far more stable and peaceful than any that preceded it.

All this is happening in a world with far more states (the League of Nations had fifty-eight members at its peak; the UN today has 193) and people (the global population has more than tripled since World War II) than ever before. Rather than fuel Malthusian competition for resources or Kaplanesque anarchy, runaway population growth has been accompanied by a drastic decline in violence. Furthermore, while some statistics regarding the rate of battle deaths take population growth into account, none attempt to capture the greater number of years people are living. Today people live, on average, about twenty years longer than they did in 1950.[16] Citizens of the twenty-first century have nearly 30 percent more time to experience warfare. Yet the odds of being killed in conflict still decline.

The New Peace is not without its skeptics and critics, the arguments of whom will be addressed below. Although it is now widely (if grudgingly) acknowledged in the academy, popular perceptions about warfare certainly do not match empirical reality. Anxiety and unease about the state of the world remain high. The bloody mess in Syria in particular has blinded many observers to the broader security trends, which remain essentially unchanged. When the current era—as dangerous as it may seem—is compared to any other, the verdict is clear: This is a golden age of peace and security, one in which fewer people are dying in warfare than ever before. The decline in violence is as empirically incontrovertible as is unipolarity. Whether the two are related, however, remains an open question, one that is hotly debated and vitally important for both the theory and practice of international relations.

## OBJECTIONS TO THE NEW PEACE

Is the New Peace an illusion? Before addressing the U.S. role in bringing about an era of (relative) international stability, we will divert a bit to address the arguments of those unconvinced by the steadily accumulating evidence. There is little point in discussing unipolarity and the New Peace if the latter does not really exist. Those only interested in the role played by U.S. hegemony can skip the next two sections. There will be no quiz.

Skeptics have raised five objections to the idea that any peace is particularly new or particularly significant. First, some have asserted that it is simply too soon to know whether these trends in armed conflict are statistically anomalous. Bear Braumoeller has suggested that a minimum of 150 more years needs to pass before we can say with confidence whether war is actually declining.[17] His work focuses on major, great-power wars, however, and excludes both minor and internal conflicts. While the New Peace is a relatively new phenomenon, perhaps too new to convince everyone, it is also so pervasive across so many measures of violence, and so potentially important, that surely it deserves serious consideration, even at this early stage.

Second, a number of scholars object to the assertion that "peace" is merely the absence of war. Johan Galtung seems to have been the first to make a distinction between "negative peace" (the absence of war) and "positive peace" (the "integration of human society," or the presence of justice, cooperation, equality, and/or other indicators).[18] The New Peace is a phenomenon of the former, leading some to suggest that its importance is exaggerated. This line of reasoning, which figures most prominently in the discipline of peace studies, suggests that the absence of violence has the potential to create complacency or even complicate efforts to address the world's various injustices.[19] While one might reasonably argue that "negative peace" has value in itself, especially given the alternative, substantial evidence suggests positive peace is on the rise as well. A major new study on the subject has concluded that a number of important indicators of human progress are, in aggregate, waxing.[20] The current era thus contains good news for every definition of peace, even if substantial global problems remain unsolved.

Third, the last few years have been marginally more violent than the ones that preceded them, leading some to suggest that the New Peace might be ending.[21] While the exact numbers are in some dispute, and even though they dropped in 2015 and again in 2016, it is true that Syria has provided a bloody exception to global trends.[22] Pinker has noted the uptick in battle deaths but also has pointed out that the overall numbers— both in absolute terms and especially in relative—remain far below those of the 1960s, 1970s or 1980s, "when the world was a *far* more dangerous place."[23] Furthermore, the other significant trends that help define the era remain unchanged.[24] Variation occurs during the New Peace, but it is variation at an extremely low level, insignificant in comparison with past experience.

The fourth objection to the New Peace holds not that the statistics are wrong but that they are not capturing the reality of modern armed conflict. According to this argument, the form taken by post–Cold War violence is different from earlier versions, which makes it harder to detect by traditional measures. In her influential *New and Old Wars*, Mary Kaldor warned of the rise of "new wars," which are less organized, less structured, and more deadly for civilians than those that came before.[25] By her widely repeated estimate, new wars result in eight civilian deaths for every one combatant, a much higher ratio than in any previous era. Old wars may be on the decline, in other words, but perhaps new wars, which are deadlier for the innocent and more disruptive to society, have taken their place.

Time and scrutiny have not been kind to Kaldor's ideas. A number of researchers have found that the ratio of civilian-to-combatant casualties has not changed markedly over time.[26] If anything, the wars of the post–Cold War era have been *less* deadly for civilians than those that came before.[27] Kaldor has now backed off some of her 1999 claims, especially the eight-to-one civilian-to-combatant casualty ratio.[28] Proponents of the "new wars" thesis are surely correct when pointing out that civilians suffer horrifically during post–Cold War conflicts, but it is hardly the case that those fighting in Biafra, Cambodia, Mozambique, and the other Cold War proxy conflicts were gentlemen strictly following the Marquis of Queensberry rules. There is nothing particularly new about how civilians experience modern wars compared to those of earlier times. If anything, combat-related mortality is probably lower today, thanks to the increase in relief-agency activity, refugee aid, and emergency medical services.[29] Worldwide attention is focused more on civilian suffering because we are far more aware of it, not because it has necessarily increased.

The final objection is more visceral than empirical. The New Peace just does not *feel* right to many people, and no amount of empirical evidence can change that impression. An enduring majority both in and out of the academy simply does not believe that the world is more peaceful than ever. The belief that the world is a dangerous, violent place has staying power beyond what the data say. People are generally very slow to change their beliefs, which are manifestations of emotion as much as intellect. Although they almost always have some basis in reality, beliefs need not pass rigorous tests to prove that they match it.[30] No amount of evidence has been able to convince some people that vaccines do not cause autism, for example, or that the climate is changing because of human activity, or that our fates are not tied to the movement of celestial bodies. As future chapters will discuss, a good deal of work suggests that confronting people with evidence that contradicts previously held beliefs actually causes them to cling more firmly to misperceptions. Ultimately, as Robert Jervis explains, "we often believe as much in the face of evidence as because of it."[31] Facts may change, but beliefs remain the same.

Rarely have popular perceptions of the international security environment been at such stark odds with reality. The suggestion that we live in dangerous times is as ubiquitous as it is mistaken. Eggheads with their "data" and "statistics" might claim that the world is much safer than ever before, but Americans know better: a 2009 poll found that nearly 60 percent of the public—and fully half of the membership of the elite Council on Foreign Relations—actually considered the world more dangerous than it was during the Cold War.[32] Donald Trump rode this wave of unfounded, irrational fear into the Oval Office. Since this is belief rather than knowledge, no amount of rational argumentation is likely to convince the various pessimists that they are wrong about their fundamental security. But wrong they remain.

The era of New Peace is hardly without problems, challenges, or lingering violence. Declining conflict does nothing to mitigate climate

change, inequality, ISIS, avian flu, cyberterrorism, or four-dollar spe-
cialty coffees. However, the number of scholars who dispute the system's relative stability should shrink as more and more relatively
peaceful years go by. Why these welcome trends are occurring is not
nearly as clear, although a number of attempts have been made to
account for it.

## EXPLAINING THE NEW PEACE

How long will the New Peace last? What is causing its pacific trends? Few
questions have larger implications for the theory and practice of international politics. Were the New Peace to prove to be more than a transient
phenomenon—if levels of conflict remain low for a sustained period of
time, enough to convince the remaining skeptics—then it would constitute nothing less than a complete revolution in international affairs,
demanding major adjustments in leading theories and models of state
behavior.[33] And some would be rendered utterly obsolete.

Thus it is rather surprising that more time has not been spent trying
to understand the forces behind the trends. Part of the problem is epis-
temological: Explaining nonevents is no easy task. Deterrence theorists
have struggled with this problem for some time. No one can say for sure
if deterrence actually works, if potential aggressors are convinced not
to attack by the potential response or if they had no desire to attack in
the first place. Nonaggression might be the result of actions taken by the
defender or simple indifference.[34] Wars are extremely low-probability
events to begin with; there are no "most likely" cases, or moments when
war could have been reasonably expected to occur that are ripe to have
their processes traced. Studies of war are fortunate enough to have ample
dependent variables upon which to choose their cases (even if doing so
should raise red methodological flags).[35] Explanations of peace present
no such obvious guideposts.

While conclusive proof for the New Peace remains elusive for now, a
number of major and minor factors have been cited over the years that
might help account for the phenomenon. First, some scholars give

primary credit to nuclear weapons, which were invented at about the same time that the great powers stopped fighting one another.[36] Faith in the pacifying effect of deterrence led a few prominent realists to suggest that an efficient way to spread stability would be to encourage controlled proliferation to nonnuclear states.[37] If states are rational actors, then the removal of the possibility of victory should discourage aggression. Perhaps the presence of nine nuclear arsenals is sufficient to generate widespread fear of war and overall systemic stability.

Second, some observers have argued that modern integrated markets contain powerful incentives for peace. While economic considerations are not the only ones that states must weigh when war looms, to the extent that they affect decisions, in this postmercantilist age they do so in a uniformly pacific direction. In the 1970s, neoliberal institutionalists argued that modern levels of economic interdependence provide strong incentives for states to resolve disputes peacefully.[38] Today's states would be far better off cooperating rather than run the risk of ruining their economies and those of their main trading partners by fighting. The globalization of production, as Stephen Brooks has convincingly argued, is a powerful force for stability among those countries that benefit from the actions of multinational corporations.[39] Furthermore, today's highly mobile investment dollars flee instability, providing strong incentives for states to settle both external and internal disputes peacefully. As Secretary of State Colin Powell once told a Ugandan audience, "money is a coward."[40] Overall, globalization has been accompanied by an evolution in the way national wealth is accumulated. The major industrial powers, and perhaps many of their less-developed neighbors, seem to have reached the rather revolutionary conclusion that territory is not directly related to national power and prestige.[41] Azar Gat has argued that the value of peace has concomitantly risen, decreasing incentives for countries to resolve their disputes through violence.[42]

Third, perhaps it is no coincidence that the New Peace rose alongside the number of democracies in the world. While the widely tested and debated "democratic-peace theory" is not universally accepted in the field, the hundreds of books and articles that have been written on the subject over the past thirty years have been sufficient to convince many that democracies rarely fight one another.[43] Since most of today's great powers practice some form of democracy, perhaps it should be unsurprising that conflict has been absent in the global North.

Fourth, a number of scholars have suggested that regimes, law, and institutions shape state behavior and can serve to inhibit aggression.[44] Some major theorists of the New Peace, including both Mack and Goldstein, give the United Nations and its peacekeeping arm primary credit for the decline in warfare.[45] At the very least, there is convincing evidence that wars do not recur with the same frequency as in the past, a phenomenon for which the United Nations can certainly take a degree of credit.

These potential explanations suffer from the same general weakness: stability exists where the influence of their independent variable is weak or absent. Neither Central nor South America has nuclear states, for example, but those regions have been virtually free of interstate war for many decades. The relative decline of civil wars and ethnic conflict around the globe since the end of the Cold War is not a product of nuclear deterrence either. Africa and other areas of the global South are experiencing historically low levels of armed conflict, which suggests that economic growth and interdependence might not be the sole determinants of peaceful choices by leaders.[46] The democratic-peace theory might help explain why there have been no intra-West wars, but it cannot account for the pacific trends among and within nondemocratic states. Poor, nonnuclear, authoritarian countries are experiencing lower levels of conflict too.

Proponents of both the democratic and capitalist peaces can never be completely sure about the direction of their causal arrows. Peace may well have preceded, and then abetted, the rise of the other factors. Democracy and economic growth might be the results of stability, rather than the other way around.[47] The rise in peacekeeping has certainly been possible only because of increased great-power cooperation. These phenomena may well be related, just not in the way their proponents suggest.

A number of other explanations for the New Peace have been proposed. Pinker discussed a series of "rights revolutions," especially including those of children and women that, in addition to several other factors, may well have contributed to the decline of war.[48] Others have suggested that demographics may be playing a decisive pacific role, either through aging populations or declining birthrates in the global North.[49] The final explanation for the decline of war combines all of the above, suggesting that they contribute to a change in the way people view conflict itself. Together these factors may have combined to remove the romance and glory from warfare, replacing it with revulsion and dishonor. Ideas, when widely held, can evolve into norms that shape state behavior.[50]

A final potential explanation exists, one that is far more commonly articulated in the policy community than in scholarship. The possibility that the United States is essentially responsible for the New Peace, either through its military power or institutional order it created, is the subject of the rest of this chapter.

## TWO VERSIONS OF HEGEMONIC STABILITY

Few ideas from academia gain much purchase among policy makers. Washington water-cooler conversations rarely center on audience costs, or expected utility, or even the self-help imperative. Occasionally, however, a concept does manage to make its way out of the Ivory Tower to influence how leaders think and how states behave. One of those rare crossovers is the so-called hegemonic-stability theory, which holds that an anarchic international system will be unstable unless one power is able to create and enforce rules. The simple, elegant theory first described the Bretton Woods international economic order, in which the strong dollar played a stabilizing role, and it has been applied to security matters many times since.[51] Hegemonic dominance eases security-dilemma pressures by decreasing unpredictability in the system. The hegemon essentially provides three services: establishment of the rules of global order, enforcement of those rules, and reassurance for the other members.[52] The logic of the theory may be uncontroversial, but the suggestion that the United States plays such a role today and brings stability to the international system is not.

Is this theory applicable to the current order? Is the New Peace the result of U.S. dominance? As explained in the introduction, the United States has not instituted a global imperium, and its attempts at hegemony—if they exist at all—extend only to a few regions. One might suggest that a desire for conceptual accuracy would encourage hegemonic-stability theorists to refer instead to a "unipolarity-stability theory." But those who have faith in the stabilizing, pacifying potential of U.S. power do not make such distinctions. They argue that the United States has indeed constructed a set of rules for the system it has sought to enforce, if in a desultory way. With substantial regional variations, the unipolar power has articulated norms that other states violate at their peril. Perhaps the United States exerts hegemonic influence, if not outright hegemony, on the system, an influence substantial enough to convince most policy professionals that Washington is responsible for post–Cold War stability.

The hegemonic-stability explanation for the New Peace comes in two distinct versions that differ over the role played by U.S. hard power.[53] To some liberal internationalists, stability derives from the institutions, rule-based regimes and law promoted by the United States, which create a positive-sum system.[54] Other states have strong incentives to cooperate, since the advantages of integrating into the established order far outweigh those of remaining outside it. This *liberal* version of hegemonic-stability theory describes an international economic and legal system with no obvious enemies, one not dependent on continued U.S. hard-power dominance. Diplomacy and economic engagement, not necessarily military power, are the primary drivers of U.S. hegemony. If and when U.S. power declines compared to its rivals, according to G. John Ikenberry, this version's primary proponent, "the underlying foundations of the liberal international order will survive and thrive."[55] The United States is still the indispensable nation, but its primary job is maintenance, not enforcement.

Others are more skeptical of the potential of institutions to shape behavior and believe instead that stability is dependent upon the active application of the hegemon's military power.[56] The second version of the hegemonic-stability explanation is based upon a different view of human nature than is the liberal, and it is less sanguine about the potential for voluntary cooperation. Actors respond to concrete incentives, according to this outlook, and will ignore rules or law in the absence of punishment for transgressions. The would-be hegemon must enforce stability, therefore, not merely establish it. Policing metaphors are common in this literature, with the United States playing the role of sheriff or globocop charged with keeping the peace.[57] Take away the police or damage their credibility, and instability would soon return. "The present world order," according to Robert Kagan, "is as fragile as it is unique" and would collapse without sustained U.S. efforts.[58] "In many instances," add Lawrence Kaplan and William Kristol, "all that stands between civility and genocide, order and mayhem, is American power."[59] Though this argument is commonly associated with neoconservatism[60]—and it will be referred to as the *neoconservative* explanation from here on—it is also accepted by a number of scholars and observers generally considered outside of that ideological approach.[61]

This version of hegemonic-stability theory more closely matches Thomas Hobbes's famous early articulation.[62] Hobbes argued that cooperation is possible only if a leviathan can make all sides believe that others will comply with the law. Even smaller-scale relations can break down without the trust that the hegemon essentially provides. If and only if smaller parties become assured that consequences would follow treachery on the part of their would-be rivals will they lower their guard enough to cooperate. Hegemonic punishment of defectors, not mutual interest, encourages cooperation.[63]

The two versions are united on this point: Unipolarity in general does not account for the New Peace but American unipolarity in particular. U.S. hegemony is essentially benevolent, according to both liberals and neoconservatives. Over the years, Washington has constructed an order that takes the interests of other states into account, one that is nonthreatening and therefore does not generate resentment and counterbalancing behavior.[64] The liberal version of this order is beneficial to all its members, who have a stake in its maintenance; the more muscular version, whether neoconservative or not, assumes that the default position of smaller states in a unipolar system is to bandwagon with the center.[65] No one seems to suggest that there is an irenic structural logic of unipolarity independent of U.S. behavior. The question is therefore not so much about the connection between unipolarity and the New Peace as much as it is whether U.S. behavior, in one form or another, has brought it about.

The hegemonic-stability explanation for the New Peace is in some ways more theoretically elegant than the others. For one thing, it does not suffer from questions regarding causal direction. While it may be reasonable to suggest that peace produced the expansion of democracy and/or economic development rather than the other way around, peace did not produce unipolarity. In fact, if the United States is indeed supplying the global public good of security, it might be able to take credit for a number of other positive trends. Not just peace but democracy, economic stability, and development might all be beneficial side effects of unipolarity.[66] A world without unipolarity, argued Samuel Huntington, "would be a world with more violence and disorder and less democracy and economic growth."[67]

A great deal is at stake here for both scholarship and practice. If hegemony is responsible for the New Peace, then its pacific trends will wane if and when the unipolar moment ends. The other proposed explanations described above are essentially irreversible: nuclear weapons cannot be uninvented, and no defense against their use is ever going to be completely foolproof; the pace of globalization and economic interdependence shows no sign of slowing, Brexit and Trump notwithstanding; democracy seems firmly embedded in the cultural fabric of many of the places it currently exists and may well be in the process of spreading to the few places where it does not. The United Nations, while oft criticized, is not in danger of disappearing. And finally, history contains precious few examples of the return of institutions deemed by society to be outmoded, barbaric, and/or futile.[68] In other words, liberal normative evolution is typically unidirectional. Few would argue, for instance, that either slavery or dueling is likely to reappear in this century. Illiberal normative recidivism is exceptionally rare.[69] If the neoconservatives are correct and U.S. hard power is primarily responsible for the New Peace, however, then it cannot be expected to last long after U.S. hegemonic decline. If liberal internationalists are right and the New Peace is largely a product of the world order that the United States has forged, then it may have a bit more staying power beyond unipolarity, but not necessarily much.

Determining the relationship between hegemony and the New Peace has importance that goes beyond the academy. Even if the unipolar moment proves more durable than many think—a subject to which we will return—it is unlikely to last forever. If the New Peace is essentially an American creation, that postunipolar future is likely to be quite a bit more violent than the present.

## EVIDENCE FOR AND AGAINST PAX AMERICANA

Since the world had never experienced systemwide unipolarity before the end of the Cold War, judgments about its relative stability are necessarily speculative. Extrapolations can be made from regional unipolar systems, like the Roman Mediterranean or Tang China, but definitive statements about systemwide stability cannot be made from one case. Still, if U.S. power is primarily responsible for the New Peace, one would expect that it would leave some clues about its effects. This section reviews three kinds of evidence regarding Pax Americana in order to determine whether an empirical relationship exists between various kinds of U.S. activity and global stability.

### CONFLICT AND HEGEMONY BY REGION

Even the most ardent supporters of the hegemonic-stability explanation do not contend that U.S. influence extends equally to all corners of the globe. The United States has concentrated its policing in what George Kennan used to call the "strong points," or most important parts of the world: Western Europe, the Pacific Rim, and the Persian Gulf.[70] By doing so, Washington may well have contributed more to great-power peace than to the overall global decline in warfare. If the former phenomenon contributed to the latter, by essentially providing a behavioral model for weaker states to emulate, then perhaps this lends some support to the hegemonic-stability case.[71] In general, Washington has shown less interest in the affairs of the global South since the end of the Cold War, and the level of violence in almost all regions has declined. The United States intervenes far less in the political and military affairs of Latin America compared to any time in the twentieth century, for instance, and the states of the region are more peaceful. Warfare in Africa is at an all-time low, as noted above, as is relative U.S. interest outside of counterterrorism and security assistance. Regional peace and stability exist where there is active U.S. intervention, in other words, as well as where there is not. No direct relationship seems to exist across regions.

The U.S. sheriff certainly appears to have enforced rules upon the great powers. Since we do not have a "control" Europe, however, one without the presence of U.S. troops and alliance commitments, it is difficult to know what is causing those states to behave. In much of the rest of the world, the United States has not been especially eager to enforce any particular rules. Even rather incontrovertible evidence of genocide has not been enough to inspire action. Washington's intervention choices have at best been erratic: crises in Libya and Kosovo inspired responses, but much more blood flowed uninterrupted in Rwanda, Darfur, Congo, Sri Lanka, and Syria.

When U.S. intervention has occurred, its wisdom and efficacy have not been encouraging. The security situation in the Persian Gulf and broader Middle East, to cite the most obvious example, would be better off if U.S. troops had stayed home.[72] In recent years, substantial hard-power investments (Somalia, Afghanistan, Iraq), moderate intervention (Libya), and reliance on diplomacy (Syria) have been equally ineffective in stabilizing states torn by conflict. The region may well be essentially unpacifiable and immune to outside policing. At the very least, it seems hard to make the case that the U.S. presence has improved matters. In this strong point, unipolarity has failed to bring peace.

To say that the United States has not always been successful in imposing peace on willing combatants would be to understate. The fruitless effort to encourage the various combatants in Syria to stop killing one another is a prominent example, and there are others. The United States also took the peacemaking lead during one of the rare interstate conflicts of the New Peace era, the war between Eritrea and Ethiopia. A high-level U.S. delegation containing former and future national-security advisors (Anthony Lake and Susan Rice) made a half-dozen trips to the region, but it was unable to prevent either the outbreak or recurrence of the conflict. Lake and his team shuttled back and forth between the capitals with some frequency, and President Clinton made repeated phone calls to the leaders of the respective countries, offering to hold peace talks in the United States, all to no avail.[73] The war did not end until the Ethiopians essentially won in late 2000. The globocop was irrelevant.

The Horn of Africa is hardly the only region where states are free to fight one another today without fear of serious U.S. involvement. Since they are choosing not to do so with increasing frequency, something else is probably affecting their calculations. Stability exists even in those places where the potential for intervention by the sheriff is minimal. Hegemonic stability can only take credit for influencing those decisions that would have ended in war without the presence, whether physical or psychological, of the United States. It seems hard to make the case that the relative peace that has descended on so many regions is primarily attributable to the kind of heavy hand of the neoconservative leviathan or that of its lighter, more liberal cousin. Something else appears to be at work.

## CONFLICT AND U.S. CHOICES

If U.S. power is the only thing holding back the forces of global chaos, then we would expect to see some variation in violence as the relative capabilities of the United States wax and wane. During the 1990s, the United States cut back on defense by about 25 percent, spending $100 billion less in real terms in 1998 than it did in 1990.[74] To those believers in the neoconservative version of hegemonic stability, this irresponsible "peace dividend" endangered both national and global security. "No serious analyst of American military capabilities doubts that the defense budget has been cut much too far to meet America's responsibilities to itself and to world peace," argued Kristol and Kagan at the time.[75] The world grew dramatically more peaceful while the United States cut its forces, however, and it stayed just as peaceful even as spending rebounded after the 9/11 terrorist attacks. The incidence and magnitude of global conflict declined while the military budget was cut under President Clinton, kept declining (though more slowly) as the Bush administration ramped it back up, and stayed steady as Obama cut back again. U.S. military spending has varied during the New Peace from a low in constant dollars of less than $400 billion to a high of more than $700 billion, but war does not seem to have noticed.

The same nonrelationship exists between other potential proxy measurements for U.S. power and conflict. No connections exist between warfare and fluctuations in U.S. GDP, or alliance commitments, or forward military presence. Europe experienced very little fighting when there were 300,000 American troops stationed there, for example, and very little after 90 percent of those troops were removed. It is hard to find much correlation between U.S. actions and systemic stability. Nothing the United States actually *does* seems to matter to the New Peace.

Absolute military spending might not be as important as relative. Although Washington cut back on spending during the 1990s, its advantage over all possible rivals never wavered. The United States has accounted for between 35 and 41 percent of global military spending every year since the collapse of the Soviet Union.[76] Perhaps perceptions of U.S. power, as well as its willingness to use it, keep the peace. Fluctuations in its enormous defense budget might be unimportant compared to how the United States chooses to employ that budget. In other words, perhaps the grand strategy of the United States, rather than its absolute capability, is decisive in maintaining stability.

Perceptions of U.S. power and the strength of its hegemony are to some degree functions of its willingness to use that power. A strong United States that chose to stand on the sidelines during crises would not encourage or enforce international cooperation. If indeed U.S. strategic choices are directly related to international stability, then variation in its choices ought to have consequences for levels of conflict. A restrained United States would presumably be less likely to play the role of sheriff than one following a more activist approach. Indeed, hegemonic-stability theorists warn that following a grand strategy that did not make global policing a priority would court disaster. The "present danger" about which Kristol, Kagan, and their fellow travelers warned is that the United States "will shrink its responsibilities and—in a fit of absentmindedness, or parsimony, or indifference—allow the international order that it created and sustains to collapse."[77] The Pulitzer Prize–winning journalist Brett Stephens predicted that an insufficiently activist U.S. grand strategy would result in "global pandemonium."[78]

Liberals fear restraint as well and also warn that a militarized version of primacy would also be counterproductive in the long run. Washington can undermine its creation over time through thoughtless unilateral actions that violate its own rules. Many liberals predicted that the invasion of Iraq and its general contempt for international institutions and law would call the legitimacy of the order into question. Ikenberry worried that Bush's "geostrategic wrecking ball" would lead to a more hostile, divided, and dangerous world.[79] Thus while all hegemonic-stability theorists expect a rise of chaos during a restrained presidency, liberals also have grave concerns regarding primacy.

If either version is correct—that global stability is provided by U.S. hegemony—then maintaining that stability through a grand strategy based on either primacy (to neoconservatives) or "deep engagement" (to liberals) is clearly wise.[80] If, however, U.S. actions are only tangentially related to the outbreak of the New Peace or if any of the other proposed explanations are decisive, then the United States could retrench without fear of negative consequences.

The grand strategy of the United States is therefore crucial to theories of hegemonic stability. And, once again, there is no evidence that U.S. choices matter much. Although few observers would agree on the details, most would probably acknowledge that post–Cold War grand strategies of American presidents have differed in some important ways. As it happens, each administration is a reasonable representation of one the four ideal types of grand strategy laid out by Posen and Ross in

1996.[81] Under George H.W. Bush, the United States followed the path of "selective engagement," which is sometimes referred to as "balance-of-power realism"; Bill Clinton's grand strategy looks a great deal like what Posen and Ross call "cooperative security" and others call "liberal internationalism"; George W. Bush, especially in his first term, forged a strategy that was as close to "primacy" as any president is likely to get; and Barack Obama, despite some early flirtation with liberalism, followed a restrained realist path, which Posen and Ross label "neoisolationism" but its proponents refer to as "strategic restraint."[82] In the lingo of political science, we have substantial variation in the independent variable, more than enough to determine its effect on the phenomenon under consideration. The result is clear (see table 1.1).

Armed-conflict levels fell steadily throughout the post–Cold War era, irrespective of the grand strategic path Washington chose. Neither the primacy of George W. Bush nor the restraint of Barack Obama had much effect on the level of global violence. Despite continued warnings (and the high-profile mess in Syria), the world has not experienced an increase in violence while U.S. behavior became more restrained. Once again, if the grand strategy of the United States is responsible for the New Peace, it is leaving no trace in the evidence.

If a correlation did exist between U.S. actions and international stability, if other states had reacted differently to fluctuations in U.S. military spending or grand strategy, then surely hegemonic-stability theorists would argue that their expectations had been fulfilled. Many liberals were on the lookout for chaos while George W. Bush was in the White House, just as neoconservatives have been quick to identify apparent

TABLE 1.1  U.S. Grand Strategy and Conflict

|  | Grand strategy | Active conflicts/year |
| --- | --- | --- |
| George H. W. Bush | Selective engagement | 55 |
| Bill Clinton | Cooperative security | 43 |
| George W. Bush | Primacy | 31 |
| Barack Obama | Restraint | 24 |

worldwide catastrophe under President Obama.[83] If increases in violence would have been evidence for the wisdom of hegemonic strategies, then logical consistency demands that the lack thereof should at
least pose a problem. As it stands, the only evidence we have regarding
the relationship between U.S. power and international stability suggests
that the two are unrelated. The rest of the world appears quite capable
and willing to operate effectively without the presence of a global
policeman. Those who think otherwise base their view on faith alone.
Hegemonic stability is a *belief*, in other words, rather than an established fact, and as such it deserves a different kind of examination.

## POLITICAL PSYCHOLOGY AND THE NEW PEACE

When it comes to the notion that U.S. power is primarily responsible for
the New Peace, the evidence is weak but the belief is strong, especially
in policy circles. The best arena to examine the proposition is therefore
not the world of measurable rationality but rather the human mind.
Political psychology can shed more light on the effects of unipolarity
than can any international-relations theory or data. Just because an outcome is primarily psychological does not make it less real; perception
quickly becomes reality for both the unipolar state and those in the
periphery. If all actors believe that the United States provides security
and stability for the system, then behavior can be affected accordingly.
Beliefs have deep explanatory power in international politics whether
their foundation is firmly anchored in empirical reality or not.

   Like all beliefs, faith in the stability provided by hegemony is rarely
subjected to much analysis. When leaders are motivated to act based
on unjustified, inaccurate beliefs, folly often follows. The person who
decides to take a big risk because of astrological advice in the morning's
horoscope can benefit from superstition if the risk pays off. Probability
and luck suggest that unjustified beliefs can sometimes inspire successful
policy choices. Far more often, however, thin intellectual foundations
lead to suboptimal or even disastrous outcomes. Surely it is worthwhile

to analyze occasionally even our most deeply held beliefs to determine which ones are good candidates to inspire poor decisions in the future.

The belief in the pacifying power of the United States is in serious need of examination. People are, after all, wonderful rationalizers, and there is much to be said for being the strongest country in the world. That status provides Americans both security and psychological rewards as well as strong incentives to construct a rationale for preserving the unipolar moment, incentives that go beyond mere selfishness. Since people enjoy being number one, they are susceptible to perceiving reality in ways that brings the data in line with their desires. It is no coincidence that most hegemonic-stability theorists are American.[84] Perhaps the satisfaction that comes with being the unipolar power has inspired Americans to misperceive the positive role that their country plays in the world.

Three psychological phenomena are deeply and immediately relevant to U.S. perceptions of the connection between power and international stability. They are mutually supportive and, when taken together, suggest that U.S. policy makers are extremely vulnerable to overestimations of their importance. The belief in the major U.S. contribution to world peace, no matter how widespread, is probably unjustified.

## THE ILLUSION OF CONTROL

Could 5 percent of the world's population enforce rules upon the rest? Would even a hegemonic United States be capable of producing the New Peace? Perhaps, but it also may be true that believers in hegemonic stability are affected by a common, nearly ubiquitous form of misperception. A variety of evidence has accumulated over the past forty years to support Ellen Langer's original observations about the "illusion of control" that routinely affects observers.[85] Even in situations where outcomes are clearly generated by pure chance, like coin tosses and dice rolls, people believe that they can exert influence over events.[86] As a result, actors—whether subjects in an experiment or leaders in a stateroom—overestimate their ability to control the external world.

One of the earliest and strongest findings of this research is that such illusions are stronger when outcomes are positive. Psychologists and sociologists have long known that while actors are motivated to take responsibility when things are going well, their perceived agency shrinks in the face of bad news.[87] People attribute failure to chance and success to themselves.[88] This is related to, but not entirely identical with, the phenomenon that Anthony Greenwald labeled "beneffectance," or the tendency of people to claim responsibility for desired, but not undesired, outcomes.[89] Illusions of control over global stability and economic growth, which are manifestly desirable outcomes, should be quite powerful.

The extensive research on the illusion has revealed two further findings that suggest Americans might be more susceptible to it than others. First, misperceptions of control appear to be correlated with power: individuals with higher socioeconomic status, as well as those who are members of dominant groups, are more likely to overestimate their ability to control events.[90] Powerful people tend to be far more confident than others, often overly so, and that confidence leads them to inflate their own importance.[91] Leaders of superpowers are thus particularly vulnerable to distorted perceptions regarding their ability to bring about preferred outcomes. U.S. observers had a greater structural predisposition than others, for example, to believe that they would have been able to control events in the Persian Gulf following an injection of "creative instability" in 2003. The skepticism of less-powerful allies was easily discounted.

Second, culture matters. People from societies that value individualism are more likely to harbor illusions of control than those from collectivist societies, where assumptions of group agency are more common. When compared to people from other parts of the world, Westerners view the world as "highly subject to personal control," in the words of Richard Nisbett.[92] North Americans are particularly vulnerable.[93] People in relatively powerful countries with individualistic societies are therefore at high risk for misperceiving their ability to influence events.[94]

For the United States, the illusion of control extends beyond the water's edge. An oft-discussed public good supposedly conferred by U.S.

hegemony is order in those parts of the world uncontrolled by sovereign states, or the "global commons."[95] One such common area is the sea, where the United States maintains the world's only truly blue-water navy. That the United States is responsible for peace on the high seas is a central belief of hegemonic-stability theorists, one rarely examined in any serious way. The maritime environment has indeed been peaceful for decades: the biggest naval battles since Okinawa took place during the Falklands conflict in 1982, and they were fairly minor.[96]

If hegemony is the key variable explaining stability at sea, maritime security would be far more chaotic without the U.S. Navy. Perhaps, however, the reason so few other states are building blue-water navies is not because the United States dissuades them from doing so but because none feels that trade is imperiled. In earlier times, certainly during the age of mercantilism, zero-sum economics inspired efforts to cut off the trade of opponents on occasion, making control of the sea extremely important. Today the free flow of goods is critical to all economies, and no state would benefit from its interruption.[97] Even in the few continued (or future) areas of maritime contestation, such as the South China Sea, riparian powers have vital interests in the unimpeded movement of goods. The Chinese worry about our ability to restrict trade through the area—what is sometimes referred to as their "Malacca Dilemma," since a substantial portion of their trade (and all of their energy imports) transit the strait—just as much or more than we do about their ability to do so.[98] Hegemonists often argue that without the U.S. presence, Iran would move to seal off the Strait of Hormuz, despite the obvious fact that doing so would be economic suicide for Tehran.[99] Kori Shake spoke for many when she warned that, in the absence of compulsion, other countries might not choose policies that align with U.S. interests; however, we can be fairly confident that they would not take steps in diametric opposition to *their own* interests.[100] In today's interdependent order, what is good for one is often (if not always) good for all. Free trade at sea may no longer need protection, in other words, because it essentially has no enemies. The sheriff may be patrolling an essentially crime-free neighborhood.[101]

Robert Dahl famously defined power as the ability to get actors to do what they would normally not.[102] If the states of the Pacific Rim, Persian Gulf, or anywhere else would be doing roughly the same things without the presence of the U.S. military, its power cannot be responsible for their actions. Oceans unpatrolled by the U.S. Navy appear to be just as stable as those with its carriers. U.S. leaders probably overestimate the degree to which they control the sea and the world at large.

## EGOCENTRIC AND SELF-SERVING BIASES IN ATTRIBUTION

People commonly misperceive the role they play in the thinking process of others. Robert Jervis was the first to discuss the phenomenon now known as the "egocentric bias," which has been put to the test many times since he wrote four decades ago. Building on what was known as "attribution theory," Jervis observed that actors tend to overestimate their importance in others' decisions. Rarely are *our* actions as consequential upon *their* behavior as we believe them to be.[103] This is not merely ego gratification, though that plays a role; actors simply know much more about their own behavior and choices than they do about the internal deliberations going on in others' heads. Because people are more likely to remember their contributions to an outcome, they naturally grant themselves more causal weight.[104] *They* act with *us* in mind, or so we believe. Three further aspects of the egocentric bias suggest U.S. perceptions are particularly susceptible to its effects.

First, once again the effect is magnified when the behavior of others is desirable. People generally take credit for positive outcomes and deflect responsibility for negative ones. This "self-serving bias" is one of the best established findings in modern psychology, supported by many hundreds of studies.[105] Supporters of Ronald Reagan are happy to give him credit for ending the Cold War, for instance. Today, since few outcomes are more desirable than global stability and nonproliferation, it stands to reason that perceptions of the New Peace are prime candidates for distortion by egocentric and self-serving biases. When war breaks out, it is not the fault of U.S. leaders, but Washington is happy to take credit for peace. The connection between these biases and the self-esteem of actors is rather self-evident.

Second, for some time psychologists debated whether self-serving biases were universal or whether their effects varied across cultures. Extensive research has essentially settled the matter: a direct relationship exists between cultural individualism and susceptibility to the bias, perhaps because individualistic societies value self-enhancement rather than self-effacement.[106] Individuals from collectivist societies tend to have their egos rewarded in different ways, such as through contributions to the community and connections to others. People from Western countries are far more likely to take credit for positive outcomes than those from Eastern countries, in other words. U.S. leaders are particularly predisposed to believe that their actions are responsible for positive outcomes like peace.

Third, self-perception appears to be directly related to egocentric attributions. Individuals with high self-esteem are more likely to believe that they are at the center of the decision-making process of others than those who think of themselves more modestly.[107] Leaders of any unipolar state may well be more likely to hold their country in high regard and more vulnerable to exaggerated egocentric perceptions than their contemporaries in smaller states. It might not occur to the lead diplomat of other counties to claim, as did Madeleine Albright, that "if we have to use force, it is because we are America; we are the indispensable nation. We stand tall and we see further than other countries into the future."[108] Her predecessor as secretary of state, Henry Kissinger, said this two decades earlier: "Without our commitment to international security, there can be no stable peace. Without our constructive participation in the world economy, there can be no hope for economic progress. Without our dedication to human liberty, the prospect of freedom in the world is dim indeed."[109] American exceptionalism makes the U.S. security community even more vulnerable to this misperception than average.

A classic case of egocentrism in action took place in Washington in December 1979, following the Soviet invasion of Afghanistan.

Documents released from Russian archives make it clear that Moscow acted primarily to remove a troublesome puppet regime in its near-abroad.[110] President Carter and his administration, however, interpreted the invasion as the first step in a grand design on the Persian Gulf.[111] Despite the fact that the United States had made no effort to deter the Soviets in Central Asia, Carter assumed that they were testing U.S. mettle. His reaction—or overreaction, labeling the invasion the "greatest threat to peace since World War II"—turned a local crisis into a global one and scuttled détente.[112]

In more recent times, many in the U.S. security community believed that the United States played a decisive role in Vladimir Putin's decisions regarding Crimea and eastern Ukraine. President Obama's various critics argued that perceptions of American weakness inspired or even invited Russian aggression. The refusal to act in Syria in particular emboldened Moscow (even though in 2008, despite ample U.S. action in the Middle East, Moscow had proven sufficiently bold to send troops into Georgia). Other critics suggested that a variety of provocative U.S. behaviors since the end of the Cold War, especially the expansion of NATO and dissolution of the Anti-Ballistic Missile Treaty, poisoned U.S.-Russian relations and led to an increase in Kremlin paranoia and eventually to the invasion.[113] So, either through weakness or bullying, we were responsible for their actions.

Egocentric misperceptions are so ubiquitous and pervasive that they generate something of a law of political psychology: We *are probably less influential in* their *decision making than we think we are.* While it may be natural for U.S. policy makers to interpret their role as crucial in the maintenance of world peace, it is very likely that Washington exaggerates its importance in the decision making of others and in the maintenance of international stability.

The effect of the egocentric bias may be especially difficult for the unipolar United States to resist because other countries do regularly take Washington's position into account before acting. But U.S. leaders, and the people who analyze them, should keep in mind that they are still probably less important to calculations made in other capitals than they believe. As a result, hegemony and the New Peace may be epiphe-nomenal, each existing alongside the other without interacting.

## OVERESTIMATED BENEVOLENCE

After three years in the White House, Ronald Reagan had learned something surprising: "Many people at the top of the Soviet hierarchy were genuinely afraid of America and Americans," he wrote in his autobiography.

> Perhaps this shouldn't have surprised me, but it did . . . I'd always felt that from our deeds it must be clear to anyone that Americans were a moral people who starting at the birth of our nation had always used our power only as a force for good in the world. . . . During my first years in Washington, I think many of us took it for granted that the Russians, like ourselves, considered it unthinkable that the United States would launch a first strike against them.[114]

Reagan is certainly not alone in believing in the essential benevolent image of his nation. People find it exceedingly difficult to imagine that anyone could interpret their actions in negative ways. Actors are well aware of their own motives and assume that their peaceful intentions are transparent. We all overestimate the extent to which others see us as benevolent.

Hegemonic-stability theorists purport to understand the perceptions of others, at times better than those others understand themselves. Complain as they may at times, foreigners know that the United States is acting in the common interest. Objections to unipolarity, even though they are at times widespread, are not "very seriously intended," wrote Kagan, since "the truth about America's dominant role in the world is known to most observers. And the truth is that the benevolent hege-mony exercised by the United States is good for a vast portion of the world's population."[115] In the 1990s, Russian protests regarding NATO expansion—though nearly universal—were not taken seriously, since U.S. planners believed the alliance's benevolent intentions were apparent to all. Sagacious Russians understood that expansion would actually be beneficial, since it would bring stability to their western border.[116] President Clinton and Secretary of State Warren Christopher were caught off guard by the hostility of their counterparts regarding the issue at a summit in Budapest in December 1994.[117] Despite warnings from the vast majority of academic and policy experts about the likely Russian reaction, the administration failed to anticipate Moscow's position.[118] The Russians did not seem to believe American assurances that expansion would actually be good for them. The United States overestimated the degree to which others saw it as benevolent.

Psychologists have long understood the significant differences in perception between actors and observers.[119] One is so widespread and common that it has come to be known as the "fundamental attribution error" in accounting for the choices made by others: actors attribute the undesirable behavior of others to *dispositional* rather than *situational* factors, even though they feel the opposite is true for their own actions. In other words, although we understand that *our* actions are highly dependent upon the situation in which we find ourselves, we believe that *their* behavior is a reflection of *who they are*, of their immutable character flaws.[120] Early in the Cold War, to cite a brief example, Secretary of State Dean Acheson had no doubts that Soviet requests for bases on the Dardanelles in Turkey were clear evidence of their aggressive ambitions, while a very similar U.S. action—fortifying U.S. installations on the Panama Canal—was an understandable response to legitimate security concerns.[121]

Actors are quick to take responsibility for positive outcomes and refuse blame for negative. This effect is directly related to the intensity of the harm: when severe, we strongly deny our culpability.[122] This is partially a defense mechanism. Actors also believe that any behavior leading to negative outcomes is inconsistent with their general character, which everybody more or less knows to be true.[123] It should be unsurprising that U.S. observers fail to perceive the same amount of damage, either direct or collateral, caused by their policies as do others.

Once again, the culture of the United States might make its leaders more vulnerable to this misperception. The need for positive self-regard appears to be particularly strong in North American societies.[124] Western egos tend to be gratified through self-promotion rather than humility and independence rather than interdependence. Americans are more likely to feel good if they are unique rather than a good cog in society's wheel. The strong need to be perceived as benevolent, though universal, may well exert stronger encouragement for U.S. observers to project their perceptions onto others.

Foreign ungratefulness always surprises U.S. leaders. In 2003, Condoleezza Rice was dismayed to discover resistance to U.S. initiatives in Iraq: "There were times," she said later, "that it appeared that American power was seen to be more dangerous than, perhaps, Saddam Hussein."[125] Both liberals and neoconservatives probably exaggerate the extent to which U.S. hegemony is everywhere secretly welcomed. Understandable disagreement with U.S. policies, rather than mere petulant resentment, motivates counterhegemonic beliefs and behavior. The international community always has to worry about the potential for police brutality, even if it occurs only rarely. The United States almost certainly frightens others more than its leaders perceive. A quarter of the 68,000 respondents to a 2013 Gallup poll in sixty-five countries identified the United States as the "greatest threat to world peace," which was more than three times the total for the second-place country (Pakistan).[126] One suspects that when post-Trump polls begin to arrive, they will show similar disquiet in the periphery.

To review, if U.S. leaders and analysts are subject to the same forces that affect every human being, they overestimate the amount of control Washington has over other actors and its importance in their decision making. And they probably perceive U.S. benevolence to be much greater than do others. These common phenomena all influence U.S. beliefs in the same direction and may well increase the apparent explanatory power of hegemony beyond what the facts would otherwise support. The United States is probably not as central to the New Peace as either liberals or neoconservatives believe.

## THE GREAT YELLOWSTONE COUNTERFACTUAL

What would the world look like without the United States? What would happen if unipolarity came to a sudden, unequivocal end? Such an outcome is not as difficult to imagine as it may seem. One of the most picturesque U.S. national parks is actually the caldera of an enormous supervolcano, which on occasion in the distant past has erupted with more force than any event in human history. Someday it will do so again. And the United States as we know it will all but cease to exist.

No volcano is more closely monitored, in anticipation of that day when seismic activity begins to increase across the park. Over the course of a few weeks—if we are lucky—telltale signs of rising magma will signal what is coming. Ground deformations, gas releases, and even small eruptions would probably precede the cataclysm, providing time for some measure of evacuations. Once the main chamber blows, a disaster of truly unprecedented magnitude would unfold. When it ends, a month or so later, the United States would find itself buried under billions of tons of ash. Decades of recovery would follow, during which time unipolarity would come to a definitive, dramatic end.

How would the system respond? Could the New Peace survive without its policeman? Good counterfactual analysis minimizes the number of both assumptions and alterations of reality. It is also obviously wise to choose relatively simple cases, ones that do not involve many potentially confounding variables.[127] The ramifications of an actual supervolcanic blast would not be contained in the United States; the massive amount of material ejected into the atmosphere would blot out the sun and cause global temperatures to drop for years. To keep this thought experiment manageable, let us imagine a natural disaster that only affects the United States, one resulting in the effective disappearance of U.S. military and political engagement with the rest of the world.

The effect of an aloof United States on some regions need not be imagined because it already exists. In South America, the U.S. Southern Command has a minuscule operating budget and no troops to speak of, despite its theoretical "responsibility" for the entire continent. The

United States maintains no significant physical presence in Africa or large swaths of Asia. A Yellowstone supereruption would presumably not change security calculations in these areas much at all.

Europe would be similarly unaffected, at least in the short term. The United States currently maintains 95,000 troops from all services in its European Command, none of whom are tasked with maintaining the internal stability of its allies. During the Cold War, U.S. troops did not involve themselves in the domestic conflicts of their host states, unlike their Soviet counterparts. Their job was always to protect Europe from without, not within. The continent is the world's most stable, its countries the most cooperative, and its people the least martial. It would probably take more than the removal of U.S. troops for ash-cleaning duties to bring back security dilemmas, arms races, and conflict. Borders have hardened, as have norms of conflict resolution. No one can know for sure, of course, but Europe does not seem to be a good candidate for chaos in the absence of the United States.

Without the presence of U.S. forces, much of the Middle East would be unstable and chaotic. With the presence of U.S. forces, much of the Middle East is unstable and chaotic. A supervolcano erupting in Wyoming would not have much impact on the security of the world's most dangerous region. Israel would be just as safe as it was before, since its marked military superiority over all potential rivals is the ultimate guarantor of its security, not U.S. troops or ships. Without the prospect of help from Uncle Sam, the failing governments of Iraq and Libya, as well as the rebels in Syria and our allies in Saudi Arabia, Yemen, Jordan, and elsewhere, would learn to become more self-sufficient. Perhaps they would even make long-term deals with their rivals. It might be good to throw them out of the U.S. nest and encourage them to fly on their own or crash. Fears of a resurgent Iran would be articulated by the usual suspects, no doubt, but both history and the realities of power suggest Tehran would find it hard to dominate its neighbors, even if it had the will to do so.

The regions that would be of most concern in such a scenario would be the peripheries of those once and potentially future great powers, Russia and China. To believers in the "deterrence model," first described by Robert Jervis four decades ago, weakness is provocative, and the post-U.S. world would seem everywhere weak.[128] Moscow and Beijing would attempt to expand their influence, and ultimately perhaps their borders, once they were assured that they would face no pushback from Washington. Perhaps gradual interference in their near-abroads, such as we have already seen in eastern Ukraine, northern Georgia, and the South China Sea, would occur with increasing frequency in the vacuum left by a U.S. withdrawal.

While such expansion cannot be ruled out, especially in the long run, large border adjustments would probably not occur in the absence of U.S. power, for least two reasons. First, the removal of American troops would not alter the calculations regarding the costs and benefits of conquest in the twenty-first century. Although absorbing neighbors sometimes paid substantial dividends in the pre–information age, today territory is unrelated to wealth.[129] The people of larger states are not automatically better off than those of small ones. India is not richer than Singapore; Russia would not benefit from invading Ukraine; China would hardly be materially better off if it ruled Taiwan. The other members of the international system might not be able to stop such adventurism militarily, but they can certainly punish it economically. The costs related to invasion and the inevitable problems that arise during occupation would outweigh any possible benefits that may accrue. Conquest in a trading system is profoundly irrational, and the incentives for peace are strong.

Rational calculations are not the only motivations for cross-border violence. As Norman Angell argued a century ago, people have to believe that war is not worth the cost before they will forswear it.[130] The quest for glory and prestige has sent many an army into motion over the centuries; Alfred Thayer Mahan responded to Angell's rationalism a century ago by pointing out that "nations are under no illusion as to the unprofitableness of war itself" but honor often compels them to fight anyway.[131] By 2017, however, those calculations have changed. It is not at all clear that glory still automatically accompanies conquest. The second reason to believe that Russia and China might not dominate their near-abroads in an essentially U.S.-free world is that the behavioral norms of the New Peace discourage aggression. Imperialism invites opprobrium, not admiration. This does not mean that such assaults could not happen—Genghis Khan was unconcerned about opprobrium, for instance, and Vladimir Putin might be too—but surely it is significant that conquest has been all but absent since the Second World War. The unipole is not the only thing restraining potential combatants; both their material and reputational interests do so as well.

If and when a catastrophic supervolcanic eruption weakens the United States, other countries would still have substantial interest in maintaining the overlapping network of international economic and political institutions that serve the interests of all members. All would want to see free trade and investment continue unmolested, whether or not the global policeman could punish violators. Most would continue to place some value on international law, human rights, and the UN system. Why any state would want to move backward to a mercantilist time of pure self-help and violence would be difficult to imagine. It is 2017, not 1717.

Volcanologists assure us that someday Yellowstone will awaken with terrifying fury. The human and material cost will be immense, but the ramifications for international security may not be as dramatic. While it might take that kind of event to settle the questions concerning hegemonic-stability theory once and for all, we can still use our imaginations to anticipate the kind of reaction that the system would have if the global 911 is taken off the hook. Even more decisively than a Trump superpresidency, a supervolcano eruption would test the New Peace and settle forever debates over the importance of unipolarity. Until then, one can only imagine what the system would be like without the United States. And the smart money would be with those who say that it would probably look pretty much the same, with very small amounts of conflict and warfare, even if few people seem to notice.

———— ∞ ————

In the end, what can be definitely said about the relationship between U.S. power and international stability? Probably not much that will satisfy partisans. The pacifying virtue of U.S. hegemony will remain largely an article of faith in some circles in the policy world. Like most beliefs, it will resist alteration by logic and evidence. Beliefs rarely change, so debates rarely end.

For those not yet fully converted, however, perhaps it will be significant that corroborating evidence for the relationship is extremely hard to identify. If indeed hegemonic stability exists, it does so without leaving much of a trace. Neither Washington's spending, nor its interventions, nor its overall grand strategy seem to matter much to the levels of armed conflict around the world (apart from those wars that Uncle Sam starts). The empirical record does not contain much support for the notion that unipolarity and the New Peace are related. At the same time, three common psychological phenomena suggest that hegemonic stability is particularly susceptible to misperception. U.S. leaders probably exaggerate the degree to which their power matters. Researchers will need to look elsewhere to explain why the world has entered the most peaceful period in its history.

The good news from this is that the New Peace will probably persist for quite some time, no matter how dominant the United States is, how much it spends on policing, or how much resentment its actions cause in the periphery. The Trump administration will put it to a tough test; if it passes, the New Peace will probably be here to stay. Its existence may well be attributable less to any security or institutions created by a hegemon than to a normative order that would exist with or without it. The people of the twenty-first century are likely to be much safer and more secure than any of their predecessors (even if many of them do not always believe it), no matter how dominant is the United States.

# 2

## UNIPOLARITY AND
## NUCLEAR WEAPONS

The ever-present threat of nuclear annihilation was one of the Cold War's less charming features. Although rational calculations from think tanks and universities suggested that deterrence would maintain a stable peace, citizens of the superpowers went to bed at night unsure if their sleep would be interrupted by air-raid sirens and a blinding flash of light. Many were resigned to the notion that, sooner or later, those sirens would sound. The average person rests better now that the "horror of nuclear," to use President Trump's words, has receded.[1]

That average person might be surprised to discover that those same think tanks and universities that seemed so calm in the face of past nuclear dangers are worried about the present. Optimism has been relatively rare in the community of defense intellectuals regarding nuclear issues since the Soviet Union collapsed. Expectations for the new, post–Cold War age have been quite negative regarding many aspects of security, and nuclear weapons have been no exception. Proliferation, instability, regional wars, and catastrophic terrorism were widely expected to be hallmarks of what soon became known as the "second nuclear age."[2]

This chapter examines the expectations, evidence, and psychology of this second nuclear age. While not all the works under discussion fit together well, they all are part of the broad renaissance in nuclear-weapons studies that has occurred since the end of the Cold War. The first section reviews the assertions commonly made during this renaissance, and the second compares them to twenty-five years of accumulated evidence. It renders judgment, to the extent possible, on the relationship between nuclear weapons and unipolarity, arguing that the second nuclear age is likely to be substantially less dangerous than the first. Why, then, does pessimism dominate? The chapter concludes with an examination of the psychological foundation of nuclear pessimism, including the puzzling nostalgia for the Cold War that pervades so much of this literature. Popular perceptions regarding nuclear weapons are once again different from those of the expert, and this time they seem more rational: The unipolar world is significantly better in almost every respect than the one that preceded it.

## THE SECOND NUCLEAR AGE: EXPECTATIONS

The moment when many people began to take seriously the possibility of fundamentally new nuclear rules came in 1998, when India and Pakistan conducted a round of tests. "Atomic weapons have returned for a second act," wrote one of this literature's major figures, Paul Bracken. For him, "1998 was the turning point."[3] Once South Asia "had broken free of Western nuclear controls," he argued, other countries in the "arc of terror" would surely follow.[4] Others mark its beginning somewhat earlier, but all those who write about the second nuclear age (hereafter SNA, when used as an adjective) attempt to describe and predict behavior regarding nuclear weapons in a unipolar world. "It is a second age," according to Bracken, "because it has nothing to do with the central fact of the first nuclear age, the cold war."[5] Taken as a whole, these analysts are a rather pessimistic lot, skeptical about the prospects for stability and nonproliferation in the absence of a superpower to balance the United States. This basic structural dynamic will lead to a number of unpleasant outcomes.

First and most obviously, the second nuclear age is likely to be marked by a great deal more proliferation than the first. According to Bracken, the "overarching theme" of the age will be the "breakdown of the major power monopoly over the bomb."[6] Unipolarity provides strong incentives for smaller states, who have no hope of balancing the United States, to pursue nuclear weapons. No matter how much effort the United States puts into non- and counterproliferation, "nuclear weapons will nevertheless spread, with a new member occasionally joining the club," predicted Kenneth Waltz.[7] "The most likely scenario in the wake of the Cold War," argued John Mearsheimer, "is further nuclear proliferation in Europe," and "it is not likely the proliferation will be well managed."[8] Instability and insecurity would spread, as would nuclear weapons, throughout the global South.[9] Since new nuclear states were almost inevitable, both Waltz and Mearsheimer felt that it was in the interest of the West to attempt to manage, and indeed even to encourage, gradual proliferation to help stabilize the system.

These chains of proliferation will lead to new, potentially unstable nuclear rivalries. Were North Korea to be accepted as the ninth nuclear-weapons state, Graham Allison warned in 2004, South Korea and Japan would build their own arsenals "by the end of the decade."[10] The second nuclear age will be "much more decentralized," with "many independent nuclear decision centers."[11] A "multipolar nuclear order" is on the horizon, if it has not already arrived.[12]

The new nuclear powers are not likely to resemble the old. The second major assumption of the SNA literature is that proliferation will reach less enlightened parts of the globe, those led by unpredictable, semirational tyrants. The old rules of deterrence may not apply, since the motivations of these actors are not only less knowable but often ruled by passions and nationalism. "The idea of budding defense intellectuals sitting around computer models and debating strategy in Iran or Pakistan defies credulity," or at least Bracken's estimation, since in these states "hysterical nationalism" overrules rationality.[13] The "overdetermined" cascades of proliferation across Asia will bring a host of new, less trustworthy actors into the nuclear camp, from rogue states to nonstate actors, all of whom will be essentially undeterrable by traditional means.[14] Their motivations will be less rational or simply less transparent to the outside world.

In the second nuclear age, not just an accidental but the intentional use of nuclear weapons by new nuclear actors cannot be ruled out.[15] Rogue states do not seek nuclear weapons for the reasons that motivated earlier proliferants. While all U.S. observers believe that Washington's arsenal exists for *defensive* purposes, to deter any attack that our enemies would otherwise contemplate, the primary use of new nuclear weapons will be *offensive*. The possibility for irrationality in new nuclear powers inspired the United States to scrap the Anti-Ballistic Missile Treaty and begin thinking about how to "tailor" deterrence to target smaller actors.[16] A nuclear Iran will use its weapons to bully or even attack, not deter. In 2017, experts warned that North Korean intercontinental ballistic missiles would be coercive, to extract concessions from U.S. allies. "North Korea's contempt for its neighbors suggests that it would hold them hostage with its nuclear weapons," wrote the widely respected ambassador Chris Hill. "Would proliferation stop with South Korea and Japan? What about Taiwan?"[17] As a result, the basic assumptions of deterrence need to be rethought.

Third, preventive wars will be much more likely in the second nuclear age than they were in the first.[18] The unipolar state is an essentially status-quo power with strong incentives to prevent nuclear proliferation, especially if it involves states with disconcertingly inconsistent relationships with rationality.[19] The process of nuclearization, always profoundly unstable, will be even more dangerous now. Since many states may be interested in developing their own nuclear programs very soon, the risk of counterproliferation wars should increase.[20]

Preemptive and preventive wars might not be the only ones becoming more frequent. The fourth characteristic of the new age expected by those who described it was an intensification of regional rivalries. The removal of the stabilizing influence of the superpowers will encourage local actors to take new steps to assure their security. Regional powers may well feel simultaneously less safe without the backing of their former patron and less constrained in their own actions. In security terms, this means that the reach of "nuclear umbrellas" has shrunk. Extended deterrence (the promise to retaliate if one's allies are attacked), some-thing upon which few NATO members could completely depend during the Cold War, is particularly hard to take seriously now that it is over. The credibility of U.S. commitments to its partners will decrease along with their strategic significance. Threats to retaliate in the periphery will not be as effective, and more regional wars—even nuclear wars—may be on the horizon.[21] As a result, many expected to see the reemergence of security dilemmas, regional arms races, and their attendant negative effects on international relationships.

Fifth, other observers have been more concerned about dangers arising from reverse vertical proliferation. The erosion of Russian spending on (and attention to) its arsenal led some to question the viability of mutual assured destruction (MAD) in the second nuclear age. The United States appears to be approaching "nuclear primacy" as a result, and the results could be destabilizing.[22] A Kremlin without full confidence in its aging early-warning radar systems might grow increasingly concerned about its vulnerability to the dreaded bolt-from-the-blue attack. "To the extent that great power peace stems from the pacifying effects of nuclear weapons," explained Lieber and Press in a widely read piece, "it currently rests on a shaky foundation."[23] That foundation grows shakier as the second nuclear age, and U.S. technology, advances. Second-strike capabilities might no longer be what they once were.[24]

Finally, contributors to the nuclear-studies renaissance worry a great deal about the potential for catastrophic terrorism. The "Managing the Atom" project at Harvard's Belfer Center leads the concerned: "If terrorists do get their hands on a nuclear device or on highly enriched uranium or plutonium," warned Graham Allison, the project's founder, "they could easily make a bomb operational within a year."[25] He and others have repeatedly claimed that anyone with a master's (or, at times, merely a bachelor's) degree in physics could assemble a nuclear weapon if they acquired fissile material. Daniel Deudney worried about "nuclear leakage" to unsavory characters, which would lead to an age of "omniviolence."[26]

Perhaps some SNA theorists knew that their rhetoric was a bit over-heated at times but rationalized their occasional use of hyperbole as a necessary tool to shock society into awareness regarding the ongoing dangers posed by nuclear stockpiles. A skeptic might suggest that perhaps some had also noted the ease with which fear sells books. Even if the SNA literature had more than one inspiration, its tone is homogenous: pessimism dominates, with most theorists arguing that the risk of nuclear use has risen dramatically in the unipolar world. As of this writing, the Doomsday Clock maintained by the *Bulletin of the Atomic Scientists* stands at two-and-a-half minutes to midnight, which is closer to Armageddon than at almost any time in the past.[27] Bracken has even wondered whether it will be "possible for countries to survive the second nuclear age."[28]

## THE SECOND NUCLEAR AGE: EVIDENCE

The removal of the Cold War rivalry has indeed had a rather dramatic effect on the world's relationship with its nuclear weapons, but not quite in the way described above. Most careful observers of international politics would probably agree that, so far, there have been no regional nuclear wars, and no cities have disappeared under a terrorist's mushroom cloud. While those SNA concerns can be dismissed without much discussion, others might deserve a bit more examination.

### PROLIFERATION

The first quarter-century of unipolarity has been remarkably good for the nonproliferation regime. As it turns out, the great powers did not take Mearsheimer up on his recommendation to aid would-be proliferators. Thus far, at least, the second nuclear age has been much less dangerous than the first.

Proliferation comes in two forms, horizontal and vertical. The former refers to the spread of weapons capability from country to country; the latter concerns the accumulation and development of weapons within countries. The superpowers tried to discourage horizontal proliferation during the Cold War while engaging in rather gaudy vertical proliferation of their own. Neither form has occurred since its end.

Two states founded the nuclear club in the 1940s (the United States and the USSR), one more joined in the 1950s (the United Kingdom), and two each in the sixties (France and China), seventies (India and Israel), and eighties (Pakistan and South Africa). In the 1990s, there were no new members, and only one has joined in the new century. The same number of states possesses nuclear capability in 2017 as did in 1990, for a net horizontal proliferation rate of zero (see table 2.1).

Three states that inherited part of the Soviet arsenal (Belarus, Ukraine, and Kazakhstan) peacefully surrendered the weapons, against the advice of some outside observers.[29] At the time of this writing, the middle of 2017, for the first time in eight decades, no country is actively pursuing nuclear weapons, which is an underappreciated development. Nuclear testing has effectively ground to a halt outside of the Korean peninsula.

Meanwhile, the number of nuclear-*capable* states continues to grow. Although enthusiasm for nuclear power waxes and wanes alongside oil-price fluctuations and climate-change fears, the process is not secret. In April 2017, 449 nuclear reactors generated power for thirty different countries.[30] All industrialized states, and quite a few less industrialized

TABLE 2.1 Horizontal Proliferation in the Second Nuclear Age

| States with nuclear weapons, 2017 | States with nuclear weapons, 1990 |
| --- | --- |
| United States | United States |
| Russia | USSR |
| United Kingdom | United Kingdom |
| France | France |
| China | China |
| Israel | Israel |
| India | India |
| Pakistan | Pakistan |
| North Korea | South Africa |

ones, are capable of building nuclear weapons.[31] But no new ones are doing it.

The supposedly landmark events that began the second nuclear age in earnest have proven profoundly unimportant. No proliferation cascades followed the 1998 Indian and Pakistani tests, which, it is helpful to recall, were only a reminder of what was already widely known: both countries had nuclear arsenals.[32] India conducted its first test in 1974, insisting that it was a "peaceful nuclear device."[33] Pakistan was unconvinced, and had developed its own weapons by the 1980s, although it refrained from testing. Domestic political calculations had changed in 1998, not international conditions.[34] The tests were irrelevant to both the nonproliferation regime and geopolitics of the subcontinent.

Only one state has acquired nuclear weapons during unipolarity, but it is a prominent one. The anxiety generated by the new North Korean arsenal and its evolving delivery system may outweigh any optimism generated by otherwise negative proliferation momentum. Perhaps it is not the quantity of proliferation that should worry us but the quality; perhaps one North Korean nuclear program is the functional equivalent, in terms of its ability to inject instability into the system, of six from Canada or the Nordic countries. In March 2017, Secretary of State Rex Tillerson announced that the era of "strategic patience" with North Korea was over and that preemptive action was a real possibility.[35] Former ambassador John Bolton is not alone in worrying that accurate long-range missiles would allow them to become a "full-fledged" nuclear state.[36] Apparently North Korea has only been a partially fledged nuclear state since 2006, when it tested its first weapon.

Since that time, however, the so-called hermit kingdom has hardly acted irrationally. Indeed, its behavior has not changed at all. Pyongyang engaged in a consistent series of aggressive actions long before it acquired nuclear weapons, including assassinating dissidents, seizing U.S. Navy vessels (and torturing captured crews), shooting down U.S. reconnaissance aircraft, sinking South Korean ships, infiltrating special forces into the South, and other misdeeds. They are no more aggressive today than they were throughout the first nuclear age.

Pyongyang (and Trump's Washington) provides strong evidence for one of the most basic lessons from Foreign Policy Analysis 101: Much more wisdom comes from watching what countries do than from listening to what their leaders say, since the latter is often primarily designed for domestic audiences. North Korean rhetoric is maniacal, but its actions are usually somewhat rational and restrained, far more so than commonly perceived.[37] The world's newest nuclear-weapons state has not used its weapons for offensive purposes and appears to be just as deterrable as all those that preceded it. It is worth remembering that the Soviet Union joined the nuclear club when its leader was at the height of his paranoid mania and in complete control of his arsenal, yet even Stalin acted rationally when it came to atomic affairs.

Predictions of further rogue-state proliferation have not been borne out by events. The most obvious example of this is Iran, whose program has been halted, at least temporarily. The controversial and awkwardly named "Joint Comprehensive Plan of Action" (JCPOA) dramatically complicated Tehran's path toward a bomb for fifteen years, and probably more, if it is renegotiated and renewed in 2030.[38] No contributor to the SNA literature anticipated that agreement or offered much hope for the prospect that Iran could be kept nonnuclear without what might be euphemistically called preventive counterproliferation. Indeed, a number of analysts called openly for a preemptive strike on Iran, an outcome they deemed preferable to trusting Tehran's basic rationality. "Iran's rapid nuclear development will ultimately force the United States to choose between a conventional conflict and a possible nuclear war," wrote Matthew Kroenig on behalf of the former option.[39] Six days before the framework for the deal was announced, former ambassador John Bolton warned that "Iran will not negotiate away its nuclear program." "Mr. Obama's fascination with an Iranian nuclear deal always had an air of unreality," he wrote. "The inconvenient truth is that only military action . . . can accomplish what is required."[40] Fortunately no such choice was necessary. The various proliferation cascades so many anticipated throughout the Middle East have been put on hold for now, at least, as the Trump era begins.

It is also surely worth noting that Iran may not have been as determined to develop nuclear weapons as has been widely assumed. Both
U.S. and Israeli intelligence believe that Tehran never made any final
decisions to nuclearize. According a 2007 U.S. National Intelligence
Estimate, which remains the assessment of the entire community, Iran
essentially abandoned its efforts to develop a bomb in 2003.[41] Tehran's
insistence that it had no active program was dismissed by those whose
judgments were based not on inside information but on distrust of Iran,
which led them to believe that they thought they understood the Islamic
Republic better than did intelligence professionals (who rarely have an
incentive to underestimate). The JCPOA might have put an end to a program that had already effectively ended.

Despite widespread concerns to the contrary, the nonproliferation
regime has proven even more robust in the second nuclear age than it was
in the first. The story is even better regarding vertical proliferation: There
are far fewer nuclear weapons on the planet after the first twenty-five
years of unipolarity. The largest arsenals shrank the most precipitously,
decreasing the overall number of warheads by over 70 percent. The United
Kingdom and France maintain far fewer weapons than they did during
the Cold War, and despite threats to build a new generation of warheads following the election of Trump, thus far the Chinese arsenal
remains essentially unchanged.[42] Only India and Pakistan experienced
meaningful vertical proliferation in the first decades of the second
nuclear age (see table 2.2).

Moscow has taken steps to address its eroding second-strike capabilities. The Russians embarked upon a nuclear modernization program in
2011, spending billions to upgrade systems and replace older weapons
with new ones.[43] This renewed activity may or may not imperil bilateral
arms-control treaties, but if it continues it should alleviate concerns that
the United States is about to achieve nuclear primacy, with all its potentially destabilizing tensions. While the capability to take out an opponent's arsenal with a bolt-from-the-blue attack has been a concern of
theorists since the dawn of the nuclear age, no state has appeared eager
to put theory into practice. Reluctance to use these weapons, whether
as a result of a taboo or merely prudent caution, is a central feature of

TABLE 2.2  Vertical Proliferation in the Second Nuclear Age

| Total warheads | United States | Russia | China | United Kingdom | France | India | Pakistan | Israel | North Korea | South Africa | Global total |
|---|---|---|---|---|---|---|---|---|---|---|---|
| 1990 | 21,392 | 37,000 | 230 | 422 | 420 | 7 | 4 | 53 | 0 | 6 | 59,534 |
| 2017 | 6,800 | 7,000 | 260 | 215 | 300 | 110 | 140 | ~80 | ~10 | 0 | 14,915 |

*Source:* Estimates of 1990 arsenals: Robert Norris and Hans M. Kristensen, "Global Nuclear Inventories, 1945–2010," *Bulletin of the Atomic Scientists* 66, no. 4 (July 2010): 77–83. Most up-to-date estimates are taken from the Arms Control Association, "Nuclear Weapons: Who Has What at a Glance," January 2017, https://www.armscontrol.org/factsheets/Nuclearweaponswhohaswhat.

both the first and second nuclear ages.[44] Improvements in targeting or intelligence have not (yet?) weakened the basic logic of MAD, which was put to the test far more often in the first nuclear era.

Nuclear experts are perpetually identifying tipping points at which the world stands. Despite a vast decrease in the number of weapons and net-zero horizontal proliferation, the world always finds itself on the precipice of disaster, only a few minutes from midnight. Fortunately, the nonproliferation regime is far less fragile than the SNA theorists feared. The pace of proliferation in the second nuclear age has thus far been substantially slower than most predicted.

## PREEMPTION AND PREVENTION

How much credit can preemption take for these negative proliferation trends? The only unambiguously preventive war of the second nuclear age—the 2003 invasion of Iraq—had nothing to do with nuclear weapons, even if it was occasionally (and disingenuously) sold that way. "We know he [Saddam Hussein] has been absolutely devoted to trying to acquire nuclear weapons," Vice President Dick Cheney said on *Meet the Press* four days before the tanks rolled. "And we believe he has, in fact, reconstituted nuclear weapons."[45] It is unclear who the vice president meant by "we," because no one in the U.S. government or security community thought that Iraq had "reconstituted" nuclear weapons in March 2003.[46] Erroneous beliefs regarding other weapons of mass destruction were among the reasons for the war, but it was not the kind of preemptive strike on a nuclear program foreseen by SNA theorists.

Iran was not the only rogue state to abandon its nuclear program without a fight. At times denuclearization occurred by choice, as with Libya, while at others nonproliferation was thrust upon states, as was the case with the inchoate Syrian program. Colonel Qaddafi's motivation for his decision to shut down his WMD programs has been the subject of ferocious and heavily partisan debate. At issue is the extent to which the war in Iraq affected his calculations: was Qaddafi concerned about being the next target of U.S. counterproliferation, or was his decision a reflection of a broader effort to remove his government from the list of international pariahs? Supporters of the Bush administration posit a direct connection between the war and the colonel's sudden change of heart. Negotiations with Qaddafi had begun some years earlier under the Clinton administration, however, leading a number of observers to conclude that Libya would have abandoned its program whether or not the war in Iraq had occurred.[47] More recent work on the issue suggests that fear of being next on the U.S. target list did affect Qaddafi's thinking and can at the very least account for the timing of his offer to disarm.[48] "Disarm" is probably not the right word, however, since Libya had nowhere near the requisite state capacity to build a bomb, and Gaddafi probably knew it. After the NATO intervention, IAEA inspectors found centrifuges and other crucial materials in their original packing crates, where they had apparently been for years.[49] Libya may have announced it would not be joining the nuclear club following the invasion of Iraq, but that was likely a conclusion it had reached some time before. For these purposes, it is sufficient to note that Libya has abandoned its program for the foreseeable future. Diplomacy worked, the nonproliferation regime held, and the rogue-state list shrank by one member.[50]

While it cannot yet be said that the 2007 Israeli airstrikes on a reactor construction site permanently removed the possibility of a Syrian nuclear weapon, the program has not restarted since the attack. Three-and-a-half years passed between those strikes and the current civil war, during which Assad presumably had plenty of time to reestablish his reactors, should he have desired to do so. Instead it appears that his government abandoned its efforts, which had not progressed very far anyway.[51] American intelligence had never been confident about Syria's desire to build nuclear weapons in the first place, in large part because additional facilities required for such an effort were not under construction.[52]

Overall, while preemption occurred in the second nuclear age, its pace is not increasing. Israel, for example, struck facilities of its Arab neighbors during the first nuclear age as often as in the second. Nonproliferation in the Middle East has come in different forms in the unipolar era, from high-level diplomacy to air strikes. But the outcomes have been roughly the same, and nightmares of a region in a "nuclear context," or a gallery of nuclear-armed rogues, have not come to pass.

## TERRORISM

Finally, despite the string of bleak and terrifying projections from a variety of experts, nuclear weapons have remained well beyond the capabilities of the modern apocalyptic terrorist. The great fear of the SNA literature, that scientific knowledge and technology would gradually become more accessible to nonstate actors, has remained only a nightmare. Nor does there appear to be a great reservoir of fissile material in the world's various black markets, waiting to be weaponized.[53]

Just because something has not yet occurred does not mean that it cannot or will not eventually. However, it is worth noting that the world has not experienced any close calls regarding nuclear terrorism. Forecasting unique events is a necessarily dicey enterprise, but one way to improve accuracy is to examine events that have already or almost happened. Given the many complexities involved with nuclear weapons, especially for amateurs (as any terrorists would almost certainly be), it is not unreasonable to expect a few failures to precede success. While it is possible that we might not know about all the plots disrupted by international law enforcement, keeping the lid on nuclear near-misses would presumably be no small task. As of this writing, the public is aware of no serious attempts to construct, steal, or purchase nuclear weapons, much less smuggle and detonate one. "Leakage" does not seem to be a problem yet. Knock wood.

The uniformly pessimistic projections about the second nuclear era have not, at least thus far, been borne out by events. Post–Cold War trends have instead been generally moving in directions opposite to these expectations, with fewer nuclear weapons in the hands of the same number of countries and none pursuing more. Why, then, does nuclear pessimism persist? What are the roots of the current fashionable unwillingness—or even inability—to detect positive patterns in nuclear security?

## PSYCHOLOGY AND THE SECOND NUCLEAR ERA

"I look back wistfully at the Cold War," said James Inhofe, the ranking Republican in the Senate Armed Services Committee, in February 2014. "There were two superpowers, they knew what we had, we knew what they had, mutually assured destruction meant something. It doesn't mean anything anymore."[54] Inhofe is hardly alone. When he was secretary of defense, Robert Gates was fond of noting that the Cold War was "less complex" than the current era.[55] Secretary of State Rex Tillerson expressed this clearly in his first major address to his department in May 2017. "In many respects the Cold War was a lot easier," he said, employing the trademark eloquence of the Trump administration.

> Things were pretty clear, the Soviet Union had a lot of things contained, and I had a conversation with Secretary-General Guterres at the UN. He described it as during the Cold War, we froze history. History just stopped in its tracks because so many of the dynamics that existed for centuries were contained. They were contained with heavy authoritarianism. And when the Cold War ended and the Soviet Union broke up, we took all of that off, and history regained its march. And the world got a whole lot more complicated. And I think that's what we see. It has become much more complicated in terms of old conflicts have renewed themselves because they're not contained now.[56]

Former chairman of the Joint Chiefs of Staff Martin Dempsey waxed nostalgic for the Soviet era over and over, repeatedly claiming that the world had become more dangerous than at any point in his lifetime.[57]

On its face, this point of view, no matter how widespread, demonstrates a significant lack of perspective. All who study international politics know—or should know by now—that the post–Cold War era has been far more stable than the one that preceded it. Even if the New Peace remains controversial, the trajectory of proliferation and nuclear issues is not. The verdict on the second nuclear age is plain and irrefutable: thus far, it has been better in most ways than the first. The world is much less dangerous than it was during the Cold War, when many thousands more nuclear weapons stood on hair-trigger alert in superpower arsenals. States might not always have been able to cooperate, or even agree, over the course of the last twenty-five years, but at no time have tensions risen to the heights reached by a dozen or more Cold War crises. General Dempsey was born in 1952, so although he missed the Berlin Airlift by a few years, he was alive for the Korean War, Cuban Missile Crisis, Yom Kippur War, Soviet invasion of Afghanistan, 1983's "Able Archer" scare, and a host of other perilous moments that have no post–Cold War equivalents. The unipolar era has not seen serious analysts urging the use of nuclear weapons on nonnuclear states, as happened in the United States in 1950 and 1954 (and in the Soviet Union in the early 1960s). It has had nothing remotely similar to China's Great Leap Forward, where as many as thirty million people perished.[58] Massive, bloody wars occurred during General Dempsey's lifetime that dwarf even the horror in Syria, some of which involved the United States. Around two million people died in Vietnam alone while the general was a teenager. The attacks of 9/11 shook this country to its core, but terrorism since has not been as dangerous to Americans as have bathtubs, cows, lightning, deer, or even the televisions that bring such frightening images into their living rooms.[59] By any reasonable measure, the Cold War was not only bloodier and less stable than the period since its end, but it was less safe for the United States.

How soon General Dempsey and so much of our national security establishment forget the consistent, nagging fear that hung over much of the Cold War, which was stronger at some times than others but could rarely be dismissed entirely: it often seemed as if the West might be *losing*. In retrospect, this seems rather silly, given the advantages of the First World over the Second in nearly every measurable category of power, but back then the concern was real. Disasters seemed cumulative, as long as one interpreted them correctly. The Chinese Civil War,

*Sputnik*, Vietnam, and other occasional setbacks fed the impression that momentum was on the other side. The ultimate outcome of the struggle was not clear, which led to a steady waxing and waning of national anxiety. Today, no such fear exists. No matter what happens during the current "war on terror," no major Western country is going to be speaking Arabic when it is over. Actual defeat is unimaginable, regardless of what timeframe one uses.[60] Today's modern industrialized state faces no existential threats.

Cold War nostalgia is particularly inappropriate regarding nuclear weapons. Almost all of those who write about the second nuclear age look back wistfully at the simpler, rational, predictable first. This claim overlooks the fact that many specialists and laymen alike were unconvinced that the Soviet leadership was rational, and some were fully convinced that it was not. Moscow sought not stability, hardliners endlessly warned, but revolution. Richard Pipes was typical when he argued that significant danger arose from the fact that "we consider nuclear war unfeasible and suicidal for both, and our chief adversary views it as feasible and winnable for himself."[61] Anyone attributing basic rationality to Soviet leaders engaged in naïve "mirror imaging," the mistaken assumption that they were essentially like us.[62] The Soviets could not even be trusted to oppose the death of hundreds of millions, as long as such sacrifice advanced the cause of communism somehow. When today's analysts remember a time when U.S. rivals were rational and predictable, they are recalling a fantasy, one that did not reflect the reality of the time.

The People's Republic of China seemed even less rational. A half-century of Chinese nuclear behavior makes it is easy to forget just how fast and loose Beijing once played with its rhetoric. Mao appeared quite sanguine regarding a global nuclear conflict, since it would result in the "total elimination of capitalism." He told Soviet leader Nikita Khrushchev in 1957 that in such a war, "we may lose more than 300 million people. So what? War is war. The years will pass and we'll get to work producing more babies than ever before."[63] His bluster turned out to be just that; since China tested its bomb, it has acted quite responsibly. This was hardly predictable in the early 1960s, when it was nuclearizing. As the historian Francis Gavin observed, "No country in the post–World War II period—not Iraq, Iran, or even North Korea—has given U.S. policymakers more reason to fear its nuclearization than China."[64] All this was enough to encourage the superpowers to contemplate large-scale preemption, even during the supposedly stable and predictable first nuclear era.[65]

The amorphous, generalized anxiety pervasive in the United States today is of a fundamentally different character and intensity than the existential dread that accompanied the Cold War. Nuclear war would have meant death not only for the individual but for civilization itself, the total annihilation of the past and future, which for many people seemed worse than mere death.[66] Threats of apocalypse permeated all layers of society, affecting the general mental health in ways that no terrorist, no matter how frightening, can match.[67] To keep their rosy memories intact, nostalgics have to forget or suppress the ever-present danger of World War III that hung over the Cold War and the utter terror and helplessness it produced.

## EXPLAINING COLD WAR NOSTALGIA

Expectations of a calamitous second nuclear age, as well as the general refusal to recognize the relative safety of the New Peace, are symptomatic of a larger, rather puzzling phenomenon. A lingering nostalgia for the Cold War has accompanied the unipolar era, a plaintive longing for an earlier, supposedly simpler, more predictable, and less dangerous time. Such nostalgia is the result of a few related phenomena working together, subconsciously making that dangerous past seem preferable to the much safer present. They are all related to one of the classic subjects in psychology: the manner in which memory operates.

As one might expect, a good deal of research has been done on how people remember. Psychologists have long known that memory is an active process, one that involves the purposeful reconstruction of events, opening the door to the influence of a variety of identifiable cognitive and motivational biases.[68] Over the years, researchers have identified many factors that shape the process of reconstruction and reinterpretation that we call our memories. This process produces noticeable patterns that, when taken together, help account for the common tendency to look back upon earlier eras with unearned positive feelings, in both SNA theorists and the general public alike.

First, psychologists describe a phenomenon sometimes descriptively referred to as *rosy retrospection*, according to which the past seems better in memory than it was in reality.[69] A strong line of research suggests that people often engage in the "active forgetting" of negative events, for a variety of reasons, and focus instead on the positive.[70] The human mind has an incentive, in a sense, to minimize the details and duration of unpleasant experiences. As a result, there tends to be a *positivity bias* to memory, which makes it easier to recall positive events or outcomes than negative ones. Our memories of the past are left rosier than our experiences of the present, and nostalgia forms.

For example, a number of studies have looked at the ways people remember enjoyable events such as vacations and festivals.[71] Participants consistently report greater satisfaction with their experiences after they return than they did while the event was taking place. They focus on the positive moments and forget those that were disappointing, frightening, or just plain boring. Lying by the pool seemed pretty good while it was happening but *great* once back in the office. The same basic dynamics may well apply to bipolar standoffs; we are more likely to focus on the good events and forget the less pleasant or terrifying ones. Rosy retrospection encourages people to remember the moon landings more clearly than *Sputnik* or Reagan's speech at the Berlin Wall more than that of Khrushchev at the United Nations. Most of all, we remember the end, that the wall fell, the Soviet Union collapsed, and the West emerged victorious.

Second, according to what psychologists call the *immediacy bias*, people experience current emotions more intensely than they do older ones.[72] The fear, dread, and pessimism of the Cold War faded long ago, while emotions generated by events of the present era remain powerful in our minds. In the argot of the field, recent events are more easily *available* in our memories than those of the past, so the emotions they engender are more *salient*. As a result, for example, more recent human-itarian crises are more likely to attract the attention of outsiders than persistent problems, regardless of the objective level of need.[73] Immediate emotions are often more powerful than older ones, which, over time, may have lost their affective edge.

The present always outweighs the past, and as a result the Cold War seems less dangerous than it was, especially when compared to current events. Temporal distance makes 9/11 far more terrifying than the Cuban Missile Crisis, Iraq appears more heartbreaking than Vietnam, and ISIS is as scary as the Soviets. Although a detached assessment might suggest that the reverse is true, people rarely make detached assessments. Current problems lead stereotypical teenagers to declare every few weeks that they are experiencing the worst day of their entire life and perhaps even seasoned generals to decide that no time was more dangerous than the present.[74]

The third explanation for Cold War nostalgia has to do with how memory operates. People might look back fondly upon that era in part because they simply do not remember it accurately. One of the hottest areas of research on decision making concerns so-called construal-level theory, or CLT, which suggests that the greater the distance from events, the higher the level of construal, or abstraction.[75] "Psychological distance" can be measured along four dimensions—temporal, spatial, social, and "hypotheticality," or the distance between reality and imagination—each of which has different effects on construal.[76] But for our purposes here, the important point is that the more events fade into the past, the more abstractly people tend to remember them. The concrete, day-to-day details are lost to time, leaving behind only overall impressions. "As we move away from direct experience of things," write the originators of CLT, "we have less information about those things."[77] The act of abstraction allows actors to retain certain features in their memories while omitting those deemed less important or less central. High levels of construal open the door to incomplete or incorrect reconstructions of memory, leaving actors with representations of the past that are "simpler, less ambiguous, more coherent, more schematic, and more prototypical than concrete representations."[78] In other words, people impose order on their memories, even if no such order existed when the events occurred. The past appears simpler, more coherent, and—whether regarding nuclear weapons or other geopolitical threats—less dangerous.

The relationship between psychological distance and construal is complicated and just beginning to be understood. A couple of issues seem clear, however, that relate to the way people remember the Cold War. First of all, affect appears to fade faster than cognitive aspects of memory. In other words, people tend remember facts but forget the intensity of emotions they generated. The terror of the Cuban Missile Crisis fades, but the general story remains. This process only accelerates as the psychological distance grows. Furthermore, in many instances, according to the "valence-dependent time-discounting hypothesis," which was an important influence on the early tests of CLT, negative emotions fade faster than positive ones.[79] Trope and Liberman use the example of houseguests: soon after they leave, we may remember both the inconvenience they produced and the good times we had with them. Over time, though, the former fades, and we recall the positive emotions more clearly and are ready to welcome new guests.[80] The research on the CLT therefore supports the notion of rosy retrospection, offering even more reason to believe that people tend to remember the positive aspects of the past more than the negative.

Finally, and perhaps most importantly, all memory of the Cold War is filtered through the lens of certainty. We know how the bipolar era ended, and we know that the world managed—through some combination of skill, luck, and inertia—to avoid a nuclear holocaust. Khrushchev blinked during the Cuban Missile Crisis. Zbigniew Brzezinski chose not to wake up President Carter when his military aides erroneously detected hundreds of inbound Soviet missiles in 1979.[81] A heroic Soviet lieutenant colonel disobeyed orders and refused to start a chain reaction after detecting a similarly false radar signature, averting an accidental nuclear war.[82] Not only did the species survive, but the West won, and communism was essentially vanquished to a few irrelevant geopolitical backwaters.

In contrast, no one knows what the future holds, either for the next would-be terrorist or the unipolar moment. One of the most robust findings in psychology, supported by behavioralists and neuroscientists alike, is that uncertainty is profoundly stressful.[83] The past might not have been uniformly pleasant, but its outcome is known, and it had a happy ending, more or less. The present carries no such guarantees. No one can say for sure what North Korea or Vladimir Putin will do, or what plots ISIS minions are conjuring, or what catastrophes the warming climate will bring. The unknown unknowns, to borrow from Donald Rumsfeld, keep people awake at night.[84]

These four psychological processes help explain why so many continue to believe that the Cold War was somehow more predictable and less complicated than the current era. Without the natural bias regarding the past commonly created by memory, more reasonable evaluations of the current security environment would be possible, regarding nuclear weapons and all other imaginable categories. Nostalgia for the past reaches beyond security studies: Donald Trump did not promise to make America great but to make America great *again*. Apparently its greatness had slipped to an unacceptably low level compared to times past. For many people, life is always better in the rear-view mirror, no matter what the facts say and no matter how strong the empirical case of those who argue otherwise.

## UNIPOLARITY AND NUCLEAR ZERO

What is the future for nuclear weapons in a unipolar world? A state that dominates most measures of power might try to minimize the importance of the few categories it does not. "Nuclear zero" would be advantageous to the United States, as former secretary of defense Les Aspin recognized shortly after the beginning of the new era. "Nuclear weapons can still be the equalizer against superior conventional forces," Aspin noted. "But today it is the United States that has unmatched conventional military power, and it is our potential adversaries who may attain nuclear weapons. We're the ones who could wind up being the equalizee."[85]

Basic logic might suggest that the unipolar power ought to favor nuclear disarmament, in order to keep the playing field tilted in its favor.

This has not been the case. Although the United States has made occasional noises about complete nuclear disarmament, and President Obama made it the topic of his first overseas address, Washington does not appear eager to lead a global movement to eliminate nuclear weapons. A number of high-profile former officials have urged the United States to move toward nuclear zero, but the potential for that occurring, especially during the Trump era, seems slim.[86] Deterrence remains a cornerstone of strategic stability in the unipolar era because, as the thinking still goes, nuclear weapons remove the possibility of victory from the calculations of potential aggressors. According to critics, disarmament would make the United States fundamentally unsafe.

Throughout the Cold War, the millions of words devoted to deterrence were all based on a series of assumptions that could never be tested. Foremost among them was the notion that the desire to attack was omnipresent, or at least occasionally present, in the superpowers. Without that desire, nothing would actually be deterred. In practice, as discussed in the previous chapter, it was never possible to determine when exactly states were deterred from attacking by guarantees of retaliation and when they were simply not contemplating aggression. Superpower peace and the existence of enormous stockpiles of nuclear weapons may be merely coincidental.[87] The current era poses particular challenges to those seeking to ascertain whether nuclear weapons are actually deterring anything. Cross-border attacks with the goal of conquest have been just as rare in regions with no nuclear weapons as in those supposedly kept secure by deterrence. Would today's leaders really contemplate assaults on their neighbors if nuclear weapons were not part of the equation? What if the world's nuclear weapons are deterring no one, because the will to attack is essentially absent? In a system where conquest has been rendered so rare as to be obsolete, deterrence would be an illusion. The New Peace has tremendous implications for deterrence theory, in other words, none of which are currently captured by the current thinking on the second nuclear age.

Abolition is not an experiment that the U.S. security community is eager to run, at least as long as the assumption remains ubiquitous that deterrence is the ultimate guarantor of safety. But thinking regarding the second nuclear age is woefully short on the implications of the New Peace and the death of conquest. It seems likely that outside of a few places where active enmity still exists, such as on the Indian subcontinent, today's nuclear arsenals deter nothing except the erosion of national pride. They may well be expensive, dangerous dust catchers with little utility outside of the minds of their designers.

✾

Theorizing about the second nuclear age seems like security studies at its best. The parameters are well defined, the puzzles clear, the expectations elegant and logical. The only problem is the evidence, which stubbornly refuses to cooperate. Proliferation has not increased, regional rivalries have not deepened, and omniviolence has not materialized. Instead, unipolarity has diminished the importance of nuclear weapons for all but a handful of states. The second nuclear age is indeed different from the first; contrary to most expectations, however, thus far it has been significantly better. The end of the Cold War has improved nuclear security in every measurable way. Many observers are unlikely to realize the extent of these improvements as long as they remain unaware of the deeper psychological biases that make the past seem better than it was.

John Mueller once described the tendency of people to romanticize the past, elevating prior ages over the present, no matter how irrationally. Human beings have a "tendency to look backward with misty eyes, to see the past as much more benign, simple, and innocent than it really was," he observed. "No matter how much better the present gets, the past gets better in reflection, and we are, accordingly, always notably worse off than we used to be. Golden ages, thus, do happen, but we are never actually *in* them: they are always back there somewhere (or, sometimes, in the ungraspable future)."[88] As big problems become resolved, he continued, "we tend to elevate smaller ones, sometimes by redefinition or by raising standards, to take their place."[89] The second nuclear age may turn out to be a golden one, but human nature might make it impossible for citizens and scholars alike to appreciate its benefits.

The unipolar era has been marked by a drastic, if quiet, decrease in both warfare and the number and significance of nuclear weapons. Why, then, are perceptions about unipolarity so unremittingly gloomy? The next chapter shifts the focus from the system level of analysis, suggesting that the most important effects of unipolarity may be on the psychology of the individual. Those seeking to understand the politics of the twenty-first century might do better consulting Freud rather than Waltz.

# 3

## UNIPOLARITY AND PERCEPTION

Security is relative. No state is ever fully safe, just as no individual is ever completely free from danger. As long as ideology, religion, and/or psychopathology inspire nonstate actors, there will be threats from within; as long as other states maintain militaries, there will be threats from without. The United States will always face danger, which is good news for its politicians and news media, neither of which ever tire of highlighting the various bogeymen lurking in the shadows.

However, when viewed comparatively, that is, when its security is considered next to that of any other state, it is hard to argue that the United States is in any serious peril. It remains surrounded by vast oceans and weak neighbors, and its power dwarfs not only all potential competitors but most realistic hostile coalitions. If any state in an anarchic system should not fear for its security, surely it is the unipolar power. By any reasonable measure, the post–Cold War system is a safe one for the United States.[1]

As the Trump election makes clear, however, Americans do not feel safe. To a far larger degree than its allies, the United States considers the world to be a very dangerous place, full of enemies and threats.[2] One belief has remained constant in both elite and popular circles since at least World War II: *We are living in dangerous times.* Many of those who make and/or comment on U.S. foreign policy maintain that the world is full of enemies and evil, so this (whenever "this" is) is no time to relax. Constant repetition of this idea has over time generated genuine belief for leaders and followers alike—and substantial fear. Although the world might have seemed a bit safer after the collapse of the Soviet Union, Americans know better: A 2009 poll found that nearly 60 percent of the public—and fully half of the elite Council on Foreign Relations—considered the world more dangerous than it was during the Cold War.[3] The 9/11 attacks clearly led to greater public anxiety and insecurity, but elevated threat perceptions predate Al-Qaeda. Though the source of that danger has evolved over the years, from communist spies to Soviet missiles to Japanese industrialists to Islamic terrorists, the United States has always detected threats in the system more serious than other countries realize. Enemies always exist, and the danger they pose never diminishes.

The unipolar state is simultaneously the safest and most fearful of all the great powers of the twenty-first century.[4] This is not a coincidence. As it turns out, perception and misperception are, in large part, functions of power. Asymmetry has important and at times counterintuitive effects on image formation. Threats are more likely to be identified, by both core and peripheral states alike, when one power essentially dominates the rest. Misperception is always common in international politics, but in unipolar orders it is the rule.

How and why have its advantages in relative power affected threat perceptions in the United States? What is the effect of unipolarity on perception, for both big and small powers? Could power actually contribute to insecurity? This chapter examines the political psychology of unbalanced power and its implications for perceptions in both big and small states. Some of the phenomena under consideration are widespread, or even ubiquitous, in the human experience and are merely exacerbated by power; others are essentially the products (or, more accurately, byproducts) of asymmetry. Unipolarity creates obstacles to empathy and fuels conspiratorial thinking, complicating international relationships, which are difficult enough to maintain without it. It encourages the growth of overconfidence in the unipole and warps its ability to assess risk. Strong countries are less likely to pay attention to the weak and more likely to objectify and stereotype them. And most of all, power affects the formation of images, especially negative ones. Implacably hostile enemies are far more likely to be identified in unipolar systems, whether or not they actually exist.

Power is not a neutral attribute, for people or for states. Its possession fundamentally changes actors—corrupting absolutely in its absolute form—shaping the way they perceive their environment and affecting behavior as a result. The deck is stacked against accurate perception in asymmetric international orders. Understanding the other side is going to be particularly difficult in the coming decades.

History contains plenty of reasons to believe that, in international politics, there is no connection between power and wisdom. In fact, the opposite may be true: The stronger a country gets, the more mistakes it seems to make. Granted, this is partially because strong-state blunders are more visible and consequential than those of the weak, and their actions are subject to greater scrutiny. Albania and Malawi probably make mistakes too, but hardly anyone notices. Certainly fewer suffer. Presidents of the United States live under a microscope: their every decision is endlessly analyzed and evaluated. Not all of Washington's errors in judgment can be chalked up to the inevitable outcome of increased attention paid to them by critics, however. Power is accompanied by predictable perils, all of which increase the chance of blunder as well as the stakes.


## POWER AND PSYCHOLOGY

Power may be at the heart of political science, but it has been subjected to surprisingly little analysis by psychologists until relatively recently.[5] Most of what is known (or hypothesized) about the effects of power on the individual is the result of research done in the last two decades. But many of the findings have been consistent, significant, and relatively uncontroversial, at least inside the field. Some also have direct relevance for the unipolar United States.

Care needs to be taken lest the findings of one field be haphazardly applied to another. Psychology and political science have different goals, rules, epistemologies, and ontologies and sometimes differ over basic terms and concepts. For one thing, the two fields do not always agree on just what power is. While both generally recognize the fundamental conceptual distinction discussed in chapter 1—that power can be a reflection of *empirical/structural elements* or *influence*—psychologists commonly assume that the two aspects are sufficiently correlated, rendering any difference unimportant. In many of their experiments, power is regarded as a psychological property more than a material one. "Power is not only the capacity to influence others," argued one of the major researchers on the subject, "it is also a state of mind."[6] The perception of relative power among subjects is crucial to these research programs, not necessarily its empirical reality. After all, much of the time roles and their relative power are arbitrarily assigned by experimenters.

Measuring perceptions of power in laboratory settings is no small task. In an influential and frequently imitated experiment, Cameron Anderson and Jennifer Berdahl asked participants to fill out a questionnaire before the experiment began and assigned scores that reflected the internal, subjective sense of power they brought into the lab.[7] Power has also been commonly "primed" by researchers, which means that subjects have been asked to recall times when they experienced a sense of strength or weakness.[8] Sometimes hierarchy is built in by dividing subjects into groups with obvious status implications, such as managers and workers or job candidates and recruiters. The best studies assign power in the many different ways common to the field and run their experiments multiple times.[9]

Fortunately for this discussion, the various techniques lead to the same general conclusions. No matter how it is constructed in the lab, power seems to shape perception and behavior in broadly consistent ways. If these insights are correct, the relative power of the unipolar United States probably affects the psyches of leaders at home and abroad in ways that are not always obvious.

## EMPATHY

The historian Henry Adams once observed that the effect of power is "the aggravation of self, a sort of tumor that ends by killing the victim's sympathies . . . one can scarcely use expressions too strong to describe the violence of egotism it stimulates."[10] Few policy makers appreciate the extent to which perceptions are affected by, and a product of, their relative power. Leaders of strong countries deal differently with weaker countries than they do with peers. Powerful subjects objectify much more readily, for one thing, treating others as means to their own ends rather than as actors with interests worthy of consideration and respect. An instrumental relationship quickly forms between the strong and the weak, one fundamentally different than those between relative equals.[11] This phenomenon is rather widely observed in the laboratory: Power leads to objectification, inhibiting understanding and discouraging empathy.[12]

Empathy, or the ability to understand the motivations of others, is not something that comes naturally.[13] People are not born with the capacity to put themselves in others' shoes; it is a learned trait, a skill honed by experience and effort. And it is not easily attained, especially in international politics. "Actors rarely appreciate the extent to which other's views are wildly discrepant from theirs," noted Robert Jervis, and the efforts they make to understand others are often woefully inadequate.[14] Even when sincere efforts are made, rarely do we understand why they act as they do.[15]

The nontrivial obstacles to empathy are exacerbated by asymmetry. Power weakens the imperative to understand the motivations of other actors. Participants in experiments consistently demonstrate empathy in inverse proportion to the arbitrary level of strength assigned to them.[16] Some neuropsychologists suggest that perceptions of power might actually affect the physical function of the brain, making it difficult for subjects to empathize even when told to make a conscious effort to do so by researchers.[17] Weak actors are simply not as important in the lives of strong ones, so the imperative to understand them diminishes.

In asymmetrical relationships, empathy must overcome insecurity in the small state and insensitivity in the large. For example, U.S. "freedom of navigation operations" (FONOPs) in the South China Sea might seem like nonviolent, harmless assertions of international rights in Washington, but they are interpreted very differently in Beijing. During a FONOP, which have been occurring since at least 1979, U.S. Navy vessels sail through various international waters in order to emphasize to riparian states that no one controls shipping twelve miles or more offshore.[18] Though over the years FONOPs have been carried out against a variety of countries, from Canada to Iran to the Seychelles, by far the most significant episodes have occurred in the Pacific Rim. To U.S. planners, such operations are reminders about the law of the sea and responses to Chinese actions. Analysts in Beijing, when not noting the hypocrisy of a state enforcing laws it has not ratified (the United States is not a party to the UN Convention on the Law of the Sea), argue that FONOPs are deliberate provocations, expressions of hegemony that carry not-so-veiled threats of violence. One side's policing action is another's provocative, unnecessary display of strength. Chinese insecurity and U.S. insensitivity make for a potentially dangerous combination.

With exalted status comes arrogance and hubris, both of which are great obstacles to empathy. Any state that achieves the level of success of the United States would have its national ego grow in kind. And since empathy is a key component in any effort to improve perception, unipolar Washington is likely to be prone to misperception and mistakes.


## ACTION ORIENTATION: THE EFFECTS OF EFFICACY AND CONFIDENCE

A basic contention of neorealist international relations is that unbalanced power leads to action, and consequently unipolar states can be expected to pursue their interests more aggressively because they face no substantial opposition. The psychological literature approaches "action orientation," or a general preference for action over passivity, from a different angle. While political scientists focus on restraints and assume similar state goals (security, prosperity, state survival, etc.), psychologists allow for much more variation in motivation. Some actors are bound to have higher action orientations than others. And the powerful have the highest of all, for several reasons.

First, perceptions of power are closely associated with *efficacy*, or the perception of the ability to affect or even control events.[19] Actors with high levels of efficacy are substantially more likely to adopt proactive approaches to problems and opportunities because they feel like their actions matter. Second, for both individuals and nations, power leads to perceptions of exceptionalism.[20] The rules do not necessarily apply to powerful people; the rich are much quicker to rationalize away antisocial behavior and suggest that laws are not meant for them. In laboratories and staterooms, powerful actors believe that they are not beholden to the same set of rules that govern everyone else and are more likely to believe that their actions are "prosocial," or in the community's interest.[21] They have earned the right to be treated differently.

Finally, and most importantly, power is closely associated with confidence and optimism, both of which contribute to high action orientations.[22] The causal direction can be questioned outside the laboratory—perhaps confidence and optimism help a person attain power—but during experiments arbitrary assignments of power have immediate effects. Confident, optimistic people are more willing to take the risks that accompany action, believing they will succeed.

While a confident, optimistic outlook can be beneficial for an individual's overall mental health, it can also lead to problems if not kept in perspective. The line between optimism and overconfidence, with its attendant perceptual distortions, is a fine one. Actions weak subjects deem too dangerous seem reasonable and achievable to the strong.[23] Overconfident people are undeterred by high likelihoods of failure. Power interferes with the ability to assess risk, in other words, making blunders more likely. As one researcher put it, "no problem in judgment and decision making is more prevalent and more potentially catastrophic than overconfidence."[24]

Many foreign-policy blunders, including not a few disastrous wars, are only explicable by positing harmful levels of optimism possessed by leaders.[25] "The consequences of positive illusions in conflict and international politics are overwhelmingly harmful," Kahneman and Renshon have argued. "Positive illusions generally favor hawkish, aggressive behavior."[26] Overconfidence causes people to underestimate risks, making the difficult appear easy and the impossible merely difficult.[27] When the risks of action are underestimated, policy makers can be in for nasty, expensive surprises.

By virtue of their power, therefore, U.S. leaders are liable to exhibit pathological overconfidence and act on its misperceptions. They are likely to feel that they can accomplish nearly anything they put their minds to, even when the odds of success are low. And they will believe that their obvious prosocial motivations allow them to be held to a different standard than their counterparts in other countries.

At no point in history was this dynamic more obvious than during the lead-up to the invasion of Iraq. The Bush administration and its allies spent most of 2002 assuring a wary public that toppling Saddam would be quick, easy, cheap, and glorious. The former Pentagon official Kenneth Adelman famously predicted that liberating Iraq would be a "cakewalk," which was the dominant message promoted by the war's proponents, even if some bristled occasionally at the use of that word.[28] The Hussein regime was a house of cards, the American people were told, one that would collapse with the slightest nudge. American troops would be greeted as liberators, not conquerors; the streets of Baghdad and Basra, according to the vice president, were "sure to erupt with joy."[29] A healthy Iraqi democracy was waiting to replace Saddam's tyranny, needing only a little push to help bring it about. Furthermore, Iraqi oil would pay for it all. Extensive postconflict planning done by the State Department prior to the war was pushed aside, since there was no need for its insights.[30] Without the gross asymmetry of power that existed between the two countries—which is the typical bilateral relationship of unipolarity—a more realistic assessment of the risks of invasion might have emerged, and the war might not have happened.

Not only do powerful actors tend to be overconfident and underestimate risk, but they are more willing to act on their underestimations than are the weak. They are more likely to do something rather than just stand there, for better or worse.

## ATTENTION DEFICITS AND STEREOTYPING

In a series of works on structural asymmetry in the Pacific Rim, Brantly Womack analyzed the role played by relative levels of attention in fostering misperceptions between China and Vietnam.[31] Hanoi places a far higher premium on understanding what is going on in Beijing than vice versa, and as a result Vietnam has many more China experts than China has experts on Vietnam.[32] This dynamic is common everywhere that power asymmetry exists: smaller actors make a much greater effort to decipher the actions of the big. The Lilliputians pay far more attention to Gulliver than he does in return. Citing "decades of research" on this, the psychologists Russell and Fiske point to "one fundamental principle: Attention follows power. The powerless are more motivated and thus more likely than the powerful to engage in effortful, deliberate, and accuracy-oriented impression formation processes."[33] Because of their position atop the international hierarchy, "Americans have little incentive to arouse their interest in less powerful countries that are more or less irrelevant to national interests and valued outcomes."[34]

Powerful actors tend to have broad interests and interact with a large number of others. As a result, they have less time for any single relationship or situation. They tend to be "attentionally overloaded," in the jargon of the profession, and can devote less time to individual issues.[35] Leaders of powerful countries must split their time among many interests, and as a result the quality of their decision making can be expected to suffer. They are more likely to employ heuristics, or mental shortcuts, the dangers of which are well known to political scientists.[36] What is somewhat less well-known is the common finding in psychology that rapid, underinformed decisions are also those more likely to be affected by biases and stereotypes.[37]

Power is directly associated with stereotyping. Strong actors do not feel the need to pay close attention to those lower on the hierarchy and are more accepting of information that confirms preexisting images.[38] This phenomenon has been observed in laboratory and real-world settings, across cultures and time.[39] The increased tendency to accept stereotypical information applies not just to views of subordinates: subjects given higher status in experiments quickly come to view out-groups more stereotypically than those given lower status.[40] This rule applies across levels of analysis, therefore, to individuals as well as collectivities. Powerful actors rely on stereotypes more in their decisions, and this creates challenges for foreign-policy making. Leaders in the United States are more likely to believe information that conforms to their previously held stereotypes than are leaders from, say, Canada. Such stereotypes can lead to the formation of images, both positive and negative, and then to their confirmation and reinforcement. Images held by U.S. leaders are likely to be stronger and less responsive to correction by new information. And Canadian perceptions are likely to be more accurate because of it.

Womack noted that inattention on behalf of the stronger state in an international relationship (what he called "state A") has two further policy characteristics: insensitivity to what the weaker state ("B") actually does and general inconsistency.[41] Policy makers in A are just not interested enough in the relationship to worry much about its maintenance. These characteristics obviously wreak havoc on the perceptions of B, for whom the relationship always carries an element of existential danger.

Peer competitors concentrate the mind. Without them, the urgency to empathize with other states and assess the accuracy of perceptions declines precipitously. The threat of nuclear exchange provided an incentive for scholars to explore the extent to which Cold War perceptions were accurate. Washington's ability to understand Moscow, which was never great, has grown even worse since the Soviet Union collapsed. Russian concerns about NATO expansion, missile defenses, and the treatment of fellow Slavs have been dismissed as atavistic, imperialistic impulses that will soon fade. The United States expressed opinions regarding the fate of tiny regions in Russia's sphere of influence that not one American in a thousand had heard of previously—Transdniester, South Ossetia, Abkhazia, the Donbass, etc.—and even fewer could find on a map. American leaders make much less of an effort to understand their Russian counterparts and as a result are repeatedly surprised when Moscow objects to its initiatives.

George W. Bush had even greater difficulty understanding the actions of an absurdly weak actor, Saddam Hussein. The dictator seemed utterly irrational and unpredictable, even when faced with certain outcomes. Saddam could not possibly have expected to defeat the U.S. military and maintain his hold on power, so why did he not take a deal and live to fight another day? This mystification was widespread. "Every time I put myself in his [Saddam's] shoes," the former chairman of the Joint Chiefs of Staff William Crowe was fond of saying before the invasion, "I start running."[42] American leaders failed repeatedly to understand what motivated Saddam Hussein, and he appears to have been uniquely delusional about their determination to remove him.[43]

The advice and intelligence leaders receive in asymmetrical relationships is often different from what they can expect regarding near-peers. The root of the problem is, once again, attention. As Womack explains, the underlying question for the experts on the smaller country B in the bigger country A is, "Why is this matter in (B) worthy of our attention?" They tend to pay heed only if the issue is connected to something bigger, a "grander concern" that involves A. "An expert arguing that (B) is part of a global conspiracy will get attention; one arguing that (B)'s actions stem from domestic factors without further ramifications will sound full of tedious, unfamiliar and uninteresting detail." For B's experts on A, however, the basic question is, "Does this development in (A) affect our vulnerability to (A)?" They have the opposite problem from A's experts on B.

> Instead of being seen (or unseen) as arcane area specialists, they
> deal with a leadership that watches (A) carefully. An expert who has

discovered a malevolent pattern in (A)'s seemingly unrelated actions, or who extrapolates a larger threat from a particular gesture, will attract attention; less attention will be paid to one arguing that (A) is pre-occupied by larger concerns and is not as concentrated on (B) as vice versa.[44]

These different perspectives greatly increase the chances for misinter-pretation and misperception.

Accuracy in perception, and therefore the quality of decision mak-ing, may well be inversely related to relative power. The "power curse" discussed by Giulio Gallarotti holds that "the greater the power, the less vigilant that nations need to be in understanding and managing . . . com-plexity."[45] Goliath did not pay sufficient attention to his challenge from David, given the complications of his power advantages (his overconfi-dence, decreased attention, and objectification of his lesser foe). Percep-tions of limited vulnerability and hubris that accompany power also complicate decision making and lead to blunders in both biblical com-bat and modern foreign policy.[46] David, on the other hand, focused on the task before him and excelled.

## PSYCHOLOGY AND THE POWERLESS

The world's Davids do not always prevail, of course. Smaller actors face their own set of obstacles to perception, all of which are born from insecurity. Powerful actors—whether bosses or unipoles—generate sub-stantial stress and anxiety among subordinates.[47] As it turns out, there is good reason for the weak to distrust the strong. Power is directly related to what is sometimes called, in the jargon of the philosopher, "assholish" behavior.[48] As actors grow in status, even in the controlled setting of the laboratory, they become increasingly antisocial. Studies have shown that powerful people are more likely to break the law while driving, take goods from others, lie, cheat, and endorse other unethical behaviors.[49] In the boardroom, people in positions of power are far more

likely—maybe as much as three times more likely—to interrupt cowork-
ers, raise their voices, "multitask" during meetings, and say insulting
things.[50] Weak states, suffering as they must at the hands of the strong,
can surely relate.

Worst-case-scenario assumptions are rational for small states. But
the research on power indicates that a healthy concern for security can
transform into a general tendency to overestimate threats. Structure
may cloud the ability of policy makers in Washington to recognize the
limits of their capabilities, but it also fosters misperception in the countries forced to coexist with the United States, where asymmetry is a
more present and greater daily reality. Respect for the strong's capabilities can easily lead to overestimation, the impression that the unipole
could bring about nearly any outcome it wanted. Assumptions of virtual U.S. omnipotence appear on both sides of its asymmetrical relationships, fed in Washington by overconfidence and elsewhere by the
persistent anxiety that unchecked power generates. Not only in Washington, in other words, is the distinction between superpower and super-
hero blurred.

Those under the impression that unipolar capabilities are essentially
unlimited hold the United States responsible for nearly every international outcome, even those that seem (to the naïve) quite inimical to the
unipole's interests. Weaker actors commonly assume that Washington
orchestrates all important events or allows them to occur through inaction. For many in the periphery, the status quo is essentially a reflection
of U.S. interests; all things are as they are because the United States wills
them. President George H. W. Bush could have deposed Saddam Hussein in the 1990s, for instance, so there had to be a reason why he did
not. His son could have brought peace to Iraq after the invasion but did
not, so Washington must have wanted chaos. President Obama's decision
to leave Assad in power is evidence of the tyrant's unspoken usefulness to
the United States. The challenge for analysts in small states is to determine why the United States wants the world to look as it does, because
clearly it could have brought about different outcomes. Overestimations
of U.S. capability, which are natural on all sides in unipolarity, help lay
the groundwork for conspiracy theories.

Conspiratorial thinking has been the subject of a good deal of recent research.[51] One of the central findings is that people who feel powerless, who feel that their destiny is essentially out of their control, are far more likely to believe that hidden forces are working behind the scenes to produce reality.[52] Those with a recent history of external control, such as people in postcolonial states, are particularly vulnerable.

The power of the unipole may be limited, but imaginations in the periphery are not. The hidden hand of the United States can be detected behind every event, especially those with negative outcomes. Nothing is too far-fetched or too malevolent. Washington is blamed for nearly every unwelcome event that befalls the regimes in Iran, Pyongyang, and Beijing.[53] External (read: U.S.) interference provides a convenient scapegoat for all manner of domestic problems experienced by the Bolivarist regimes in Latin America.[54] In Turkey, the belief that the CIA orchestrated the July 2016 coup attempt is commonly held in government, press, and popular circles.[55] The election of Donald Trump, who promotes any conspiracy theory that will benefit his image, has only served to exacerbate perceptions of U.S. perfidy. Trump's campaign assertions that Barack Obama was the "founder" of ISIS merely confirmed what many across the Arab world already suspected.[56]

Not all conspiratorial thinking is wrong, of course. The United States does work to undermine other governments at times and has been involved with many actual conspiracies over the years. As a result of this history and the psychological effects of asymmetry, there is little that the unipolar United States can do to ease minds in weaker states. Its capabilities will feed assumptions that the hand of the unipole can be seen everywhere, if only one knows where to look. U.S. policy makers are used to dealing with foreign misperceptions regarding their actions, the pace of which is not likely to slow as long as no other power can provide balance to the system. The essentially uncheckable power of the United States is going to produce perceptions in the periphery that differ substantially from those of the center.

Unipolarity complicates perception in a number of complex, undetectable, and interrelated ways. Many international relationships that could be stable and cooperative, especially in the era of the New Peace, instead remain challenging and tense. The likelihood of pathological, negative-image formation actually increases in cases of extreme asymmetry. Enemies, whether real or imagined, are more likely to rise in a unipolar world.


## UNIPOLARITY AND IMAGE FORMATION

The most deeply studied, important, and pernicious form of misperception is the "enemy image." During the Cold War, political scientists and psychologists spent a good deal of time describing the effects of negative assumptions regarding the motivations of others on decision making.[57] Leaders do not react to other states, strictly speaking, but to the images they hold of those states.[58] Those images, which tend to be constructed around certain ideal types (friend or foe, ally or rival), act as heuristic devices that help individuals organize and prioritize information. Images are often related to objective facts or truth, but they are not equivalent.

Self-images are almost always positive, since *we* know that *we* are trustworthy and peaceful; we can never be too sure about *them*, however. International politics breeds suspicion. Leaders know that no global police will rescue them from aggressive neighbors, so they are responsible for looking out for themselves and the interests of their people. This "self-help" imperative renders policy makers especially sensitive to threats and encourages them to assume the worst in their rivals in order maximize their chances for safety. The simplest explanations for the actions of others often do not receive proper vetting as long as other, more nefarious motivations cannot be ruled out. Leaders who hold negative images of their rivals are quick to assume that other states are plotting all sorts of malevolence, which can over time poison relations and lead to unnecessary, unwanted conflict.[59]

Partially because of misperception, therefore, enemies may be somewhat natural in international politics. Some psychologists have further suggested that the creation of enemies may be necessary for individuals to function.[60] George Kennan wrote once that people "need to think that there is, somewhere, an enemy boundlessly evil, because this makes them feel boundlessly good."[61] People may need to believe that they are good in order to give life order and meaning, and good cannot exist without evil. If actors need enemies to serve their self-image, evil will always be discovered, whether or not it actually exists.

Once established, negative images become self-reinforcing, acting as filters for new information and casting suspicion on all enemy actions. People interpret signals from enemies in negative ways, often ignoring positive messages entirely. In the early years of the Cold War, for example, President Eisenhower proposed a deal that would have allowed each side to conduct aerial reconnaissance over the other's military installations, hoping to alleviate concerns about sneak attacks and to build mutual confidence and trust. Khrushchev and his advisors, however, viewed this "Open Skies" initiative as the opening gambit of a nefarious espionage plot and rejected the proposal.[62] Nothing Washington could have done would have changed these perceptions, which had solidified in Soviet security circles. Many in the United States, of course, felt the same way about the USSR. When Moscow announced that it would be cutting troop levels in 1956 as part of an effort to reduce tension, Secretary of State John Foster Dulles was not impressed. Those troops might be more valuable to the Soviet cause in industry or agriculture, he thought: "It's a fair conclusion that I would rather have them standing around doing guard duty than making bombs."[63] Everything the enemy does is evidence of evil intentions. As a result, few things persist as long in international politics as negative images. "His signals," explained Jervis, "cannot change his image."[64]

The pace of scholarship on the enemy image slowed considerably after the collapse of the Soviet Union, perhaps in part because the urgency to understand its dynamics decreased alongside the risk of nuclear war. In addition, there seemed to be little left to do; the image was well described by this first generation of political psychologists, to the point that its existence was relatively uncontroversial. By the mid-1990s, few scholars spent time seeking to understand the effect that enemy images had on post-Soviet international politics.

This is not to say that research on misperception came to a complete halt. Since the end of the Cold War, a few scholars have tried to take the topic in new directions, identifying other images that might explain nuance overlooked by previous research. A recognition of asymmetry— and the belief that enemies need to be somewhat symmetrical—was at the heart of Richard Herrmann and Michael Fischerkeller's attempt to go "beyond the enemy image."[65] Replacing the enemy in their taxonomy were new images that included the *imperialist, barbarian*, and *dependent*, all of which are determined by relative power and cultural status. Over the course of a decade, the framework essentially became the cutting edge of research on images in international politics.[66] Other scholars have attempted to describe an entirely new image, the *rogue state*.[67] The enemy image itself had been left behind.

This is not necessarily a welcome turn of events. The logic of behind the new taxonomy's central distinguishing criteria is underexplained. Why *power* and *culture* are the most important variables in explaining perception and strategic behavior rather than, say, *proximity* and *history* is not clear. The way those criteria are measured is also problematic: How does one determine cultural superiority or inferiority, even in perception? No doubt there are individuals in Iran who deem their culture inferior to the liberal West, just as there are Americans who see their nation as backward compared to the more liberal Europeans. But do these voices speak for the majority? Very few cultures consider themselves markedly inferior to others; perceptions of cultural superiority are far more common, if only as a way for measurably weaker nations to maintain self-respect. The Chinese could reassure themselves in the nineteenth century, for example, that although the British had superior weaponry and forced them to import opium, they were still atavistic cultural barbarians.

The new taxonomy is also methodologically suspect. While its images are purportedly arrived at deductively (based on theory), in reality, like most new ideas in international politics, they have been constructed using inductive inference (based on observations). The same evidence is used both to construct and confirm the existence of the proposed images. A tautology lies at the heart of the framework, in other words, that fundamentally weakens its explanatory power.

The value added by the Herrmann-Fischerkeller framework to our understanding of state behavior is limited. Most importantly, the logic behind the oft-expressed insistence that only equals can be enemies has never been adequately supported. Rather than new images, what is needed in the post–Cold War world is an understanding of how power affects behavior toward enemies. The image the United States holds of Iran today could be quite similar to how it perceived the Soviet Union a generation earlier, and its actions are different only because it is less constrained. Herrmann and Fischerkeller were identifying not new images but behavioral manifestations of the old one under new structural conditions. The enemy did not change; power did.

Rejecting the common post–Cold War image taxonomies hardly closes off avenues for useful observations about perception under conditions of substantial asymmetry. In fact, it declutters the intellectual landscape and allows the investigation to move forward, in perhaps more fruitful directions. There is still a great deal of value in the enemy image, far more than in any proposed updates. Understanding its dynamics, as well as vigilance against its pathological effects, is just as important for current leaders as it was for their predecessors.

## UNIPOLARITY AND THE ENEMY IMAGE

How are perceptions affected by drastic power imbalances? Are enemies more or less likely to be identified by states in unipolar systems? Psychologists tell us, rather logically, that power is inversely related to threat perceptions: as relative power decreases, detection of danger increases.[68] Unlike many other results from the lab, however, this one does not seem to translate well to the stateroom. It does not appear true that the growth of U.S. power has led to a decrease in its perception of threats. In fact, quite the opposite has occurred, for reasons that relate more to structure than to psychology.

As it turns out, a state's perception of threat is directly related to power: as capabilities grow, so too does the enemies list.[69] As Jack Snyder has explained, for history's most powerful states, "the preventive pacification of one turbulent frontier usually led to the creation of another one, adjacent to the first."[70] New enemies are always just over the horizon, awaiting discovery. Since the end of the Second World War, the United States has been simultaneously the world's premier power and its supreme worrier. It has consistently detected more danger in faraway corners of the world than any other state, including its closest allies. Washington could find little support for its contention that the vital interests of the West were at stake in Southeast Asia in the 1960s, for example, or in Central America two decades later, or in Iraq in 2003. The U.S. experience is not atypical; perception of threat expands with power, for at least four reasons.

First, great powers define their interests more broadly than do weak states. They participate in global as well as regional politics and take positions on many more issues as a result. Unipolar powers take this phenomenon to an extreme, identifying more interests—as well as threats to those interests—than any other state in the system. "Most countries are primarily concerned with what happens in their neighborhoods," as Jervis has explained, "but the world is the unipole's neighborhood."[71] Today the United States is the only country that participates in the geopolitics of every continent and takes positions in their disputes. Great powers have broader concerns than do smaller, and a "hyperpower" should have the broadest of all.[72]

Prior examples of this dynamic are not hard to find. Two millennia after its collapse, it is easy to forget the extent to which insecurity motivated Roman imperial expansion. Many of Rome's most prominent conquests, from Gaul to Dacia to Iberia, were driven not only by the desire for glory but also the sincere belief that untamed populations along its widening periphery represented threats to the empire.[73] Cicero spoke for many when he explained that many Romans felt expansion was thrust upon them as part of a project to rid themselves of "frightening neighbors."[74] The fact that most of these neighbors were manifestly weaker did not matter; as its power grew, so too did Rome's insecurity. On this notion, known to historians as "defensive imperialism," Joseph Schumpeter is probably unsurpassable:

> There was no corner of the known world where some interest was not alleged to be in danger or under actual attack. . . . Rome was always being attacked by evil-minded neighbors, always fighting for a breathing space. The whole world was pervaded by a host of enemies, and it was manifestly Rome's duty to guard against their indubitably aggressive designs. They were enemies only waiting to fall on the Roman people.[75]

The most powerful, and in many ways safest, society in the ancient world was never convinced that its security was assured as long as potential enemies existed anywhere.

Similar fears haunted the great European powers of the premodern and modern eras as well. The enormous size of the Spanish empire, which at its height encompassed a quarter of the Earth's land area, meant that its leaders could always detect a threat lurking somewhere. In 1626, King Philip IV lamented that "with as many kingdoms and lordships as have been linked to this crown, it is impossible to be without war in some area, either to defend what we have acquired or to divert our enemies."[76] Madrid spent itself into decline trying to address the many dangers it faced, whether real or imagined.[77]

Great Britain also exhibited a high level of insecurity throughout the eighteenth and nineteenth centuries, which heightened its desire to expand its influence. As the boundaries of the empire expanded, new dangers consistently materialized. British politicians and strategists felt that turbulence on colonial borders "pulled them toward expansion," in the words of a prominent historian of the era.[78] The notion that the empire could not be safe until all potential threats were addressed encouraged unnecessary forays into Afghanistan, Uganda, Zululand, the Crimea, and other places that served only to sap British strength.

Unipoles are by nature status-quo states. The second reason that threat expands with power is the fear that systemic disruptions could result in hierarchical alterations, that is, disruptions of status. For the power on top of the mountain, movement can only occur in one direction. Instability and conflict anywhere can appear to be the first steps toward systemic chaos and unpredictable status shakeups. The unipolar power can be expected to perceive threats quickly, therefore, often where other powers do not, and be more tempted to get involved in far-off turbulence that has the potential to challenge the system's stability.[79]

Maintenance of the status quo, or preservation of the "unipolar moment," has been a central if often unstated goal of U.S. grand strategy since the end of the Cold War.[80] The goal has not always been unstated: the infamous and still classified 1992 Defense Planning Guidance made opposing the rise of peer competitors a central focus of its recommendations.[81] Successive administrations have not been as explicit about their status concerns, but none has shown a willingness to cede the top spot in the international hierarchy. As a result, unipolar powers are likely to view other states as potential challengers and be wary of their intentions. Actors atop hierarchies are apt to be protective of their exalted status and quick to perceive challenges, whether any exist, under the assumption that others are seeking to replace them. Unipoles inhabit an inherently insecure position and are by nature suspicious and distrustful of those beneath.

Rich people worry a great deal about security. They build tall fences, install motion detectors, and hire private security guards to protect themselves and their belongings from the throngs of have-nots they assume are plotting to take what is theirs. Wealth creates insecurity in individuals, and it seems to do so in states as well. In today's international system, the United States has the most and worries the most. After all, to borrow Robert Kagan's memorable metaphor, the enemy of the outlaw is the sheriff, not the saloonkeeper.[82] Power and perceptions of insecurity are related, as counterintuitive as it may seem, since strong states believe themselves to be the primary targets of those malevolent forces lurking in the dark corners of the world.

Lost status threatens more than just a state's security. Since it is to a large degree an intangible asset, the defense of status necessitates the use of intangible means.[83] Perception of unipolarity *is* unipolarity, to paraphrase an old saying about power. Unipolar countries are especially conscious of insult and willful disregard of their position in the hierarchy. They are more likely to be concerned for their honor, in other words, and will be quick to perceive challenges to it. Status is a social asset; it exists because the community believes it exists. The United States can be expected to try to retain its standing, primarily through defense of its credibility and honor, for as long as possible, whether or not it is rational to do so.

The final reason to expect that the power of the United States should be accompanied by intensified perceptions of threat is psychological, not structural. Not only do the powerful rely on stereotypes more than the weak, but those stereotypes are not neutral. As actors grow in power and status, their evaluations of others, especially subordinates, become increasingly negative.[84] There is also some evidence, though admittedly not as robust, that power affects the tendency to dehumanize others, muting reaction to their entreaties and/or suffering.[85] These and the other obstacles to empathy make asymmetric relationships fertile ground for the growth of enemy images.

## ASYMMETRY AND THREAT: CAPABILITY VERSUS INTENT

One of the reasons why Americans overestimate danger is that, in general, people are not good at assessing risk. Daniel Kahneman and Amos Tversky won a Nobel Prize in economics for their work explaining that human beings have a hard time with numbers and respond much more powerfully to images.[86] The average person is essentially incapable of grasping the implications of being one of roughly 320 million Americans. When a few are killed by the ISIS sympathizer du jour, televised images make the danger appear immediate, overwhelming the comfort that an assessment of the empirical odds might bring. Perceptions of safety are casualties of the various heuristics preprogrammed into the human mind.

Were we rational beings, we would understand that threat is a function of capability and intent. Those enemies with the intention to harm us but no capacity to do so are not dangerous; likewise, actors capable of harm without the desire to do so pose no threat. To oversimplify:

$$THREAT = CAPABILITY \times INTENT$$

This equation is meant not to provide the basis for higher-level calculation but merely to emphasize that the relationship is multiplicative: If either capability or intent is zero, threat is also zero.[87] The enemy image interferes with this calculation, in different ways depending on the polarity of the system. During the Cold War, many observers equated threat with capability, while today many commonly assume that threat is essentially intent's equivalent.

In bipolar systems, or at least in roughly equal relationships, the danger of misinterpreting intent encourages a focus on an adversary's capability. To U.S. planners, Soviet capabilities were always more transparent than their intentions. Many strategists warned that prudence demanded a focus upon those capabilities, since intent was a matter of speculation. Often the two were assumed to be essentially equivalent because capabilities provided insight into intent. The Soviets always appeared to possess more military power than they needed for a purely defensive strategy, which implied that they were considering something more. For planning purposes, threat was often assumed to be roughly equivalent to material power during the Cold War, and the focus on intent was minimized.[88]

In the post–Cold War era, that assumption has been reversed: While the hostile intent of enemies, from Saddam Hussein to Iran to ISIS, seems clear (at least to some), their capabilities are negligible. But as if threat were a constant, perceptions of danger have hardly diminished. Today's enemies are said to be dangerous, even though they have very little capability to harm the United States, because their hostility implies that someday they will develop sufficient means. Thus Israel's prime minister can warn U.S. leaders that Iran's meager military capabilities should still frighten us because they are "bent on world domination."[89] Where there is a will, eventually there will be a way. The desire of post–Cold War enemies to do harm creates danger, irrespective of their capabilities. Since intent remains inherently unknowable, today's calculations are entirely subjective and even more susceptible to pathological images than when the Soviets were a plausible bogeyman with measurable kinetic potential.

When intent becomes the equivalent of threat, perceptions of danger are bound to rise. The hostile intent of enemies is clear and eternal, which guarantees that they will someday pose enormous threats to the unipole's interests, even if they do not now. Such thinking leads logically to the conclusion that enemies need to be attacked or preempted, preferably long before that far-off day when they develop the capability to cause harm. And it suggests that U.S. perceptions of their hostility are unlikely to diminish, no matter what dangers are actually present in the security environment.

Most of the time, even dire enemies find ways to coexist. When negative images dominate relations between peers, whether great or small, tension is typically high but aggression risky.[90] The Soviet Union and United States were certainly enemies, but rational calculations of cost and benefit assured that the Cold War never got hot. Unequal relationships affected by the misperception, however, are likely to prove more unstable. When the enemy image arises in asymmetric dyads, where neither balance nor deterrence is a realistic possibility, the risk of war is high. Few things are as dangerous as an unrestrained, unduly paranoid unipolar power.

After Iraq's invasion of Kuwait in 1990, George H. W. Bush quickly came to see Saddam Hussein through the prism of the enemy image. The Iraqi dictator was not merely a rival but a devil, "a man of evil standing against human life itself," in the president's words.[91] In the time between the wars, there was nothing Saddam could have done to change that perception in influential circles in Washington. In return, he maintained consistently hostile perceptions of U.S. intentions, interpreting all initiatives through a negative lens.[92]

Saddam also overestimated U.S. intelligence capabilities. As Charles Duelfer and Stephen Benedict Dyson explain in a remarkable 2011 article, the Iraqi dictator assumed that the omniscient United States knew he possessed neither WMD nor connections to Al-Qaeda. Saddam could not imagine that the unipole was actually scared of him, and thus he interpreted George W. Bush's rhetoric as bluster and bluff. He refused to believe that an attack was imminent, and told his subordinates that Bush's words were actually intended for North Korean ears. Unfortunately for him, the enemy image was so deeply embedded in the other side that it was essentially impossible for the Iraqi dictator to get off the hook. Diplomatic feelers were rebuffed, denials ignored, and when inspectors could not find evidence of WMD, it was interpreted as proof of Saddam's dishonesty.[93] Unipolarity helped the United States identify Iraq as an enemy and equate its intent with threat. In the absence of a plausible balancer, war was almost inevitable.

Similar instability can be expected any time that enemy images form in Washington for the foreseeable future, since all its relationships will be profoundly asymmetrical. Peace treaties and nuclear deals might delay conflict, but unless images change—or unless balance and deterrence come to the relationship—cycles of crises are quite likely to continue until the unipolar power feels safe. And given the persistent nature of images, that often means bad news for the smaller state.

Unipolarity makes misperception of enemies simultaneously more likely and more dangerous. Unnecessary conflict is quite possible if U.S. leaders prove unable to separate pathological images from actual hostility. Improving perception, which should always be a goal for leaders, is particularly urgent for those involved with U.S. foreign policy. The next chapter provides some limited guidance for those trying to perceive the world more accurately, by offering a set of common indicators of the presence of pathological, overly hostile views of the enemy.

# 4

## IDENTIFYING THE ENEMY IMAGE

The United States is hardly the only country that suffers from a chronic misperception of enemies, but its power guarantees that pathological U.S. images will be more common and far more consequential. Can its perception be improved? Can leaders learn to recognize the symptoms of misperception and control its pathological effects? Recent research suggests that the answer may be no. As it turns out, correcting perception, which psychologists sometimes refer to as "debiasing," is a very tall order.[1] People are loath to examine, much less alter, their beliefs. Even obviously erroneous facts often prove immune to all efforts to disprove them. Researchers have found that attempts to correct false impressions often backfire and end up reinforcing instead of undermining confidence in preexisting, incorrect information.[2]

Beliefs and perceptions are even more resistant to change than mere facts because of their close connection to identity. Tolstoy memorably observed that even intelligent people "can very seldom discern even the simplest and most obvious truth if it be such as to oblige them to admit the falsity of conclusions they have formed, perhaps with much difficulty—conclusions of which they are proud, which they have taught to others, and on which they have built their lives."[3] The people of the United States are unlikely to be convinced that they are fundamentally safe, for example, or that credibility is not worth fighting for, or that international competition leads to problems.[4] A great deal of depressing experimental evidence exists to suggest that debiasing is nearly impossible.[5]

Nearly impossible, however, is not impossible. While correcting misinformation will not alter beliefs immediately, over time the constituency for reason can grow.[6] False beliefs, even false collective beliefs, cannot persist forever in the face of sustained, rational assault. The process rarely results in sudden epiphanies, like that of Saul on the road to Damascus, but rather gradual and nearly imperceptible evolutions.[7] Individuals often recognize that a change in their beliefs has occurred only after the fact and resist admitting even to themselves that their minds are evolving while it is happening. Young people are generally more susceptible to the possibility of change and senior members of any generation much less likely to admit that their long-held theories might be wrong. This is particularly true for senior scholars, as Thomas Kuhn pointed out in his study of paradigms, because they rarely prove eager to adjust the belief systems that have served them well for so long. Junior members of any field are much more likely to adopt new ways of thinking because they are not as invested in the old and may gain a certain bit of pleasure in tearing down the old shibboleths.[8] Experimental evidence agrees.[9]

Collective debiasing might actually be easier than it is for individuals. Organizations can institute policies that, by altering structure, eventually affect agents. Cultures are more malleable in hierarchical organizations than they are in heterogeneous societies; those at the top might not be able to shape the beliefs of their members, but they can affect what they think about and how they act. Techniques such as devil's advocacy or "red-teaming," in which a subgroup is appointed to argue against the majority whenever feasible, can force members of organizations to confront and defend their positions and assumptions.[10] Those beliefs based on weaker foundations should find it difficult to survive. Over time, beliefs often come to align with actions, since people do not tolerate inconsistency for long.

Governments face far more challenges in implementing society-wide debiasing than do corporations. Even if improved popular perception is desired by those in power—leaders often share their society's biases and sometimes benefit from their existence—monolithic messages from the top are hard to sustain. But it is not impossible, if the will is present, along with sagacious leadership.

One area where debiasing may be successful is in the formation of images. Since they are not necessarily connected to emotion, alterations of images do not necessarily lead to identity crises. All actors, especially leaders, have an incentive to minimize misperceptions in their decision-making processes. In foreign policy, few factors impoverish decisions as much as the enemy image, which also produces consistent, identifiable, and repetitive patterns of thought and action. A description of indicators might help actors recognize these patterns and understand when their perceptions need reexamination. Images may prove to be like mirages or illusions: once they are recognized, perceptions of reality are never quite the same again.[11] Or at least that is the hope that motivates this chapter.

## INDICATORS OF THE ENEMY IMAGE

Enemy images are not always irrational. Rivals do exist, some of whom do secretly plot to destroy their opponents. While overestimating the belligerence of rivals can lead to misperception, underestimations can be fatal. Leaders holding an unjustified "inherent good-faith" image of others can be in for unpleasant surprises, as Stalin found out in 1940 when Hitler's tanks rolled into a stubbornly unprepared Soviet Union. The next year, Japanese bombers informed Franklin Roosevelt that he had been underestimating threats in the Pacific. Misperception in either direction can lead to national disaster, to either Pearl Harbor or Iraq. Few things are more important for national leaders, therefore, than accurate perception of the intentions of others. While unverified trust is rarely prudent, neither is constant worst-case-scenario planning, since that can also lead to counterproductive policies. Actions made to maximize safety can waste resources and bring about outcomes those policies were intended to prevent.

Although the "amount and quality of self-conscious judgment employed in decision-making can be increased," Robert Jervis wrote in 1976, "no formula will eliminate misperception or reveal which image is correct."[12] Perhaps not, but we may be able to approach such a formula in an indirect way by identifying common indicators of pathological images, in the hopes of creating a soft metric for more systematic evaluation. Leaders may not find it possible to eliminate the enemy image, but they can certainly take steps to recognize its presence and minimize its effects. The misperception of enemies, whether international, domestic, or interpersonal, tends to follow an established pattern. The risk of unnecessary war in any situation is directly related to the extent to which either side finds itself believing the following indicators. None is always wrong, of course. But when enough appear together, there is a high chance that the enemy image is at work and the hostility of rivals is being overestimated—and disaster could be on the horizon.

## INDICATOR 1: OUR DIFFERENCES ARE FUNDAMENTAL AND "EXISTENTIAL"

The most basic indicator of the presence of the enemy image is the belief that the other is not merely a state pursuing its interests but a fundamentally different sort of actor. Since we are good and trustworthy, it follows that those who are different may well be the opposite. The enemy's *nurture*—history, ideology, culture, and/or religion—outweighs our common human *nature*, creating mutually incomprehensible worldviews. What we think is basic to rationality, morality, and humanity simply might not apply to them. As a result, our differences are existential (which in popular discourse has essentially come to mean "irreconcilable" rather than the more traditional "threatening the existence of"). Our enemy hates us for *who we are*, not *what we do*. Our very existence threatens them, and our actions cannot change that. Enemies do not evolve, at least not in important ways; theirs is a permanent nature, born in their innate, immutable national characteristics (and flaws). Mutually agreeable peace, now or in the future, is a utopian fantasy absent significant evolution on their part.

Religious differences make fertile ground for such perceptions. Their faith (or lack thereof) has conditioned their identity in ways very different from ours. "Soviet Communism starts with an atheistic, Godless premise," said Eisenhower's secretary of state John Foster Dulles, the literature's paradigmatic example of a leader beholden to a pathological negative image. "Everything flows from that premise."[13] The apparent fanaticism of Iran's dominant Shia clerics might affect their views on an apocalyptic showdown with the West. "With these people's apocalyptic mindset, mutual assured destruction is not a deterrent, it is an inducement," wrote the influential Princeton historian Bernard Lewis on behalf of many. "It is a quick free pass for the true believers to heaven and its delights and dispatch of the rest to hell."[14] States with higher levels of religiosity are more likely to identify enemies across the various fault lines of faith. When two exceptionally religious countries find themselves on opposite sides of issues, as have today's United States and Iran, spirals of misperception are quite likely.

## INDICATOR 2: THEY DO NOT VALUE HUMAN LIFE LIKE WE DO

"The Oriental doesn't put the same high price on life as does a Westerner," General William C. Westmoreland told the documentary filmmaker Peter Davis. "Life is plentiful. Life is cheap in the Orient."[15] As it turns out, all the enemies of the United States have felt the same way. Clearly the Japanese did not value human life like we did during the Second World War.[16] Communists valued their ideology over people, and Putin inherited their cold indifference.[17] Such accusations are now more commonly leveled at the Muslim world, from Afghanistan to Gaza, where suicide bombers are taken as evidence that *they* simply do not care about life to the same extent that *we* do. At the same time, in many parts of the world, NATO's willingness to drop bombs from the sky is seen as evidence that its leaders place insufficient value on human life. The enemy culture has destroyed its ability to sympathize with others, which is a trait central to our character. The impetus for this misperception is not hard to determine: Westmoreland needed to believe that life was cheap in the Orient because it is easier to fight dehumanized enemies. The supposition that they do not value life like we do, which can be supported by a selective reading of evidence in any conflict, helps convince actors that they are on the side of righteousness. It is common, perhaps universal, and universally wrong.

The enemy's cavalier attitude toward humanity extends even to extinction. Deterrence might not work against our enemy because its leaders do not necessarily fear a nuclear holocaust and may even initiate one. During the Cold War, a variety of analysts argued that the Kremlin did not believe in mutual assured destruction and felt that nuclear war could be waged and won.[18] Former secretary of defense Caspar Weinberger, for example, believed that enormous suffering at the hands of the *Wehrmacht* had hardened Soviet leaders. He consistently argued that the United States faced an adversary who did not share its abhorrence of war, even the nuclear variety.[19] The Soviet civil-defense program and force structure led many observers to doubt that Moscow believed in strategic stability destruction at all.[20] At the same time, the Soviets worried that Washington might believe it could fight and win a nuclear exchange. Weinberger made occasional jokes about this, which were broadly misinterpreted in Moscow. So too was a widely circulated comment by a Reagan administration official that all the United States had to do was build enough bomb shelters to emerge victorious in a nuclear war.[21] We know now that neither side seriously contemplated launching a bolt-from-the-blue attack and that deterrence was accepted by both superpowers.[22] Doubts to the contrary were misperceptions fed by the enemy image.

To some observers, post–Cold War enemies of the West appear equally undeterrable. The Anti-Ballistic Missile Treaty was scrapped in 2002 on the premise that rogue states are inherently unmoved by fear of retaliation and cannot be expected to act rationally. The enmity Iranians feel toward the United States and Israel is so great that it may well outweigh their desire to live, which is why the regime might use any nuclear weapons it develops. Leaders in Tehran might prove sufficiently irrational to bring down their civilization in a blaze of suicidal glory, unleashing a religiously inspired doomsday plan that would pit their one or two weapons against states that have hundreds.[23] When we find ourselves believing that our enemies are unable to recognize the most basic tenets of rationality, misperception is likely at work.

## INDICATOR 3: THEIR WORD CANNOT BE TRUSTED; NEGOTIATIONS ARE A WASTE OF TIME

Shortly after the Cuban Missile Crisis, the Soviets made a series of proposals designed to cool superpower tensions. Marine Commandant David Shoup found little reason to accept anything the Soviets said. "It's hard for me to believe," said the general, who was a member of Kennedy's Joint Chiefs of Staff, "that their philosophy of lying would be subject to any sudden reversal to a philosophy of telling the truth." The rest of the administration apparently agreed, citing as evidence the lies that the Soviet foreign minister Andrei Gromyko had told the president during the Cuban Missile Crisis.[24] The word of the United States was trustworthy, on the other hand, despite the fact that in the previous few years a steady stream of lies had emanated from the White House regarding the U-2 affair, bungled attempts to assassinate Castro, and other misadventures. On April 12, 1961, Kennedy told the press that "there will not be, under any circumstances, any intervention in Cuba by U.S. forces."[25] Five days later, the invasion at the Bay of Pigs began, and Kennedy's ambassador to the United Nations, Adlai Stevenson, denied to the world that the United States had anything to do with it.

Leaders lie all the time in international politics.[26] The main difference between our lies and theirs is that we remember theirs, believing they reflect our rival's true character. Ours are unfortunate reactions to particular situations, always understandable in context, and certainly not indicative of who we really are. This is essentially the "fundamental attribution error" discussed in chapter 1, or the tendency of people to emphasize dispositional rather than situational factors in interpreting the behavior of others but do the opposite in their own case.[27] The error in perception is nearly universal and deeply pathological.

Perhaps it goes without saying that there is little reason to negotiate with untrustworthy actors. Diplomatic overtures to enemies are not only pointless but dangerous, since they can lull us into a false sense of security while having little effect on their overall hostility and perfidy. Enemies cannot be expected to honor commitments. When the United States began arms-control discussions in earnest with the Soviets, the enemy image led many to doubt their potential for success. "When we sit down to negotiate with the Soviets, we negotiate for peace," argued Weinberger, "they negotiate for victory."[28] The Harvard historian Richard Pipes explained to the many leaders he advised that the Soviets viewed arms control as a tactic to restrain, and ultimately divide, the West.[29] Negotiations are just another weapon in the enemy's endless struggle against us.

The same refrain accompanied the bargaining with Iran over its nuclear-weapons program. Israel's prime minister Benjamin Netanyahu told the U.S. Congress in 2015 that since Iran could not be trusted, any deal would be by definition a bad deal. Forty-seven GOP senators agreed and followed the speech up with an open letter to Tehran designed to scuttle the talks. On the other side, Supreme Leader Ayatollah Khamenei reportedly told his diplomats that "you are fools if you think the Americans will live up to anything they promise."[30] We bargain in good faith; they do not. Nothing they say can be believed, since their words are unrelated to their intentions.

## INDICATOR 4: THE ENEMY REGIME IS SIMULTANEOUSLY DANGEROUS AND FRAGILE

Leaders misinformed by pathological enemy images are predisposed to believe that the people in rival states do not really support their evil government. Our disagreement is with the enemy regime, not its people, whom we suspect are basically good and more or less like us.[31] Their government, therefore, is much weaker than it appears. The political psychologist Ralph White observed that "nations tend to overestimate the insurrectionary possibilities (with implied friendliness toward themselves) in countries whose governments they strongly dislike," citing as examples the U.S. confidence in revolution in Cuba and the Soviet Union's similar outlook for the capitalist world in its early years.[32] Later U.S. policy makers would be convinced that their troops would be greeted as liberators in Iraq and that the Iranian people would welcome the overthrow of their government.

At the heart of the inherent-bad-faith image, therefore, lies a paradox: evil regimes are simultaneously terrifyingly powerful and essentially fragile. No matter how evil they may be, with the right amount of effort on our part, they can certainly be overcome. Indeed, it probably would not take much to topple the enemy regime, since its legitimacy is built on sand. The two parts of the paradox are directly related: the greater the evil, the stronger its inherent vulnerability. Dulles saw signs everywhere of the Soviet Union's internal weakness and felt that it was perpetually on the verge of collapse.[33] Former Reagan administration official Michael Ledeen has argued for three decades that while the government in Iran represents an existential threat to the United States, overthrowing it would be a simple affair.[34] And we have already reviewed how destructive it was to consider Saddam Hussein's regime a grave threat that would be a cakewalk to remove.[35]

Given its internal weaknesses and fundamental insecurity, the enemy is always thought to be particularly responsive to forceful measures. Throughout the Cold War, many analysts remained sure that despite its military prowess, the Soviet Union would retreat whenever confronted by a resolute United States because its leaders could not risk upsetting their precarious domestic economic and social balance.[36] Likewise, if only the Obama administration had supported the 2009 "Green Revolution" in Iran—even verbally—it might well have succeeded.[37] A few years later, opponents of nuclear diplomacy argued that compromise was unnecessary, since with more pressure the regime would have had no choice but to comply with all the demands of the West. A "better deal" was possible because of fragility in Tehran. The enemy regime is always a house of cards on the verge of collapse, which makes it vulnerable to our pressure—but it is also insecure, desperate, and thus even more dangerous.

## INDICATOR 5: THEY ARE REALISTS AND ONLY UNDERSTAND THE LANGUAGE OF FORCE

One of the iron rules about perception in international politics is that the other is a "realist." We have *principles* that drive our decisions, but they act almost exclusively in pursuit of their *interests*. This is particularly true for any state with which we have even a mild rivalry or any reason at all to suspect its motives. Many Western observers consider Vladimir Putin to be particularly ruthless and single-minded in pursuing power and interest, for example. The Chinese at the beginning of the twenty-first century are commonly portrayed as being the paragons of *realpolitik* in their policies, whether in Africa or Latin America or their nearby seas.[38] Arabs routinely reject any explanation for U.S. policy in the Middle East that does not begin and end with the pursuit of oil.

Since our rivals are realists, it follows that the main goal of their foreign policy is to increase their power at the expense of ours. Central to the enemy's eternal nature, therefore, is deep-seated cultural dissatisfaction with the status quo. *We* are interested in maintaining the world as it is; *they* always want to change the balance of power in their favor. To use the terms of art in international relations, they are "revisionists," but we are a "status-quo" power.[39] Throughout the Cold War, U.S. leaders were easily convinced that international communism had an expansionary nature but overlooked similar aspects of their support for the aspirations of freedom-loving people everywhere. "Soviet leaders are first and foremost offensively rather than defensively minded," declared the infamously inaccurate intelligence-oversight committee nicknamed "Team B," while the United States obviously favored defense.[40] Likewise, Soviet leaders felt that the United States "was not satisfied with the nuclear balance and continued to seek strategic superiority," according to a contemporary analysis, and "had not rejected the idea of pre-emptive war."[41] Today, many U.S. leaders believe that Putin plans to alter the map of post–Cold War Eurasia and reassemble the USSR. Likewise, Tehran does not take an understandable, legitimate interest in the affairs of its neighbors but actively undermines them as part of a plan to dominate its region. Unipolar powers, who are structurally predisposed to favoring the status quo, are particularly susceptible to the belief that others are revisionists.

A general policy prescription follows logically from this ubiquitous assumption that the other is monomaniacally focused on power: strength must be met with strength. Leaders commonly believe that their rivals only respond to force, grit, and determination.[42] As senior Truman administration advisor Clark Clifford explained to the president, "the language of military power is the only language which disciples of power politics understand."[43] *Realpolitik* has essentially robbed the enemy of its ability to understand nuance and subtlety or to care about anything except its national interest. Thus the eternal, endlessly repeated prescription when dealing with enemies is that they "only understand the language of force," as opposed to, presumably, a language of words.

As it turns out, every enemy or rival of the United States in the last half-century, from the North Vietnamese to the Sandinistas to Saddam Hussein, has "only understood" force. In 1986, President Reagan announced a "victory in the global battle against terrorism" after sending a message "in the only language Khadafy seems to understand," which was in that case an air strike that killed the Libyan leader's fifteen-month-old daughter.[44] Madeleine Albright, Richard Holbrooke, and other U.S. officials consistently argued throughout the 1990s that the various Balkan leaders, especially Serbia's Slobodan Milosevic, only understood the language of force.[45] Since the Soviets were the greatest Cold War enemy, U.S. leaders from Truman onward consistently felt that Moscow displayed the least ability to grasp diplomatic subtleties.[46] Even some of our most seasoned diplomats have agreed: In his famous "Long Telegram," George Kennan wrote that Soviet power was "impervious to logic of reason" but "highly sensitive to the logic of force."[47]

The enemy image reduces rivals to unidimensional caricatures who respond only to demonstrations of brute power. Cooperative approaches are not only a waste of time but counterproductive, since they signal weakness to realist enemy actors always on the lookout for opportunities to increase their power. Forceful measures have a far greater chance of success.

## INDICATOR 6: OUR VARIOUS ENEMIES
## WORK TOGETHER

The enemy image blurs distinctions among those we distrust. All our enemies, as it turns out, work together. Their hatred for us overpowers any differences they may have and binds them in an unholy alliance. The egocentric bias assures that we are, as ever, the primary determinant of their behavior.

Many people considered communism a monolithic force throughout the Cold War, even after the Soviets and the Chinese began fighting each other in the late 1960s. "International communism is in effect a single party," explained Dulles, notwithstanding the ample evidence may have existed to the contrary.[48] "There isn't any difference in totalitarian states," according to President Truman. "You call them Nazi, Communist or Fascist, or Franco, or anything else—they're all alike."[49] After 9/11, President Bush believed that Al-Qaeda and Iraq were brought together by their common hatred of the United States. "In my judgment," the president said in October 2002, Saddam "would like to use Al-Qaeda as a forward army."[50] In 2014, as the conflict with ISIS began, the lines separating the various actors in the Middle East opposed to U.S. policies again began to fade. Hezbollah, Hamas, Iran, Al-Qaeda, and ISIS were all part of the other side, with distinctions, perhaps, but not differences. Michael Flynn, who had a brief but glorious run as President Trump's first national security advisor, wrote that Al-Qaeda and ISIS are part of an alliance that includes Russia, Iran, China, North Korea, Cuba, Venezuela, Syria, and a host of others united by a shared hatred of freedom.[51]

Not only is evil always united, it also generally has an epicenter. "There seems to be a curious American tendency," observed Kennan toward the end of his life, "to search, at all times, for a single external center of evil, to which all our troubles can be attributed, rather than to recognize that there might be multiple sources of resistance to our purposes and undertakings, and that these sources might be relatively independent of each other."[52] During the Cold War, the root of the world's ills was obvious, and today it appears equally plain for many observers. Iran has become to the twenty-first century what the Soviet Union was for the second half of the twentieth: evil's epicenter, the origin and supporter of the world's problems, from terrorism to radicalism to proliferation. The road to victory in the war on terror, therefore, goes through Tehran. The perception is mutual; for many Iranian analysts, most of what's wrong in the world can be traced back to Washington's machinations.[53] Defeating the enemy essentially removes evil from the world, a goal for which no amount of urgency can be sufficient.

The inability—or unwillingness—to distinguish between rivals is a hallmark of what the social psychologist Milton Rokeach once labeled a "closed belief system."[54] People with such a personality tend to merge all their "disbelief systems," or those beliefs they automatically and unthinkingly reject, into one category. It becomes natural for such people to conflate Islam with fascism ("Islamofascism"), or Osama bin Laden with Saddam Hussein, or Nazis with communists. An internal memo circulated in the early months of the Trump administration linked the regime's various enemies—the mainstream media, academia, the "deep state," globalists, bankers, the Democratic leadership, the GOP leadership, Islamists, and "cultural Marxists"—into one huge, malevolent conspiracy.[55] Rokeach and his colleagues also found that correlations between closed belief systems and anxiety are always positive. The world such people inhabit is perpetually dangerous and terrifying.[56]

People with closed belief systems are more susceptible to negative images. The notion that our rivals work together intuitively appeals to some people more than others. Conversely, it is clear that, once established, enemy images interfere with the ability to detect division in their ranks, leading to the perception that the world is populated by hostile coalitions devoted to undermining our security and way of life. The resulting vicious cycle is difficult for reason and empathy to penetrate.

## INDICATOR 7: THEY ARE SUPERIOR STRATEGISTS WHO TAKE THE "LONG VIEW"

Jervis observed that, for a variety of reasons, "actors tend to see the behavior of others as more centralized, disciplined, and coordinated than it is."[57] People are aware of their own internal deliberations and divisions but see only the outcomes of decisions made elsewhere, which makes other actors seem unified and strategic. In addition, given their particular cultural predisposition, rivals seem perfectly willing to put off the achievement of their goals for generations if necessary. Unlike us, enemies have the gift of patience.

Authoritarian states in particular appear to have an advantage over democracies when it comes to making strategy. Unencumbered by public opinion, oversight, or constitutions, dictators can run efficient policy processes. They have no meaningful disagreements over national interests and objectives and can quickly settle upon the most efficient means to pursue those ends. U.S. policy makers sometimes seemed jealous of the freedom of action that tyranny afforded Soviet leaders and warned of the strategic advantages it created. As a result of centralized decision making, enemy policy is always more calculated and unified than ours can hope to be.

Enemies are superior long-term planners as well. While our leaders rarely think beyond the present crisis, theirs combine wisdom with cunning and patience. To use the common metaphor, they play chess while we perpetually respond with checkers. The Soviets were by nature patient, long-term strategists, according to many U.S. observers. Team B warned that the first item emphasized by Soviet doctrine was "unflagging persistence and patience."[58] Moscow was willing to wait decades or even generations for the collapse of the West, confident in its eventual victory.[59] Post–Cold War enemies have been equally far-sighted and sagacious. Western leaders faced the chess master Vladimir Putin, whose forays into Ukraine and the U.S. election were clearly all part of an as-yet-mysterious master plan. The Chinese are commonly considered equally good strategists, far superior to those in the West, planning two, three, or four decades into the future on a regular basis.[60] Islamic fundamentalists might not be remotely close to achieving their goal of a reestablished caliphate, but that should provide cold comfort: they are willing to wait many years to see it come to fruition. President Trump denounced the Iran nuclear deal by explaining that "they think in terms of 100-year intervals, not just a few years at a time."[61]

Enemies also excel at implementation. While we often botch even our best-laid plans, they are masters at producing their intended results.[62] Once the enemy image has taken hold, "each party attributes to the other a degree of omniscience and omnipotence that he knows is manifestly impossible in his own situation," wrote Raymond Bauer more than a half-century ago. "It is often assumed that if 'the intentions of the Soviet leaders' can be deciphered, these 'intentions' can almost automatically be assumed to be implemented."[63] The enemy is somehow immune to accidents, chance, blunders, and bureaucratic inefficiency, the kinds of things that we know often plague us. Or, as Jervis bluntly put it, "like confusion, stupidity is rarely given its due."[64]

Finally, unlike us, enemies control their proxies. While our allies think and act independently, the subordinates of our enemies are merely tools in their kit. During the civil war in Syria, the U.S. leaders knew they could exert little influence on the decisions made by the various antigovernment groups but were convinced that President Assad essentially took orders from Moscow. President Trump believed that the Chinese could make Kim Jong Un behave and "easily" solve whatever problems North Korean ICBMs posed.[65] Thus it has always been, from Vietnam through El Salvador to the present day: our allies barely listen to us, but theirs are willing pawns in their overall global designs.

Our fear of their strategic superiority often finds expression in rhetoric and inspires a series of key terms that can be considered indicators in themselves. Most commonly, the enemy image inspires us to believe that we have *principles* or enduring values but that they have an *agenda* or secret, ulterior motivation. No document makes this distinction more clearly than NSC-68, the famous top-secret policy document prepared by senior Truman administration officials in 1950. NSC-68 spends a good deal of time explaining the fundamental differences between the two superpowers, referring repeatedly and endlessly to the "design" of the Kremlin and the "purpose" of the United States.[66] The difference in terminology is important and indicative of the enemy image: whether in domestic or international politics, "agendas" or "designs" are secret and shrouded in dishonesty; "principles" or "purposes" are noble, transparent, and admirable. Obviously, we engage in the latter. These terms should be considered warning signs of the presence of pathological images.

## INDICATOR 8: THEY UNDERSTAND US BETTER THAN WE UNDERSTAND THEM—AND THEY KNOW WE ARE RELUCTANT TO USE FORCE

Largely thanks to their superior strategic capability, our enemies understand us far better than we understand them. Pipes argued during the Cold War that Soviet strategists had an enormous advantage over their counterparts in the West because they emerged "from the background of an international revolutionary movement," which meant they "always had a keen interest in Western societies."[67] Today, since many senior Iranian leaders have spent time in the West, they appear to have an edge in comprehending our strengths and weaknesses. Our understanding of enemies—outside of a small coterie of experts—is always rudimentary at best.

As explained in chapter 1, actors routinely overestimate how benevolently they are perceived by others. As a result, we believe the enemy knows that our intentions are essentially benign and that we are not going to attack. In effect, the enemy image convinces its host to believe that the normal, natural distrust that states feel toward one another is not present in its rivals, because *they* know *we* are rational and trustworthy. Ronald Reagan argued in 1983 that "Soviet leaders know full well there is no political constituency in the United States or anywhere in the West for aggressive military action against them."[68] In the same year, the Defense Department official Richard Perle lamented to Congress that they "can be quite confident in the Kremlin that the United States is not going to launch an aggressive war against them," while "we can have no such confidence."[69]

In practice this means that enemies are essentially immune to the kind of insecurities that lead to "security dilemmas," the well-known phenomenon in which insecurity drives states to take actions that decrease the security of their neighbors.[70] They are offensively, not defensively, minded; *their* actions are not caused by anything *we* have done, for they know our intentions are peaceful.

Since they have nothing to fear from us, enemies commonly exhibit a mismatch between stated policy ends and means: they always overspend, devoting far more resources toward their military than their minimal defense concerns would warrant. Weinberger told Congress in 1982 that the Soviets

> do not need a new intercontinental bomber to defend the Soviet Union, and it is not being produced because of a fear of the United States. It is being produced in keeping with their plan to secure worldwide military superiority and domination. . . . The Soviets do not need an aircraft carrier to defend the Soviet Union . . . they do not need the increased number of divisions to defend the Soviet Union . . . they do not need all the additional fighters and bomber aircraft and all the armored fighting vehicles and all the ICBMs . . . to defend the Soviet Union.[71]

A generation later, Russian actions were equally suspect, since Putin had no legitimate security concerns in his periphery. Russian protests regarding NATO expansion—though nearly universal—were not taken seriously, since U.S. planners believed that Moscow understood the alliance harbored no offensive motivations.[72] "Russia objectively has never enjoyed greater security in its history than it has since 1989," argued Robert Kagan in 2015. "Who would launch such an invasion?. . . For the first time in Russia's long history, it does not face a strategic threat on its western flank. . . . Neither Chinese nor Russians can claim that a sphere of influence is necessary for their defense."[73] It is also not possible for those viewing Iran through the prism of the enemy image to believe that its nuclear program might be inherently defensive in nature, since Tehran must know that the United States is not going to attack. Iranian leaders must have understood that the United States had no stomach for another war in the Middle East.

The enemy image makes it all but impossible for leaders to recognize "spiral-model" dynamics, where states can be essentially locked in a mutually destructive cascade of tension, arms buildups, and potential conflict.[74] Since our enemies understand our benevolence—and use it to their advantage—we know that their decisions are essentially unrelated to our actions.

## INDICATOR 9: IT TAKES A FOREIGN-POLICY "EXPERT" TO UNDERSTAND THEIR TRUE NATURE

Often specialized expertise is required to recognize the true intention of enemies. Following the death of Stalin, journalists and casual observers were more likely to perceive evolution in Soviet motivations and behavior than were experts.[75] Sovietologists were always far more skeptical of the potential for fundamental change in the Kremlin, no matter who was in charge, from Lenin to Gorbachev.[76] "Amerikanists" in the Soviet Union, whose models of the United States were predicated on eternal hostility, were no better in detecting nuance in American behavior.[77] Since the Cold War's end, former hardliners on have been loudest in attributing Putin's aggression in his near-abroad to eternal Russian cultural characteristics visible only to the specialist.[78]

Moscow is not the only center of an eternal national nature. No words or actions will alter the image of the Iranian regime that many American elites hold. Henry Kissinger warned the Senate Armed Services Committee in 2015 that Iran "reflects a history of empire," which was "one of the major themes" of its strategic culture, at least until the nineteenth century.[79] Why the Parthians and Sassanids are more relevant to modern Iranian foreign policy than the last two centuries, which contain no examples of attempted conquest, was left unclear.

Experience and expertise ought to provide foreign-policy elites the tools to form better, more accurate perceptions than those of the masses. Often this is the case: regional experts in particular are usually better at empathizing with those in the areas they study and are less likely to form unduly negative impressions. But in general the foreign-policy expert class tends to be more susceptible to the effects of the enemy image than the average person, which is a counterintuitive point in need of some explanation.

First of all, so-called experts are under social pressure to identify enemies. In the U.S. system—and probably elsewhere—hawkishness and suspicion of others is a prerequisite for being taken seriously in elite foreign-policy circles. Little professional credibility is gained from being the outlier counseling caution, patience, and benefits of the doubt. Suspicion is the mark of the professional. Elites formed negative images of Iran much faster than did the general public in 1979, for instance.[80] A generation later, the eminent foreign-policy observer Leslie Gelb became a proponent of the invasion of Iraq because, as he admitted later, "of unfortunate tendencies within the foreign policy community, namely the disposition and incentives to support wars to retain political and professional credibility."[81] Relevance and credibility in elite circles reward negative images and punish apparent appeasers.

Second, those with more knowledge about foreign affairs are less likely to change their opinions of others. As mentioned above, experimental evidence indicates that new information has a much harder time altering the long-held beliefs of the expert than the more malleable views of the neophyte.[82] The endowment effect (according to which people ascribe more value to things they own, such as their beliefs) strengthens over time.[83] This is particularly true for negative perceptions, which have even stronger staying power. Experts are under pressure to be consistent in their theories and judgments and thus rarely change in fundamental ways. The elite class is more likely to develop enemy images, in other words, and less likely to change them in the face of new information.[84]

Not all members of the elite foreign-policy class are equally susceptible to pathological perceptions. Certain characteristics within the "marketplace of ideas" increase the likelihood that their hosts will harbor distorted enemy images. Around the world, for example, political ideology is strongly linked to risk perception. People who hold right-of-center views have a greater predisposition to believe that the world is a dangerous place than do those on the left.[85] Conservative parties everywhere identify enemies more readily than their competitors. Suspicion of outsiders and paranoid politics is so central to right-wing populism, from the National Front in France to the Danish People's Party, that it can be considered one of the defining features of the movement. Soviet conservatives were consistently much more hostile toward the United States than were Moscow's liberals.[86] Fortunately for their mental health, conservatives are also more likely to believe that enemies can be readily defeated by the forces of good, in part because of their interesting tendency to envision opponents as physically small and weak.[87]

In American politics, neoconservatives consistently detect greater numbers of enemies, and therefore higher levels of threat, than other analysts.[88] "Neocons" were among the most concerned about the implacable, eternal hostility of the Soviet Union and a host of post–Cold War actors, from Saddam Hussein's Iraq to Iran to China.[89] Many early neoconservatives were converts from Trotskyism, which they claimed granted them unique insight into communism's inherent evils. To understand why the Soviet mind was fundamentally different from the American, one needed to study its seemingly obscure antecedents. Pipes, a Sovietologist of Polish extraction, claimed he was one of the few capable of decoding Moscow's intentions. "Soviet military literature, like all Soviet literature on politics broadly defined, is written in an elaborate code language," he wrote. "Buried in the flood of seemingly meaningless verbiage, nuggets of precious information on Soviet perceptions and intentions can more often than not be unearthed by a trained reader."[90] Similarly, a host of "experts" on Islam popped up after September 11 to explain the evils of that religion to the uninitiated.[91]

Expertise creates fertile ground for the enemy image, as does conservative politics. Conservative experts, therefore, run the highest risk of misperceiving the hostility of other states. When such people are decisive in opposite capitals, the corresponding risk of mutual misperception, spiral dynamics, and war is at its highest.

## INDICATOR 10: THEY ARE NAZIS

Finally, if there is one ironclad indicator of the presence of a pathological enemy image, it is the comparison of rivals to Nazis. The enemy is not just evil; it is always 1938, and we are perpetually at Munich. Often both sides of a dispute are convinced that they face the modern incarnation of Hitler. The Cold War pitted the Hitlers in the Kremlin against the Hitlers in the White House, as does the current dispute over Ukraine. The state-controlled Russian media overflows with comparisons of the United States and its Ukrainian puppets to 1930s fascists.[92] It is never hard to find someone in a position of influence equating Iran with the Nazis in the United States, and the Iranian press commonly makes the same comparison in reverse.[93]

The most common use of the ubiquitous Hitler analogies are rhetorical, to support policy decisions already made. The George H. W. Bush administration paved the way for war against Iraq in 1991 with a steady stream of Hitler talk: between the invasion of Kuwait and the onset of Operation Desert Shield, there were 228 articles published in the *New York Times* and the *Washington Post* that made reference to Nazis in one way or another.[94] At other times, policy makers appear to believe their own rhetoric. In the Pentagon during the lead-up to the 2003 Iraq War, Secretary of Defense Donald Rumsfeld understood the Ba'ath party in Iraq to be essentially a reincarnation of the Nazis. His deputy, Paul Wolfowitz, expressed his view of a proposal to integrate Sunnis into the postwar settlement on an internal memo simply with "They are Nazis!" In the feverish assessment of the Pentagon's number-three official, Douglas Feith, Saddam was worse than Hitler because he was in office far longer.[95]

The intellectual and moral sloppiness of comparing rivals to Hitler is well known, but recourse to that analogy continues unabated. When

Nazis haunt decision makers, folly follows. Nazi references are the clearest indicator of implacable hostility on our part, whether merited or not, and is a clear warning that the enemy image is at work. The analogy is a symptom of muddled thinking, shallow (or dishonest) reasoning, and pathological heuristics.

⚬⚬⚬

Sometimes there is inherent bad faith on the part of other actors. Sometimes they really are plotting against us, probing for weaknesses, and biding their time to strike. Some do have a secret, nefarious, long-term master plan. It is certainly not the case that all enemy images are misperceived. Prudence might suggest erring on the side of caution, mimicking the paranoia of Churchill rather than the faith of Chamberlain.

Danger does not only exist on one side of that equation, however. The overestimations of hostility that accompany the enemy image are far more common, and they inspire unwary leaders to enact unnecessarily belligerent, costly, counterproductive policies. The challenge is to separate truly devious actors from those just pursuing national interests, those with whom deals can be cut and accommodations made. Not all enemies are existential. Many can be mollified, or even simply be monitored and resisted, without ever succumbing to the kind of pathological fear that some of them probably hope to create.

While Robert Jervis is undoubtedly right that policy makers will never be able to consult a magic formula to assess the accuracy of their perceptions, the preceding indicators can signal pathological misperception. They are not all false, at least not on all occasions; the presence of one or two of these factors indicates nothing in particular. But policy makers, especially those of unchecked unipolar powers, should be aware that these beliefs have been indicators of misperceived hostility in the past and have inspired unnecessary belligerence, counterproductive policies, and, at times, national ruin.

# 5

## UNIPOLARITY AND STRATEGY

The great works of strategy were not written with unipolarity in mind. This is not a coincidence; for action to be *strategic*, it requires an opponent or at least other actors pursuing goals that may or may not come into conflict. The other, or a rival, differentiates strategic thinking from mere planning. One does not need a strategy to pick the kids up from softball practice, or to find the eggs in a grocery store, or to get a project done before vacation, since there is no one trying to prevent it from happening. A plan is sufficient. If, however, interaction with another actor with opposing preferences is likely, then a strategy is necessary. One can begin a strategic activity like chess with a game plan, but the opponent's moves are going to require adjustment along the way. No plan survives contact with the enemy, wrote the Prussian strategist Helmut von Moltke.[1] Or, to paraphrase more a recent strategist, everyone has a plan until they get punched in the mouth.[2] It is the reaction to that punch that differentiates the good strategists from the bad.

National security is also an inherently strategic endeavor. The system contains many other actors, some of whom will have interests that occasionally conflict with those of the United States. Washington has to take into account the reactions of others as it pursues its goals, which means that it must always think strategically, no matter how much or how little danger it believes it is in.

Unipolar powers face no peer rivals and have no existential threats, especially in an era of relative peace and security. How, then, can strategy be formulated? What has the collapse of the Soviet Union done to U.S. strategic thinking? This chapter looks at the effect of the end of the Cold War on the development of strategy. It discusses the identification of ends and means, as well as perceptions of threat, which have evolved in rather unpredictable and underappreciated ways since the last U.S. rival imploded. As it turns out, it is not easy to think strategically in a unipolar world, either for the state in the center or those in the periphery.

Large threats concentrate the mind and attract attention. The relative insignificance of post–Cold War danger has hindered the formulation of good responses. Could threat severity and strategic wisdom be inversely related? Since the collapse of the USSR and general decline in global violence, the United States has muddled along, rudderless, committing blunders large and small. Until its strategic community comes to recognize the nature of the system in which it operates, such blunders will continue, and true victory in the Cold War will remain elusive.

## STRATEGY AND THE UNIPOLAR POWER

Any struggles the United States might have had in formulating strategy since the Cold War ended are not to be blamed on a lack of effort. One could make the case that more attention is paid to strategy in the current era, especially inside the federal government, than ever before. Since 1986, when Congress mandated the production of annual "national security strategies," official U.S. documents have proliferated uncontrollably. The vast majority of these bureaucratic products are bland, vapid statements of the obvious and the uncontroversial.[3] One wonders how the Cold War was won without a *National Security Strategy, National Military Strategy, National Defense Strategy, Quadrennial Defense Review, Quadrennial Diplomacy and Development Review,* or reports about the "Joint Vision" and "Joint Operating Environment," much less the lesser "strategies" dealing with virtually every imaginable subject, from counterterrorism to cyberspace and from the Arctic to sub-Saharan Africa. The labor-hours that go into the production of such documents are apparently insufficient to make much intellectual headway into the challenges that unipolarity poses. Despite the sincere efforts of those in and out of government, the formulation of strategy has proven to be more challenging since the collapse of the Soviet empire than it was while a Third World War appeared possible.

The first characteristic one notes about the new documents and their attendant popular and academic literatures is the belief that the world remains a dangerous place. Threats are everywhere, and the United States is the only country that can address them.

## THREATS

The U.S. strategic community's initial reaction to the collapse of the Soviet Union, like the first stage of grief, was denial. As if responding to some Law of Conservation of Enemies, new dangers were always right around the corner, just waiting to be discovered. What had been second- and third-order threats—rogue states, terrorism, failed states, proliferation, "superempowered individuals," economic crises, or merely chaos itself—quickly rose to primary status, keeping the level of perceived danger constant.[4] Since those minor threats were more numerous than the singular USSR, the world seemed to have become a *more* dangerous place. James Woolsey's vision of a large dragon replaced by "a bewildering variety of poisonous snakes" was widespread.[5] Secretary of State Madeleine Albright lamented that "we must plot our defense not against a single powerful threat, as during the Cold War, but against a viper's nest of perils."[6] A very senior military officer preferred this formulation a decade later: during the Cold War, the United States was locked in a room with a cobra, but afterward it had to deal with a limitless number of bees.[7] Creators of such metaphors tended to overlook the fact that there had always been snakes and bees in the world, but no one paid them much attention in the presence of the dragons and cobras. Terrorism and the other threats of the twenty-first century were not new, but the amount of time U.S. leaders now had to devote to worrying about them grew substantially once the Soviets were gone. Background problems were moved to the foreground and elevated to replace what had been a much larger threat emanating from Moscow.[8]

By nearly any measure, the threats of the current era are minor compared to those of any other country at any other time. Global armed-conflict levels are at historic lows. Terrorism is a problem but hardly an existential threat, and it is not increasing in its severity or frequency.[9] The number of failed states is not increasing, and the threat posed by them remains minimal.[10] The New Peace does not contain great dangers for strong countries. The strongest is the safest.

The global diminution in violence is occasionally acknowledged but rarely taken seriously among the community of strategists. Colin Gray spoke for the majority when he dismissed the pacific trends out of hand. For decades, Gray has argued that nothing of fundamental importance to international politics ever changes, that there is nothing new under the sun, and that history shows that bad times inevitably follow good. As the 1990s came to a close, Gray argued that "all truly transformational theory about international politics is, and has to be, a snare and a delusion . . . humankind faces a bloody future, just as it has recorded a bloody past." "The cold war is over, but does it really matter?" he wrote in 1993.[11] New wars, big and small, loom on the horizon, even if it may be hard for the average person to see them or even imagine them.

While grieving people eventually move past denial, many U.S. strategists appear stuck in that initial phase. Even the few works that address the implications of essential threatlessness (or at least the absence of an enemy) on strategy deny that increased safety accompanies the collapse of rivals. In her *Power in Uncertain Times*, Emily Goldman argued that "relative to the Cold War context," the United States now confronts "a *greater number* of threats, *greater diversity* in the types of security actors that can threaten our interests, and a *more interdependent* world in which rapidly emerging technologies quickly diffuse and are exploited by others in unanticipated ways."[12] A Soviet-free world is not necessarily a more secure world, in other words. Goldman then went on to identify a series of precedents for the strategic situation in which the United States finds itself. Her examples, which include Russia and England between the Crimean War and World War I as well as the United States and England between the world wars, are not well chosen. The states in her cases all faced real threats or, at least, rival great powers willing to pursue their interests with force. The inclusion of the interwar era is particularly bizarre, since the latter half of that era was dominated by an expansionist empire in the Pacific and a rising, revisionist power in Europe. These periods were hardly analogous to the post–Cold War United States, which has little to learn from them. While the past may contain some examples of societies that enjoyed virtually threat-free environments thanks to geographic isolation, no great power in more recent times has been able to formulate strategy in a danger-free context. Widespread denial has guaranteed that few have spent much time considering what greatly reduced levels of threat should do to foreign policy or grand strategy.

One can hardly blame threatlessness for pathological strategic thinking if no one perceives the system as threatless to begin with. Perhaps there is a minimum threshold of danger people need to perceive in order to function; perhaps there is something unique in the nature of the United States that magnifies the small threats until they appear big. Or perhaps unipolar powers are predisposed to detect dangers others do not. Whatever the reason, the United States *fears more* than other great powers today, much to the detriment of its ability to think clearly about strategy.

The list of tangible threats in the post–Cold War system may seem insufficient to justify the United States' consistently high levels of military spending. Fortunately for those who fear major cuts to the budget, the intangible, vague, unknowable dangers that fecund Pentagon imaginations can devise are limitless. If one theme unifies two decades of U.S. strategic thinking, it is that the post–Cold War era is one marked by complexity, uncertainty, and "unknown unknowns." And as the Romans used to say, *omne ignotum pro magnifico*, everything unknown is taken as great. Vague dangers can appear great and quite frightening— as long as they are not considered in any real depth.

The threat to defense spending posed by the absence of threats to the country was first addressed by a group of analysts at RAND in the early 1990s. James Winnefeld and other "uncertainty hawks," in the words of Cal Conetta and Charles Knight, pioneered the belief that the new system was not in fact any safer, appearances and evidence to the contrary not-withstanding.[13] "Out with the old, in with the ?????" and "Certitude vs. Uncertainty" were among Winnefeld's self-explanatory subheadings.[14] "Uncertainty is the dominating characteristic of the landscape," wrote Paul Davis, the editor of a 1994 RAND volume on defense planning that focused on the dire challenges posed by the collapse of the lone threat to American security.[15] It did not take long for U.S. national-security-strategy documents to pick up the theme. "The real threat we now face," according to the 1992 *National Military Strategy*, "is the threat of the unknown, the uncertain."[16] The message has been consistent, in both official and unofficial outlets, for more than two decades. The 2005 *National Defense Strategy* elevated uncertainty—rather than, say, stability—to the position of the "defining characteristic of today's strategic environment."[17] In 1997, Secretary of Defense William Cohen said that "while the prospect of a horrific, global war has receded, new threats and dangers—harder to define and more difficult to track— have gathered on the horizon."[18] At a press conference five years later, in the days leading up to the war in Iraq, his successor warned about "unknown unknowns," which are the threats that "we don't know we don't know," which "tend to be the difficult ones."[19] Uncertainty hawks are now prevalent in the United Kingdom as well. The 2010 UK National Security Strategy, titled "A Strong Britain in an Age of Uncertainty," claims that "today, Britain faces a different and more complex range of threats from a myriad of sources" and that "in an age of uncertainty, we are continually facing new and unforeseen threats to our security."[20] Such claims are rarely—if ever—questioned, much less subjected to any kind of scrutiny. That the world today is somehow more complex and therefore less predictable or knowable has become a belief accepted on faith, with no need for further justification.

The claims of uncertainty hawks contain a number of consistent elements. First and foremost, one of the more frightening aspects of unidentifiable threats is that little can be known about their relative intensity levels. Unknown unknowns might be rather benign, catastrophically severe, or somewhere in between. For many observers of U.S. foreign policy, the possibility that unseen threats are exceptionally dangerous simply cannot be ruled out. "At present, Americans confront the most confusing and uncertain strategic environment in their history," writes the prominent historian and strategist Williamson Murray. "It may also be the most dangerous to the well-being of their republic."[21] Known knowns can be measured, understood, and combated; those left to the imagination quickly expand to ominous proportions. "To make any thing very terrible, obscurity seems in general to be necessary," Edmund Burke noted centuries ago. "When we know the full extent of any danger, when we can accustom our eyes to it, a great deal of the apprehension vanishes."[22] The dangers posed by unknown unknowns, perhaps because of their obscurity, tend to appear unlimited and especially terrible. *Omne ignotum pro magnifico.*

Second, in a related point, since the present is so uncertain and frightening, these analyses tend to downplay the dangers of the past, as if threats are strategically meaningless unless presented comparatively. The message is clear: the current era is *more* complex, uncertain, and unknowable than earlier ones. Richard Haass, who would go on to be the State Department's director of policy planning, worried in 1997 that "the world in the wake of the Cold War . . . promises to be terribly complex, more so than what came before."[23] Official U.S. government publications unanimously agree: the global security environment presents an "increasingly complex set of challenges," according to the 2012 *Defense Strategic Guidance*, compared to those that have come before.[24] Nostalgia for the Cold War, explicable once rosy retrospection and the positivity bias are understood, is quite common in official U.S. strategic documents. The United States moved from a "time of reasonable predictability to an era of surprise and uncertainty," claimed the 2006 *Quadrennial Defense Review.*[25] Although the assertion that the Cold War was predictable might surprise those who waged it, to the strategists who came afterward the struggle against the Soviets seems to have been relatively uncomplicated, even quaint.

Uncertainty and complexity have technological roots. The third theme of this literature is that the proliferation of science and engineering increases the potential mayhem future enemies can perpetrate. The evolution of technology is ominous not only for U.S. national security but for the peace and stability of the world. The National Intelligence Council predicted in 1996 that "accelerating rates of change will make the future environment more unpredictable and less stable."[26] Weapons proliferation is the most troubling, but other, seemingly benign scientific research can be destabilizing as well. The 2006 *Quadrennial Defense Review* recommended that the United States shift its emphasis toward potentially catastrophic or merely "disruptive" technologies that future enemies might employ.[27] Few topics obsess U.S. planners as much as "cyberwarfare," or the potential of a computer-based attack on the Western interests, which resulted in the creation of the U.S. Cyber Command in 2010.[28] "The world is applying digital technologies faster than our ability to understand the security implications and mitigate potential risks," warned a report of the U.S. intelligence community in 2013. "Compounding these developments are uncertainty and doubt as we face new and unpredictable cyber threats."[29] Technological change has always been accompanied by increases in anxiety and predictions of ill effects to come.[30] Since the speed of that change has never been greater, it should perhaps come as no surprise that anxiety is high as well.

Fourth, the rise of intangible threats has found a receptive audience in the American strategic community in large part because of its concern, perhaps even obsession, with surprise attack. A powerful, somewhat unreasonable fear of surprise has been a central part of U.S. strategic culture since at least Pearl Harbor.[31] The attacks of 9/11 helped remind the security community that dangers can come literally out of the blue. Arnold Wolfers observed decades ago that "nations tend to be most sensitive to threats that have either experienced attacks in the recent past or, having passed through a prolonged period of an exceptionally high degree of security, suddenly find themselves thrust into a situation of danger."[32] Periods of apparent calm are not comforting to those societies conditioned to believe that danger often materializes out of nowhere, without warning. A seemingly safe world, where the sources of those inevitable surprises remain obscure, can seem more frightening than one with obvious threats.

Finally, the obsession with the intangible prevents proper consideration of what is probably the most important force-planning question: How much is enough? How many supercarriers are enough to address the complex future, for instance? How many F-22s, cyberwarriors, spy satellites, or combat brigades does the United States need to keep its people safe from unknown unknowns? A security environment characterized primarily by drastic unknowables offers no guidance to those seeking to construct military forces. When danger is limited only by the imagination, states invariably purchase far more than they need, wasting money on weapons systems that will never be used, to address threats they do not yet perceive.

As long as human rationality remains bounded, flexibility will remain central to any sagacious grand strategy. Planning decisions must, however, take probabilities into account while establishing priorities. While anything is possible, if we are to believe the cliché, surely not everything is plausible. Imaginary danger is limitless, but real danger is not. Despite the assertions of the uncertainty hawks and no matter what fear-laden rhetoric emerges from Trump's White House, the current strategic environment has proven not only rather stable and predictable but benign. No new strategic threats have arisen out of the blue, whether small groups of psychotics (it is helpful to remember that Al-Qaeda was hardly new to international intelligence services before 9/11) or major peer competitors. The latter in particular cannot possibly emerge without giving fairly substantial warning. In the real world of national security, serious threats do not materialize out of thin air. The serious problems of tomorrow, should they emerge, will give plenty of warning.

Goldman wrote that "unlike the prior interwar period, the uncertainty engendered by the end of the Cold War shows few signs of abating."[33] In this she is essentially correct, even if her analysis is backward. The lack of identifiable, tangible, immediate threats to U.S. security has caused strategists to look toward intangible, unidentifiable, future dangers, which is a tendency that shows little sign of changing. This age of uncertainty, however, is an age of relative safety. Until the day arrives when U.S. strategists are forced to replace vague threats with concrete ones, the basic security of the United States is assured.

## THE TURN INWARD

What would a chess player do if his or her opponent simply stood up and left the table? Would it make sense to continue playing with the same amount of effort, concentrating instead on the capabilities of his or her own pieces, in case a new opponent came along? Planners in Washington apparently think so, since that is essentially how the United States has acted since the collapse of the Soviet Union. Rather than alter its outlook or level of preparation to match the evolving dangers of the world, America merely changed the direction of its strategic gaze, turning its focus inward rather than outward. The resulting unipolar conception of strategy takes no other side into account (since none exists), which has drastically and counterproductively altered the way the United States plans and constructs its military.

The most basic effect of this turn inward has been on the way that strategists regard their central concept. Although there never has been a universally accepted definition, strategy has traditionally incorporated some conflict, or at least its potential, against a foe.[34] The need to take the actions of the other into account is what makes an action strategic. In the late 1980s, U.S. strategists began to redefine the term, severing the traditional link between strategy and the enemy. One of the first strategists to do so was Arthur Lykke, of the Army War College, who wrote in 1989 that strategy is better thought of as how (the ways) states use their power (their means) to pursue their objectives (ends).[35] Risk arises when those three components are not properly balanced. The actions of others barely register in Lykke's conception. To be strategic, one needed only to ask three questions, all of which could be answered with little regard for rivals: What is to be done? How is it to be done? What resources are required to do it?[36]

Since Lykke wrote, this conception of strategy (which has become known in some circles as the Lykke model) has become ubiquitous in the U.S. strategic community. Its simplicity has had particular influence in U.S. war colleges, which are the nation's primary centers of teaching and thinking about strategy. "In essence," summarized Mackubin Owens of the Naval War College, in 2007, "strategy describes the *way* in which the available *means* will be employed to achieve the *ends* of policy."[37] No longer is interaction and the attempt to react to and influence the other the essence of the concept; no longer does Washington need to ask itself what its enemies or rivals are likely to do in response to its actions. As long as ends are properly identified and ways and means sagaciously chosen in their pursuit, the mission has been accomplished. "The challenge for the strategist," write Derek Reveron and James Cook, is not to take the potential actions of others into account but to "coordinate the various levers of national power in a smart or coherent way."[38] To those with a bit of historical perspective, such as the eminent strategist Lawrence Freedman, this new but well-established conception "barely counts as strategy."[39] Other critics have charged that the simple, formulaic conception (ends + ways + means = strategy) discourages creativity and leads to the perception that once both sides of the equation are brought into balance, the mission of formulating strategy is accomplished.[40] Despite its ubiquity, the Lykke model has impoverished strategic thinking in a country already too willing to ignore the rest of the world. "Strategy" that fails to take other actors into account is a contradiction in terms and misinforms the decisions based upon it.

The second result of the turn inward has been a fundamental alteration of the Pentagon's approach to force planning. The United States used to follow what was known as a "threat-based" model, which made priorities of assessing the capabilities of potential opponents, anticipating their likely actions, and devising ways to counteract them. Military forces would have shrunk along with threats in the wake of the Soviet collapse, had this traditional force-planning construct been followed. Instead, the construct was changed.

According to former secretary of defense Donald Rumsfeld, after the Cold War a new approach was necessary, one that "focuses less on who might threaten us, or where, and more on how we might be threatened and what is needed to deter and defend against such threats."[41] For over twenty-five years, the Department of Defense has followed a "capabilities-based" approach to force planning, in which the actions of rivals— or even their existence—are essentially irrelevant. Decisions on what capabilities to develop, and what weapons systems to support them, are now determined by perceived weaknesses in U.S. defenses that, if apparent to us, could be exploited by some future enemy. What enemies can do now is not as important as what we can imagine them doing in the future. How the country might be vulnerable is at issue, not who might be able to exploit those vulnerabilities. Post–Cold War force planning proceeds as if peer competitors were continually probing the U.S. armor for weakness, whether or not such competitors actually exist.

As a result of capabilities-based planning, the United States is now adding a new generation of attack submarines to its fleet, even though the older generation—which remains the best in the world—was never used in the role for which it was designed. The mere fact that no other navy has even one supercarrier will not stop the United States from replacing each of its ten with all-new, thirteen-billion-dollar models. The Air Force was determined to add new generations of both air-superiority (F-22) and ground-support (F-35) fighters, no matter what the rest of the world did. Stealth ships, upgraded battle tanks, and space weapons may someday be useful, we are told, even if they are not now.

This transformation in approaches to force planning did not occur accidentally or without debate. In the early 1990s, Les Aspin, who was the chairman of the House Armed Services Committee, championed the continuation of the traditional planning models, arguing that by using their logic a great deal of money could be saved in the absence of a major threat. Secretary of Defense Dick Cheney opposed him, arguing that focusing on identifiable dangers (or the lack thereof) rendered the United States vulnerable to those as-yet-unidentified threats that might arise in the future.[42] Cheney urged the United States to create and maintain the best military it could, rather than be limited by challengers of the present or foreseeable future. After all, a high jumper does not stop trying to achieve greater heights just because the competition cannot keep pace.

Capabilities-based planning was another notion championed early on by analysts at RAND. Winnefeld and some of his colleagues led the way in encouraging the Department of Defense to break away from the "tyranny of scenario plausibility." Once freed from the tyrannical intellectual constraints imposed by reality, the analyst would be able to recognize all sorts of potential trouble. "The scenarios that are over the horizon—yet nevertheless make a sudden preemptive strike on today's comfortable assumptions—lie in the category of unanticipated surprises," they wrote.[43] The Pentagon seized upon capabilities-based planning with enthusiasm, in part because it helped justify the continuation of enormous defense budgets but also because it fit nicely with a defense posture focused (or unfocused) on uncertainty. RAND's Davis emphasized that "the notion of planning under uncertainty appears in the very first clause" of his definition of capabilities-based planning because "uncertainty is fundamental, not a mere annoyance to be swept under the rug."[44] The approach "has the virtue of encouraging prudent worrying about potential needs that go well beyond currently obvious threats."[45] Worrying about needs that go beyond threats is only prudent to those following the inward-looking, capabilities-based model that has come to dominate Pentagon planning since the end of the Cold War.

The "Millennium Challenge" exercise from the summer of 2002 is a nice example of capabilities-based planning in action. The war game, which was one of the biggest in the history of the U.S. military, gave all the services a chance to test the new technologies that had rolled off the high-tech assembly line over the preceding years. Given the date, one might assume that the fictional enemy would have been Iraq or one of the other members of the "Axis of Evil," or perhaps even China or Russia. None of those had the potential to give U.S. capabilities a test rigorous enough, however, so the foe chosen for the game was the country with the second-most-sophisticated military in the world: Israel.[46] The United States spent $250 million simulating a war against the Israelis, an event even the most optimistic Palestinians would probably consider rather unlikely. But Pentagon planners had successfully avoided the tyr-anny of scenario plausibility.

Capabilities-based planning also led directly to one of the most noto-rious force-planning failures in American history. The United States went into Iraq with the army it had, to paraphrase Secretary Rumsfeld, not the army it needed. Had force planners been concentrating their energies on external threats rather than internal capabilities, they may well have thought about the possibility that irregular enemies might not use high-tech means to challenge U.S. power in the wars to come. Unfor-tunately, the long list of weapons that were in the U.S. arsenal did not include much that would defend against "improvised explosive devices," for example, armed personnel carriers with heavily armored under-carriages. The Army would have to wait until years of combat had passed and thousands of lives were lost before the Pentagon acted in response to that real, pressing threat.

No rational planner would suggest that the U.S. military should cease striving to remain the best that it possibly can be, no matter what other states are doing. The task of the strategist, however, is to assess realistic risks and allocate scarce resources according to the most likely threats of the future. Capabilities-based planning makes insufficient effort to assess probabilities, and as a result entails enormous costs, both budget-ary and in opportunity, for the United States.

## CONFLATING MEANS WITH ENDS

Since the new conception of strategy now common in U.S. defense cir-cles emphasizes matching ends, ways, and means, one might assume that at the very least those components have been well considered in the post-Soviet era. Unfortunately, this has not proven to be the case. Another effect of threatlessness on U.S. defense planning has been a habitual conflation of means with ends, often in ways that can quickly become dangerous. A collection of concepts traditionally recognized as ways to accomplish goals—influence, presence, credibility, even alliances—have all too often become the ends of policy in themselves, raising the possibility of conflict in the process.

The first example is one of the most pervasive. "Influence" in foreign capitals has always been a goal of states, but, in times of both peace and crisis, it has historically been pursued as a means with which to pursue a nation's interests. Today, influence is increasingly pursued for its own sake, under the apparent perception that it will be useful someday, even if its current utility is rarely considered, much less articulated. Once freed from tangible outcomes—or strategic purpose—the quest for influence can dramatically expand the scope of U.S. involvement abroad.

The massive U.S. investment in security cooperation and assistance, for instance, is largely intended to increase its influence. By one count, the United States deploys troops to more than 150 countries for a variety of purposes, one of which is certainly to influence events, whatever they may be.[47] The 1992 *National Military Strategy* justifies global deployments by explaining that they "lend credibility to our alliances" and "promote U.S. influence and access."[48] What exactly such influence hopes to accomplish is rarely discussed, since it is not really at issue. Influence is valuable in itself and is pursued for its own sake.

There is also a danger of conflating means and ends regarding "access." Instead of being a tool or capability that could allow for the realization of national goals, access has become an end, primarily by naval and air-force strategists. New capabilities and tactics have been developed to assure it, such as the U.S. Navy's Freedom of Navigation Operations discussed in the previous chapter. The United States sails everywhere just to show it can—because the ability to access every inch of international waters is now apparently a vital national interest.[49]

Once the end was identified, Pentagon strategists dutifully set about developing ways and means. The result was a new organizing concept for the Pacific, the so-called Air-Sea Battle, which was specifically designed to counter potential Chinese efforts to employ the dreaded "antiaccess/area denial."[50] Although details of the concept remain classified, at essence Air-Sea Battle encouraged greater cooperation between the Navy and Air Force in order to deny China the ability to deny U.S. ships access to its littoral seas. The 2012 *Defense Strategic Guidance* warned that "state and non-state actors pose potential threats to access" and pledged that the United States "will seek to protect freedom of access throughout the global commons."[51] The development of Air-Sea Battle as well as that of its successor, the descriptive if awkward Joint Concept for Access and Maneuver in the Global Commons, makes it clear that access has been awarded a value all its own.

Economic access has been an enduring U.S. interest in Asia, dating back to Commodore Perry's mission to Japan and the Open Door policy in China. In these instances access was valuable because it opened markets, which were the real goal of the policy. Today's strategists refer to economic benefits as an afterthought rather than as the central purpose of policy making. Why Beijing would decide to cut off international trade and essentially bring its economy to a grinding halt is unclear but irrelevant. Obviously freedom of action has enormous tactical and operational importance, but that freedom is meaningless in the absence of larger strategic ends. Unipolar Washington values access for its own sake rather than as part of a broader strategy to protect free trade.

Another vital interest of the United States, at least as defined by the willingness to spill blood in its pursuit, is credibility. According to the conventional wisdom in the policy world—one that, it deserves noting, is nearly unanimously rejected by scholars—credibility earned through displays of resolution can help states achieve goals in the future by affecting the calculations of others.[52] During the Cold War, the United States fought to preserve its credibility with regularity, in the belief that it was sending messages regarding its determination to defend its interests to the Soviet Union, allies, and those countries on the fence.[53]

The evidence overwhelmingly indicates that lost credibility is far less harmful than widely believed. When the Reagan administration pulled U.S. troops out of Lebanon following the 1983 barracks bombing, to take but one of many examples, hawks were predictably apoplectic. "If we are driven out of Lebanon, radical and rejectionist elements will have scored a major victory," Secretary of State George Shultz said in briefings on Capitol Hill. "The message will be sent that relying on the Soviet Union pays off and that relying on the United States is a fatal mistake."[54] Michael Ledeen was more explicit: "Our defeat in Lebanon will encourage our enemies, in the Middle East and elsewhere," he wrote. "In all probability, we shall pay a disproportionate price for our Lebanese failure," from the Middle East to Central America, where Soviet-sponsored guerrillas would be encouraged, with disastrous results. As always, U.S. allies and potential friends would be powerfully disillusioned, including the Egyptians, whom Ledeen felt would "increasingly distance themselves from the Camp David agreement."[55] Fortunately for the United States, Soviet influence in the Middle East did not increase, their guerrilla allies did not change their behavior, and the Egyptians did not abandon their treaty commitments. The fears generated by lost credibility proved baseless, as they usually do.[56]

The obsession with credibility outlived the Soviet Union, despite that today no enemy stands poised to take advantage of irresolution. No "second world" exists to offer an alternative power center toward which allies or third parties can tilt.[57] While it is far from clear that it ever had any real utility, credibility is certainly meaningless when there is no enemy to receive the messages the United States tries to send. Today the logic behind the national obsession, or what Stephen Walt calls the "credibility fetish," is rarely articulated or examined.[58] Credibility is pursued for its own sake, not so much as a tool to make future interests easier to address but as an interest in itself.

The final example of means conflated with ends involves one of the centerpieces of the U.S. security structure. Despite predictions from the Ivory Tower, NATO not only survived the collapse of the Soviet Union but grew.[59] Expansion had liberal and realist supporters, all of whom agreed that in order to survive NATO had to change, in both its missions and composition. For liberals, expansion represented a way to stabilize countries in the former Soviet bloc and integrate them into Europe.[60] The relatively few realist supporters appreciated the consolidation of gains from the Cold War, just in case future Russian leaders ever had ideas about rising again. Expansion helped give the alliance a new raison d'être, a way to reverse the negative momentum that could easily arise following the loss of its former purpose. To use the phrase common at the time, NATO had to "expand or die."[61] The alliance that had once been a primary tool to address the goal of keeping the Soviets out of Western Europe (and the Americans in, and the Germans down, in Lord Ismay's well-known formulation) was in the 1990s transformed into an end in itself.[62] Colin Powell summarized this thinking, and the confusion of means with ends, in the title of a 2004 piece in *Foreign Affairs*: "A Strategy of Partnerships."[63] Partnerships no longer served the goals of the strategy; they *became* the goals of the strategy. Commitments are now an end in themselves. In a rather devastating critique of John Ikenberry's work, Richard Betts wrote that "for most statesmen, multilateralism is a means," but for many liberal internationalists, "it is an end itself."[64] President George W. Bush's foreign policy was objectionable to this school of thought because it often leaned toward the unilateral, especially when it came to the war in Iraq. And the Trump administration appears intent on making many a multilateral-minded strategist miss the Bush era.

When there are no pressing goals to accomplish or threats to be countered, inertia assures that means previously employed take on the appearance of ends. As a result, U.S. policy makers may feel pressured to fight the Chinese over access, or to intervene in Syria to preserve credibility, or to expand NATO further to maintain the viability of the alliance. Or they might well combine these new ends and intervene to preserve the credibility of NATO, as they did in Kosovo.[65] The elevation of means into ends in the absence of threat may be understandable, but that does not make it wise. Without tangible referents, these intangible concepts are at the very least strategically pointless and often far worse. Blurring the distinction between means and ends has confused U.S. strategic thinking to the point that, in some cases, it has made unnecessary confrontation more likely.

## THE PSYCHOLOGICAL EFFECTS OF LOW STAKES AND HIGH COMPLEXITY

Perceptions of danger and complexity have very definite effects on decision making. The relationship is nonlinear and easily oversimplified, since a series of other factors—stress, time constraints, experience, etc.—come into play. But experiments have consistently found two variables routinely associated with less systematic decision-making strategies: low stakes and high complexity.[66]

Counterintuitively perhaps, people in situations of relatively low threat tend to rely more on heuristics, analogies, and metaphor when making choices (sometimes referred to as "noncompensatory" strategies, since they tend to ignore information relevant to choices and avoid tradeoffs).[67] High-risk situations appear to foster more rational, systematic decision making: danger focuses the mind. The stakes, not the relative perceptions of danger, are decisive; even if today's policy makers are unconvinced that the world is less dangerous than it was during the Cold War, they are certainly aware that the stakes were higher a generation ago. Unlike President Kennedy in October 1962, twenty-first-century presidents can be assured that no matter what choice they make, the republic is likely to survive. Their decisions are less troubled by the stress of the potential apocalyptic consequences of mistakes, and as a result they are more likely to employ mental shortcuts when making decisions. Rationality suffers as the stakes fall.

Complexity promotes less-systematic decision making as well. A wide variety of studies have demonstrated that there is a limit to the amount of cognitive confusion people will tolerate before shifting to less rational, "effort-saving" decision-making strategies.[68] It is difficult to evaluate systematically the pros and cons of any issue when the list of compounding factors grows high. People tend to go with their gut rather than their head when problems get too complicated. Policy makers convinced that they live in complex times are less likely to employ optimal decision-making strategies and are therefore more likely to make the kind of mistakes that accompany these less optimal strategies.

Taken together, these two findings suggest that the kinds of biases, motivated and otherwise, discussed throughout this book are more likely to affect calculations of decision when stakes are low and perceptions of complexity high. That these conditions obtain in the post–Cold War world makes for a dangerous combination, one likely to lead to poor decisions and strategic error.

## THE FORMULATION OF POST-SOVIET POLICY

Threatlessness has had other, more predictable effects on the formulation of foreign and national security policy, a few of which are worthy of brief mention. Elimination of the traditional strategic imperative has elevated what might be considered astrategic considerations in the policy process. In those states where no central, all-encompassing enemy demands the focus of strategists, internal factors become more important in foreign policy making.[69] Political, bureaucratic, and psychological influences on U.S. behavior become more important as national-security concerns decrease.

Members of Congress worry less about the potential negative impacts of parochial or ethnic-oriented influences on policy. As long as national security is not threatened, they are free to promote the interests of lobbies and contributors without fear of serious consequence. As a result, a variety of domestic lobbies have enjoyed a much greater degree of influence on foreign policy in the post–Cold War, low-threat period.[70] The United States tilted decisively toward Armenia in the early 1990s, for example, as its diaspora asserted itself. During the Cold War, national interests occasionally clashed with the interests of the Israel lobby; today, lawmakers compete to become AIPAC's most obsequious friend. In the absence of urgency from without, decisive influence comes from within. The United States finds itself obsessing over trivia, such as formal recognition of the 1915 massacres in Turkey as a genocide, or irrationalities, such as the continuing, pointless embargo on Cuba.[71]

The unipolar era could be read as a twenty-five-year-long case study in organizational behavior. As anyone familiar with Morton Halperin's work would have expected, the protection of resources became a central concern of the massive defense bureaucracy originally constructed to fight the Soviets.[72] In the 1990s, defenders of the budgetary status quo argued that the United States needed to be prepared to fight two simultaneous regional conflicts, which coincidentally would require approximately the same level of spending that occurred during the Cold War. Without that capability, which came to be known as Two

Major-Theater Wars (or, since nothing exists until it has an acronym, 2MTW), potential enemies might take advantage of a situation where U.S. forces were tied down elsewhere to launch their own offensives. The two theaters under consideration were kept officially vague but widely acknowledged to be the Middle East and northeastern Asia. If the United States had to deal again with Saddam Hussein, this thinking went, the North Koreans might well take advantage of the opportunity to attack southward. The mere fact that such a scenario had never happened before or that this is generally not why countries decide to invade their neighbors did not seem to bother supporters of this argument, whose primary purpose was to avoid the dreaded "peace dividend" that might have been logically expected to follow the removal of the main threat to the West.

Fiscal imperatives will drive security decisions when not challenged by those of national security. Military spending, for instance, is commonly described in terms of percentage of GDP, usually in order to argue that the United States is not spending as much as it could, or even to imply an optimal level for proper force planning. Often the connection is made quite explicitly, as in 2009 when Senator James Inhofe (R-OK) introduced a bill that would have committed the United States to devote 4 percent of its GDP to defense in perpetuity, an idea endorsed by a large number of analysts.[73] The bill died, but the sentiment lives on, and the metric has become widely accepted.

The unipolar world does indeed contain threats, as it turns out, just not threats to the security of the United States. It is the military budget that has been under siege, and its defenders have reacted with arguments that seem logical as long as they are not subjected to much sustained strategic analysis. When otherwise serious analysts argue that a certain level of spending must be maintained without reference to the external environment—essentially advocating spending for its own sake, as a value in itself—or to how the U.S. economy performs, for that matter, then all pretenses toward strategy have been abandoned. Such arbitrary, spectacularly astrategic goals for U.S. military spending would not be needed if the world were not a relatively safe place.

Finally, personality rises in importance as structural imperatives ease. Temperamental and psychological traits of presidents have greater influence on U.S. policy when unconstrained by external forces. Presidents vary somewhat in their ability to empathize, for example, which has an immediate effect on their choices. President Obama made frequent efforts to understand others and was sometimes criticized for doing so. Suggesting that American exceptionalism was not substantially different from Greek or British exceptionalism, which he did on his first trip to Europe in 2009, might have been empathetic, but it was not patriotically correct. At the other extreme, his successor appears to suffer from a pathological behavioral malady that produces an insuperable obstacle to empathy, one that increases the unipole's natural tendency to disregard others. President Trump displays the classic symptoms of Narcissistic Personality Disorder, or NPD, and so will U.S. foreign policy as long as he is in office.

Diagnosing an individual from afar, based only on a public persona, carries obvious analytical perils. For a psychiatrist, it is also explicitly forbidden: the "Goldwater Rule" of the American Psychiatric Association (APA) states that "it is unethical for a psychiatrist to offer a professional opinion unless he or she has conducted an examination and has been granted proper authorization for such a statement."[74] It thus falls to political scientists to point out that, while no concrete diagnosis can be made, Trump certainly appears to display the symptoms of NPD. According to the APA's current *Diagnostic and Statistical Manual of Mental Disorders*, the disorder is marked by a "pervasive pattern of grandiosity, need for admiration, and lack of empathy" indicated by five (or more) of the following:

1. Has a grandiose sense of self-importance (e.g., exaggerates achievements and talents, expects to be recognized as superior without commensurate achievements).

2. Is preoccupied with fantasies of unlimited success, power, brilliance, beauty, or ideal love.

3. Believes that he or she is "special" and unique and can only be understood by, or should associate with, other special or high-status people (or institutions).

4. Requires excessive admiration.

5. Has a sense of entitlement (i.e., unreasonable expectations of especially favorable treatment or automatic compliance with his/her expectations).

6. Is interpersonally exploitative (i.e., takes advantage of others to achieve his/her own ends).

7. Lacks empathy: is unwilling to recognize or identify with the feelings and needs of others.

8. Is often envious of others or believes that others are envious of him or her.

9. Shows arrogant, haughty behaviors or attitudes.[75]

The self-esteem of narcissists "is almost invariably very fragile," according to the manual. "They may be preoccupied with how well they are doing and how favorably they are regarded by others. This often takes the form of a need for constant attention and admiration." That self-esteem is enhanced "by the idealized value that they assign to those with whom they associate. They are likely to insist on having only the 'top' person (doctor, lawyer, hairdresser, instructor) or being affiliated with the 'best' institutions but may devalue the credentials of those who disappoint them." Furthermore, they "may constantly fish for compliments, often with great charm."

Many of Trump's baffling actions before and after the election become far more understandable once viewed through the prism of psychopathology. The narcissist's insecurity renders him or her "very sensitive to 'injury' from criticism or defeat. Although they may not show it outwardly, criticism may haunt these individuals and may leave them feeling humiliated, degraded, hollow, and empty. They may react with disdain, rage, or defiant counterattack." And they will be temperamentally unable to empathize.

One of the few who have considered the implications of NPD for politics is the psychologist Jerrold Post, who has argued that narcissists require "excessive admiration" and have a need for constant attention and praise. Doubt rarely enters their mind, since "dogmatic certainty with no foundation of knowledge is a posture frequently struck" by those with the disorder. Because they are so deeply ensconced in themselves, narcissists have an especially difficult time understanding others, whether adversary or ally. Finally, the disorder makes it difficult to accept advice, since to do so would be to admit flawed knowledge or insufficient wisdom. "It is difficult for the narcissist," according to Post, "to acknowledge ignorance and accordingly to seek or accept information or constructive criticism of his ideas."[76] If Trump truly has NPD, he will be incapable of any fundamental evolution. The disorder is not generally treatable, much less curable, since narcissists do not accept the suggestion that anything is wrong with them.[77]

Narcissism in staterooms is not exactly unprecedented. According to Post, "if individuals with significant narcissistic characteristics were stripped from the ranks of public figures, the ranks would be perilously thinned."[78] While other leaders may well suffer from the same disorder, none lead unipolar powers. For as long as Donald Trump is president, official U.S. empathy for other states will be even rarer than it otherwise would be.

Overall, the internal characteristics of the U.S. system, as well as those of its leaders, will play an unusually large role in its decision making as long as the United States is relatively unthreatened by outside forces. Its policy will be a reflection of its inner self, warts and all, for the duration of the unipolar moment.

—— ∞ ——

The Soviet Union did not survive the Cold War, but neither did the American ability to think clearly about strategy (to the extent such an ability ever existed). The greatest benefit of unipolarity—relative safety—carries disadvantages as well. The overall effect of the removal of its enemy has been detrimental to the formulation of U.S. grand strategy. Attempts to chart a way forward in an era of essential threatlessness have suffered from a variety of underconsidered, shallow, and dangerous ideas that have come to dominate national-security policy for more than two decades. As a result, the United States worries more—and spends more—than is necessary to achieve its goals.

During the Cold War, threat helped create an enormous strategic community; now that the Cold War is over, the enormous strategic community has helped create threat. Those who worry about the uncertainty, complexity, and undetectable dangers evince a clear nostalgia for the simpler times that came before, when all the United States had to worry about was an aggressive, totalitarian enemy with millions of troops and thousands of nuclear weapons. Those with less selective memories, however, might recall that the Soviet Union was not only tangible and unpredictable but much more dangerous to Western interests than the "unknown unknowns" that apparently now keep U.S. planners awake at night.

The United States won the Cold War but somehow feels less safe. Washington would do well to remember the advice of one of its clearest thinkers, George Kennan: "In so far as we feel ourselves in any heightened trouble at the present moment, that feeling is largely of our own making."[79] This present moment is less troubled than any that have come before, even if we do not always seem to realize it.

# 6

## UNIPOLARITY AND GRAND STRATEGY

T he demilitarization of Europe," argued Secretary of Defense Robert Gates in February 2010, "has gone from a blessing in the 20th century to an impediment to achieving real security and lasting peace in the 21st."[1] President Obama echoed such sentiments six years later, telling the *Atlantic*'s Jeffrey Goldberg that "Free riders aggravate me."[2] And during the 2016 presidential campaign, Donald Trump repeatedly questioned the utility of any alliance in which only one member paid its full share.

Gates, Obama, and Trump gave voice to a complaint common in U.S. strategic circles: U.S. allies are irresponsibly weak and content to let the unipole shoulder the lion's share of the burden associated with global security and promoting freedom and democracy around the world. According to this view, passive free riding on the back of the U.S. taxpayer is not only morally and strategically unacceptable but dangerous to long-term international stability. European weakness in particular, Gates warned, could provide "temptation to miscalculation and aggression" by hostile powers.

Neoconservatives and other hawks have taken the lead in castigating these poltroon allies. Robert Kagan argued that "Europe is turning away from power," so much so that it often seems as if—echoing a popular romance book—"Americans are from Mars and Europeans are from

Venus."[3] The ordering is no accident; Kagan insinuates throughout his entire piece that the Europeans have effectively self-effeminized and are dependent upon the men of the United States for protection in a hostile world.

A different explanation is available, if rarely discussed. Perhaps the Europeans and Japanese are not merely passive consumers of U.S. security guarantees; perhaps instead the decisions they have made with regard to their own defense are instead part of active, coherent, logical, rational grand strategies. Perhaps they are not shirking their international responsibilities as much as interpreting the threats of the post–Cold War world in a profoundly different way than are policy makers in Washington. The choice to pursue strategic restraint on the part of major U.S. allies is less an abnegation of international responsibilities, according to this interpretation, and more a conscious response to declining threat. Far from being irresponsible international actors, perhaps these and other countries are acting quite rationally in a world virtually absent of serious danger.

This chapter is about grand strategy, that is, the highest level of strategic thinking in which nations engage, in the United States and elsewhere. It begins with a review of how the great powers in the U.S. orbit have devised their grand strategies in the unipolar era. As a rule, Washington's European and Asian allies detect far less threat in the system and have adjusted their behavior accordingly. The chapter then examines some aspects of U.S. grand strategy and ends with a discussion of some of the as yet underappreciated, underexplored opportunities that unipolarity offers Washington. American grand strategy certainly can be improved moving forward, which would minimize the chances of repeating the tragedies that marked the beginning of the unipolar era.

## GRAND STRATEGY AND THE PERIPHERY

The overwhelming majority of the literature on grand strategy focuses on that of the United States.[4] Yet smaller powers are strategic too; in fact, a good case can be made that since the end of the Cold War most U.S. allies have been following a far more coherent and consistent grand strategy than has the United States, where more than one observer has wondered whether any such strategy exists or even can exist.[5] By contrast, the states of Europe and Northeast Asia have for years followed a clear strategic path, that of *restraint*.

Strategic restraint is a well-known option in U.S. debates. The most useful description remains that of Eric Nordlinger, who fifteen years ago recommended a strategy built on three pillars: "minimally effortful national strategy in the security realm; moderately activist policies to advance our liberal ideas among and within states; and a fully activist economic diplomacy on behalf of free trade."[6] Most of the major allies of the United States appear to be adhering quite closely to this prescription.

First, the Europeans and Japanese participate very minimally in traditional security matters. This disinterest should not be interpreted as incapability, however: together the twenty-eight EU member states have a GDP comparable to that of the United States (around $19 and $18 trillion, respectively) and a far greater population (514 to 323 million, as of July 2016).[7] The major U.S. allies rarely demonstrate much desire to expand their military capabilities, however, acting as if they have very different perceptions of threats and the best way to confront them. Although many have made pledges to President Trump to increase their spending, as of this writing the average non-U.S. NATO member devotes 1.46 percent of its GDP toward defense.[8] Their militaries are now primarily structured to address what some call "social work," which is important, both domestically and internationally, but not directly related to their security.[9] In fact, most of the ventures that the Europeans and Japanese have been involved in since the collapse of the USSR have not been primarily related to their own material interests. Security rationales sometimes have been invented to accompany modern crises, such as those in Bosnia, Kosovo, and Libya, all of which were primarily humanitarian interventions.

The fact that the English and French were the primary forces behind the operation in Libya demonstrates that they have not completely given up on the use of force. But they and the other major European allies do not seem to feel that a large military or overseas presence is the best way to address the remaining systemic threats they detect, like terrorism, proliferation, and the occasional atavistic tyrant. The intelligence and counterterror services of the European countries are in some ways more intrusive and robust than those of the United States, but their conventional militaries are much smaller. The historian James Sheehan summarizes the obvious, in a work descriptively titled *Where Have the Soldiers Gone?*: "Europe at the beginning of the twenty-first century is economically strong but uninterested in transforming this strength into military power."[10]

Second, clearly these states remain vigorously engaged in international trade and economics. In fact eighteen of the world's twenty "most globalized" countries in 2016 were in Europe, according to the Swiss Economic Institute.[11] These states appear to believe that the market does not need protection and that prosperity is no longer dependent upon active military intervention abroad. Multinational corporations today can generally access the entire world without much fear of undue harassment from host governments, who have strong incentives to provide a healthy, well-regulated environment for prosperity to flourish. Threats to free trade still exist from a variety of criminal predators, but their solution, according to this point of view, hardly requires costly military action. If and when local law-enforcement agencies prove incapable of protecting the businesses that operate in their territory, modern multinationals surely have the resources either to provide it for themselves or move out. In other words, the allies have reached the conclusion that Microsoft does not need the Marine Corps. Great powers no longer have to use force to guard their economic interests. Today's market takes care of itself.

Third, the major U.S. allies contribute to worldwide social-work campaigns. Strategic restraint counsels two points about humanitarian and developmental assistance: first, that their (usually fairly modest) burdens should be shared and performed in conjunction with the rest of the industrialized world; second, that they should not be conflated with security or political aid. Foreign humanitarian assistance is cheap, relatively speaking, and often carries benefits for both the donor and recipient. Under its Common Security and Defense Policy, the European Union has raised and deployed rather modest forces for peacekeeping and peace-enforcement operations. Japan has begun to raise troops for these purposes as well, although it has more commonly made financial contributions. These countries, which are some of the world's richest, have proven quite willing to share the various multilateral burdens, from Kosovo to Mali to the Congo, usually through international institutions. Strategic restraint does not entail indifference to the world's problems or denial of international responsibilities, but it does reject the notion that any single state bears responsibility to police the world.

Thus restraint is hardly isolation. No serious analyst of foreign affairs thinks that states should wall themselves off from the rest of the world, à la Tokugawa Japan. A restrained state continues to trade, participate in international organizations, and play a role in humanitarian relief efforts. It merely defines threats, interests, and obligations narrowly and arranges security commitments and military spending accordingly. Restraint has not prevented U.S. allies from contributing to the pursuit of a more just, free, prosperous, and liberal world order. "The power that European states do project internationally," observed Sheehan, "is economic, cultural, and legal, the outward expression of the values and institutions that matter most in their relations with one another and with their own citizens."[12] In the end, that the European and Japanese are following a grand strategy of strategic restraint is not as controversial as why they are doing so. Their choice is obvious, but its inspiration is not.

## EXPLAINING RESTRAINT: THREAT, HEGEMONY, AND FREE RIDING

Are U.S. allies underestimating the dangers in the security environment? Kagan thinks so. According to him and many other U.S. analysts, small countries detect few threats because of their military weakness, rather than the other way around. "The incapacity to respond to threats leads not only to tolerance," he argued. "It can also lead to denial."[13] Their low level of capability encourages U.S. allies to downplay dangers, leading to an almost utopian view of a benign international system. If nothing can be done about evil, the argument goes, then perhaps it is natural to pretend it does not exist. Is the heightened U.S. threat perception more accurate and therefore more rational, as Kagan clearly believes? If it is true that the system contains myriad dangers, then eternal armed vigilance would clearly be warranted. If instead those dangers are not terribly dire, then perhaps the kind of strategic choices the Europeans have made might make more strategic sense.

Kagan misunderstands the genesis of grand strategy, reversing the causal direction of the process he is describing. Though he would have us believe that capability drives threat perception, history suggests he has it exactly backward. The first lesson of International Relations 101 is that states in an anarchic, self-help system must address their security first and foremost. Only an insane or deluded strategist would allow low capability to render dangers ignorable or hope to make them go away entirely. If leaders in Berlin or Tokyo detected threats in the system, these rich states would certainly build large military forces to defend themselves. In other words, U.S. allies do not deny threats because of their low capability; allied capability is low because they do not perceive serious threats.

Perceptions of threat are highly correlated with support for internationalist grand strategies. The more danger the analyst perceives, the more deeply he/she feels a necessity to be involved in political affairs abroad. It is no coincidence that those with the highest perceptions of threat to the United States—the neoconservatives—also espouse the most muscular, activist grand strategy. Kagan's assumption about the unconscious motivations of effete Europeans is understandable, since he and his fellow neoconservatives see the world as a dangerous place where good is waging a constant combat against evil. He begins with his conclusion—that the Europeans are underestimating the threat—and searches for reasons, rather than exploring the possibility that they may be more accurately assessing the security environment. While Kagan will probably continue to believe that European strategists address their security by wishing threats away, it is more logical to suggest that they simply do not perceive as much danger as do many of their counterparts in the United States. The first line of the 2003 *European Security Strategy* reads, "Europe has never been so prosperous, so secure nor so free."[14] The opening sentence of the U.S. *National Security Strategy* released three years later struck a quite different tone: "America is at war."[15] It goes on to describe a tumultuous, dangerous world, one where the United States has to lead an effort to "end tyranny," since "the survival of liberty at home increasingly depends on the success of liberty abroad."

Restraint is a rational response to a low-threat international security environment. Perhaps the Europeans and Japanese are not irresponsible, effeminate, free-riding dupes but instead are following a distinct grand strategy, one that makes far more sense in this golden age of peace and security than the path the United States has chosen. For making this choice to be restrained, they do not seem to be paying any serious price. They are no less secure, prosperous, or free.

Why do U.S. allies detect less threat than does the United States? Are they allowed to relax because of the presence of U.S. security guarantees? Is U.S. hegemony responsible for the restrained path followed by its allies? Perhaps, but it is also possible that their decreased relative power counterintuitively allows them to perceive threats in a different, more accurate way. The New Peace, rather than hegemony, might be inspiring restraint in the periphery.

If U.S. security guarantees were the primary explanation for European and Japanese restraint, then these countries would be demonstrating a degree of trust in the intentions, judgment, and wisdom of an ally that would be without historical precedent. If the system was dangerous, relatively speaking, then relying entirely on the generosity and sagacity (or, perhaps, the naiveté and gullibility) of Washington would be the height of strategic irresponsibility. Indeed, it is hard to think of another time when similar choices were made. When have capable members of an alliance essentially disarmed and allowed another to protect their interests?

It seems more logical to suggest that the major allies of the United States simply do not share its perception of threat. Whether the issue is

Islamic fundamentalist terrorism or rogue actors like Saddam Hussein and Hugo Chávez, the United States detects higher levels of danger than any other state. During the Cold War, the pattern was the same: United States feared an attack by the Warsaw Pact far more than did its West European allies, who presumably had more to lose if such an event occurred; it worried about the influence of communist China more than South Korea, Japan, and the ASEAN states; and its obsession over the potential pernicious influence of Castro and the Sandinistas dwarfed that of the region's smaller states.[16] Despite the fact that the other members of the system are demonstrably weaker than the United States and are therefore more vulnerable to a variety of threats, they do not seem to worry about their safety nearly as much as does Uncle Sam. If there were as much danger as Secretary Gates and so many in the U.S. national-security community insist, then the grand strategies of the allies would be quite different. They would not rely on Washington as their only protector.

The U.S. allies have never been entirely convinced that they could rely on its security commitments. Extended deterrence was never entirely reassuring, since many Europeans doubted the United States would indeed sacrifice New York for Hamburg. In the absence of the unifying Soviet threat, their trust in U.S. commitments for their defense would presumably be lower—if in fact that commitment was at all necessary outside of the most pessimistic works of fiction.

For hegemonic-stability logic to be an adequate explanation for restrained behavior, allied states must not only be fully convinced of the intentions and capability of the hegemon to protect their interests. They must also trust that the hegemon can interpret those interests correctly and consistently. Recent events should be adequate to demonstrate that the allies are not always convinced that the United States demonstrates the highest level of strategic wisdom. In fact, they often seem to look with confused eyes upon our behavior and are unable to explain why we so often deem it necessary to go abroad in search of monsters to destroy. They participate in our adventures at times, but usually minimally and reluctantly. It is worthwhile to recall the egocentric bias, which suggests that U.S. policy makers almost certainly overestimate their own importance. Rarely are *our* actions as consequential upon *their* behavior as we believe, or, at the very least, Washington is probably not as central to the myriad decisions in foreign capitals that help maintain international stability as it thinks it is.

The significance of Trump's election for long-term international politics is not yet clear, but it certainly reinforced a message that had been communicated loud and clear since the Soviet implosion: the global policeman, though well-meaning at times, is hardly infallible. Long before Trump's investiture, Washington had demonstrated a healthy capacity for post–Cold War error. Gambling national security on the whim of an unpredictable unipolar power would appear to be the height of strategic recklessness, even for close allies.

While it is not yet possible to know for sure why the major allies of the United States have followed much more restrained paths, it should be clear soon. If the Trump administration, with its pronounced skepticism toward NATO and affection for the Putin regime, does not cause major strategic adjustments in European capitals, then it will be hard to argue that U.S. actions are responsible for their restraint. If indeed faith in U.S. strategic sagacity led to the withering away of defense budgets from London to Tokyo, then once that faith is shaken—something President Trump is almost certain to do at some point—then they should change their outlook. If grand strategies remain mostly unadjusted during the Trump years, then probably a wholly different perception on the extant threats in the system—in other words, of the New Peace—is driving their behavior. As with many of the theories and puzzles in international politics, the New Peace itself, and the strategic behavior of the actors in it, are about to be put to a grand, four-year (or eight-year) test.

## UNIPOLAR GRAND STRATEGY

Power clouds perception. Weak states are structurally positioned to perceive events more accurately, since they are not subject to the kinds of pathologies that bedevil the strong. The less powerful are hardly unconcerned with their security—far from it—but they are often more rational about it. They may prove able to keep threats in better perspective and adjust to them accordingly. There is wisdom in their grand strategies, in other words, which the United States ignores at its peril.

The combination of the New Peace and unipolarity allows the United States to consider a different path. It can cut back on military spending and engagement without fear of economic consequence, since robust, unfettered international trade is today in the interest of all states. Risks can be minimized by investing in what Richard Betts called a "mobilization strategy," which would hedge against unknowable future threats by "developing plans and organizing resources now so that military capabilities can be expanded quickly later if necessary."[17] Surely it is worth asking how much benefit proactive, internationalist grand strategies offer in a world with low levels of threat. And unipolarity provides the opportunity to ask such questions in relative safety.

While unipolarity's effect on the quality of U.S. strategic analysis has been negative, its influence on quantity has been unquestionably positive. The post–Cold War era has been very good to those who make their living devising or debating U.S. grand strategy. A cottage industry analyzing the postcontainment choices facing the United States emerged before the ashes of the Soviet Union had fully cooled. And those choices were quite broad, since unipoles have a wide array of grand strategic options, all of which have been identified and discussed in no small amount of detail.[18] The last thing the world needs is another review. Despite twenty-five years of effort, however, no unifying vision for post–Cold War grand strategy has yet been articulated. We have not found the new Kennan.

The deluge of post–Cold War analyses share one major point in common: Almost all strategists, from the most interventionist to the least, believe that prolonging the unipolar moment will maximize security and prosperity for the United States. That unipolarity is in the national interest is a given; it is an underlying assumption, not a proposition in need of defense. Debates over grand strategy concern how best to defend the status quo, not why, and which means will approach that end most effectively, not whether it is worth approaching in the first place. The most efficient ways to ward off balancing, that is, to dissuade the rise of military competitors, are at issue. Rare is the grand strategist who recommends that Washington willingly cede its position atop the international hierarchy.[19]

Advocates of primacy clearly value the unipolar moment, but many who espouse its opposite—strategic restraint—oppose primacy because of the threat it poses to U.S. status. Many restrainers believe that the way to retain top status is to cut spending and avoid the kinds of commitments that can lead to overstretch, blowback, and decline. They propose different ways to achieve the same strategic end. Grand strategists have drastically different assumptions about the best way to preserve U.S. power, but they do not disagree on the ultimate desirability of doing so. They are all primacists, in a way; few wish to see U.S. dominance come to an end. But there is no agreement on how best to avoid it.

A series of less considered opportunities afforded by unipolarity go beyond restraint. Power provides a great deal of safety, for one thing, especially in a relatively peaceful era. As a result, the United States can be patient in almost everything it does. It can survive almost any blunder; the idea that any of its actions are necessary, therefore, is an illusion. The connection between spending and security, which is taken as gospel in some quarters, can be reexamined. Unipolarity allows a great deal of strategic flexibility, which is an underappreciated strategic asset in its own right. Finally, and perhaps most importantly, it would behoove all U.S. leaders to realize a simple rule of all human interaction: in any system, the tone and norms of behavior are set by the strongest members. The following sections address each of these ideas in more detail.

## STRATEGIC PATIENCE

Few disasters have been as unequivocal as the landing of a ragtag group of exiles at the Bay of Pigs in 1962. As the scope of the failure became clear, President Kennedy asked his aides a question that many wondered at the time and since: "How could I have been so stupid to let them go ahead?"[20] A good part of the reason for his acquiescence was that he did not have the time to give the matter any deep consideration. By one reckoning, he and his advisors could never spend more than forty-five consecutive minutes on the issue.[21] They were busy people, and Cuba was only one item on a long list of foreign-policy concerns that were embedded in an even longer list of general items requiring presidential attention. If presidents of the 1960s were absurdly busy people, their successors are probably worse off, with more demands for fundraising that condense even further the time they can devote to foreign policy.

While snap judgments are sometimes required during foreign-policy crises, better decisions usually follow a period of sustained analysis. Critics and their various allies in the media may interpret instant reactions as strong leadership and deliberation as a sign of weakness, but what can appear to be indecisiveness is often in reality the result of an underrated strategic virtue: patience. Unipolar powers have the great gift of time, which should allow them to think things through. They can afford to take their time. It is almost always better to consider the potential costs and benefits for the major choices than to give in to the urge to get them off the desk quickly.

During their time as the undisputed unipolar power over the Mediterranean, the Romans understood that time was usually on their side and that to rush was to risk. Rather than attack Armenia immediately after it rebelled in AD 62, for example, Nero's forces took a full year to build a road to its border to facilitate their logistics. A few years later, the Romans took years to build a ramp up a mountain to assault the fortress at Masada. They lost nothing by taking it slowly.

The United States can usually afford to be similarly patient when making its foreign-policy choices. Unlike small countries, great powers have a large margin for error. The weak must employ worst-case assumptions about their potential adversaries because misjudgments can prove fatal. The United States, on the other hand, should have no such fear because there is no first blow that it cannot absorb (barring a suicidal, apocalyptic nuclear assault from Russia, which is unlikely, to say the least). Power reduces, rather than expands, risk; it ought to *improve* decisions because it provides the space and security for deliberation and contemplation. Better choices come from leaders who ignore the pressures of politics and the twenty-four-hour news cycle, insisting instead upon patience. The determination to act slowly might not always improve decisions, but much of the time it will, without posing any substantial risk to the United States.

Events sometimes demand rapid action. President George H. W. Bush could not delay the U.S. reaction to the coup in the Kremlin in 1991, for instance, and his son had to act immediately to respond to the financial crisis of 2008. But usually modern leaders can afford to take their time. History does not generally reward quick responses, since they run a higher risk of being underconsidered and/or affected by emotion or misperception. Given enough time, many problems solve themselves; those that do not can be dealt with in due course.

## NECESSITY IS AN ILLUSION

The perception of necessity, of having "no choice" in any given situation, is the ultimate salve for the policy maker's conscience. The terrible burden of decision making is lifted when no alternatives exist. Unfortunately, however, necessity is always an illusion for the unipolar power. The United States has a degree of freedom in its foreign-policy choices greater than any other state in history, since it is (relatively) safe and will be able to survive any decision, no matter how ill-advised and counterproductive. Advisors who tell a future president that there is "no choice" in any given situation should be shown the door, for they are either attempting to force a decision of their liking or betraying a fundamental misunderstanding of power (or, most likely, both).[22] Claims of necessity prevent coherent analysis of options and make rational choices less likely. Washington has options, including the option to do nothing, in nearly every imaginable foreign-policy situation.

The illusion of necessity helps policy makers sell decisions as well as make them. National leaders, the public is told, simply had no choice. Even the 1983 U.S. intervention in Grenada was "forced on us by events," according to President Reagan, who claimed that he had no other option but to act strongly and decisively.[23] Thus it is not only decision makers who must guard against arguments of necessity: the public must beware, as well, and be prepared to reject any suggestion that leaders were compelled to act a certain way. Such justifications make for powerful rhetoric, but in an age of relative stability, events never compel the United States to do anything. Once again, inaction may not always be the wisest course, but it is always a possible one.

## MILITARY SPENDING AND SECURITY

The foreign-policy community resists restraint in large part because of the widespread assumption that military spending is directly related to security. The more we spend, the safer we are; therefore, the sagacious leader will keep throwing money at the Pentagon, to create the impression that it keeps the country safe. Increasing the defense budget was not a trivial component of Making America Great Again, even if the details were always a bit unclear.

The experience of Japan and Europe belies this notion. These great powers are no less great, or less safe, than the United States, despite their stubborn insistence on cutting back on defense spending. More than a few smaller states have had this experience as well. Costa Rica, which abolished its standing army in 1948, is but the largest of a score of countries without military forces that do not seem to be suffering as a consequence.[24] It bears repeating that no UN member, no matter how small, has disappeared against its will. If Putin's actions toward Ukraine demonstrate that borders have not fully hardened, it remains true that conquest is dead. In the age of the New Peace, state survival is assured, no matter how much is spent on defense.

This brings us to the second of this book's two equations:

$$\text{Military Spending} \neq \text{Security}$$

Too many hawks act as if the law of diminishing marginal utility does not apply to defense. There comes a point—a point that the United States long ago reached—at which more tanks, more nuclear weapons, and more attack submarines do not translate into more safety. Purchasing above that point is wasteful and, perhaps, counterproductive. A central task of force planners needs to be determining where that point is, for all U.S. weapons systems. The answer to the classic strategic question—*how much is enough?*—has a definite answer, one that is often much less for a unipolar power than most seem to think.

## FLEXIBILITY, RISK, AND COOPERATION

Asymmetries in power imply asymmetries in risk. Foreign policy is a worst-case-scenario business, it is often said, and therefore it behooves leaders to assume the worst in their rivals. This is particularly true for peripheral powers in a unipolar order, since their existence is never assured. They have much less margin for error than does the stronger country. Iranian leaders have strong incentives to assume the worst in U.S. actions and plan accordingly, since one instance of underpreparation stemming from underperceived hostility could lead to national ruin. Cooperative initiatives are unlikely to emanate from the periphery.

Geopolitical risks for the unipolar power are far lower. The United States can afford to take chances and soften its worst-case assumptions, since the potential costs of error are far less dramatic. Strong countries accept far less risk through cooperation, since the defection of smaller powers cannot hurt them to any great extent. Stability and progress in asymmetrical bilateral relationships have to come from the top, in other words, or they are unlikely to come at all. Policies too risky for other states can be pursued by the unipole, safe in the knowledge that existential national catastrophe will not follow.

Leading cooperative ventures will not come naturally to the United States. As the old saying goes, power is the ability to not compromise. From corporate boardrooms to the UN Security Council, strong actors are much more likely to demand acquiescence from the weak rather than seek to arrive at a mutually agreeable position. Strength discourages concession and cooperation at the negotiating table, making lasting agreement less likely. As a result, powerful countries end up becoming involved with more disputes, and use their military power more often, than smaller ones. Countries tend to be more belligerent as their relative power grows. The United States is therefore especially susceptible to the belief that its problems should be solved by compulsion rather than negotiation. It may occasionally compromise when it is clearly in its interest to do so, but no one should be surprised that Washington stands virtually alone in opposition to action regarding climate change, child soldiers, the International Criminal Court, landmines, cluster bombs, discrimination against women, the Law of the Sea, and a long list of others. To paraphrase Thucydides, the strong sign what they want and the weak conciliate as they must. Why should great nations waste time—and demonstrate weakness—by searching for mutually accepted solutions, when they can impose their will and force their rivals into humiliating concessions? Such thinking can rapidly lead to counterproductive policy choices, making strong states their own worst enemy. U.S. leaders should resist the uncooperative instincts that the unipolar structure stimulates.

In the argot of security studies, unipolar powers are free to focus on absolute gains. They need not demand equal return on their various international investments, for they have less to fear from the relative gains made by others. The United States can make the first move toward normalizing diplomatic relations with Cuba whether or not it receives much of anything in return. Cuba does not, and will not, present a threat to U.S. security. The United States can also enter into trade deals without much concern for the disproportionate gains made by far smaller states. The Trans-Pacific Partnership would not have led to the rise of peer competitors, even if Vietnam or Malaysia benefited more than the United States. Unipolar powers have more possibilities for flexibility in their choices than states involved in competition with peers.

## LEAD BY EXAMPLE

The strongest actors in any system set the tone for the rest. They establish the norms and the limits upon acceptable behavior, becoming the example that all others follow. If a hostile, sexist work environment develops inside a firm, it is the fault of the management. If an academic department is ridden by pathological rivalries and personality clashes, do not blame the assistant professors. And if a system of states is marked by clashes, conflict, and opportunistic violence, it is because of the rules established by its great powers.

While it may be beyond the capability of any single state to set rules for the entire world, behavioral norms do not arise out of the ether. Just as organizations come to reflect the personality and style of their management, unipolar international systems over time reflect the positive and negative characteristics of their central powers. The United States does more to shape today's system than is often realized, usually for the better. One need only imagine a different country at the apex—the Soviet Union, or Hitler's Germany, or modern China—to appreciate the importance of the normative order promoted by Washington. Respect for international borders, for instance, is not a norm states are born respecting. The world is generally better off having the United States as the unipolar power than any other possible option. But that can change, if U.S. behavior changes over time.

By demonstrating to the world that force is indeed a last resort, even for the strongest, most capable state in history, the United States could do more to promote peace than it would through any misguided attempts at global policing. And it would waste far less blood and treasure in the process.

———— ≈≈≈ ————

Grand strategy's failures are always more obvious than its successes. Far more time has been devoted to criticizing what the United States has done wrong since the end of the Cold War than to praising what it has done right. Successful foreign policy is unremarkable; the day-to-day maintenance of healthy relationships with other great powers does not attract headlines, but neither is it simple. Those who run U.S. foreign policy toil in an often thankless job, where failure is spectacular and success boring. Criticizing is always easier than creating.

Still, few would deny that there is room for improvement. Today the United States is one of the very few holdouts against strategic restraint. While the rest of the world cuts back on its spending, one outlier soldiers on, alone and unthreatened. Perhaps the United States is unique in accurately comprehending the dangers that still exist in the international system; perhaps, however, it could learn something from the behavior of the other members. The conclusion of the many is probably more accurate than the conclusion of the one. Since the logical default option of the United States should always be to spend less, to get the maximum amount of security at the minimum cost, surely it is worth at least attempting to see whether the Europeans and Japanese are right.

Although great insecurity has traditionally accompanied great power, this need not be the case. Presumably better policy and increased security would arise from a rational, realistic assessment of threat. Insecurity, whether real or imagined, tends to lead to expansive, internationalist, interventionist grand strategies. The more danger a state perceives, the greater its willingness to go abroad in search of monsters to destroy. The "preventive" war in Iraq is the most obvious consequence of the inflated U.S. perception of threat, but it is hardly the only one. This particularly American pathology is in need of diagnosis and cure, lest Iraq be not a singular debacle, as Barry Posen has warned, but "a harbinger of costs to come."[25]

# UNIPOLARITY AND ITS
# CONCLUSION

U nipolarity cannot last forever. Whether its demise is imminent
or decades away is an open question, but even the most optimistic observers do not believe the international system has
reached its final stage of evolution. At some point, either in the lifetime
of this book's readers or long after they have left, the United States will
cease to dominate the world in quite the same way it currently does.

What will the effects of this decline be? Scholars of international
politics rarely agree on anything, but on this point widespread consensus exists: The postunipolar world will be worse, much worse in some
ways, than the current order. The only disagreement is over the extent
of the calamity. Former national security advisor Zbigniew Brzezinski
predicted that the world would turn "violent and bloodthirsty" without
the stabilizing presence of U.S. hegemony, with "outright chaos" created by new attempts to build regional empires and redress old territorial claims.[1] The British economic historian Niall Ferguson foresaw a
posthegemony "dark age" in which "plunderers and pirates" target the
big coastal cities, terrorists attack cruise liners and aircraft carriers
alike, and the "wretchedly poor citizens" of Latin America prove unable
to resist the Protestantism of U.S. evangelicals. Following multiple
nuclear wars and plagues, the few remaining airlines would be forced
to suspend service to all but the very richest cities.[2] Robert Kagan is

more blunt: U.S. decline would lead to World War III.[3] Even inveterate critics of the United States fear declining U.S. power, if for somewhat different reasons. Immanuel Wallerstein believes that the irreversible decline of U.S. hegemony, which began in 1970, is likely to lead Washington to adopt aggressive measures to maintain its status. Out of this desperation, abject geopolitical chaos will ensue.[4]

What unites all these views—and the more sober analysts who hold somewhat less terrifying visions of the postunipolar world—is general pessimism. Perhaps this is a reflection of the sense of doom that always accompanies systemic shifts. It is worth recalling that many observers of international politics were not terribly sanguine about the prospects for post–Cold War stability, only to be proven wrong by the outbreak of the New Peace.[5]

Even relative decline might prove catastrophic. According to what is alternately called the "power-transition theory" and the "Thucydides trap," unequal national growth can be profoundly dangerous.[6] Systems in which one dominant member is growing more slowly than a rising challenger are often unstable. The state on top becomes unnerved by the growth of the apparent challenger, which in turn begins to assert itself and demand the respect it feels it deserves. War often results. This is broadly the situation in which the Greek city-states found themselves in the fifth century BC, when dominant Sparta faced a rising Athens. What made the Peloponnesian War inevitable, wrote Thucydides, was the "growth of Athenian power and the fear which this caused in Sparta."[7] More than a few people have drawn parallels between the slow growth of the United States and the rapid rise of China and wondered whether power can peacefully transition from one country to another.[8]

This conclusion looks forward a bit, contemplating that day when unipolarity ends. How soon will it arrive? What are the probable consequences? Why do so many fear it so much? The following sections speculate about the durability of the current system and discuss the debates over decline. They address the roots of our fear of lost status, which run deep in the American psyche. The book concludes on an optimistic note, which is exceedingly rare for works imagining the world after the unipolar moment.

## THE DURABILITY OF THE UNIPOLAR WORLD

No topic related to unipolarity excites the average analyst more than decline. How durable is U.S. dominance? Is multipolarity on the horizon? Is U.S. power already in retreat? It has become quite fashionable to declare that the current order has already reached the end of its life expectancy and that U.S. power is in the process of relative decline. The nagging fear that other powers are catching up (or have already caught up) to the United States is as old as Washington's superpower status. Declinism, as the school of thought came to be known, first appeared in the late 1950s and has repeatedly reemerged with metronomic regularity since.[9]

Fears of decline inevitably accompany great power.[10] Almost as soon as the United States became a superpower, a variety of observers declared that its status was slipping. The first big wave of declinism was led most prominently by Henry Kissinger, who warned in 1962 that "fifteen years more of a deterioration on our position in the world such as we have experienced since World War II would find us reduced to Fortress America in a world in which we had become largely irrelevant."[11] At least four more waves of declinism would crash upon Cold War shores, the most significant of which began in the late 1970s and lasted through the mid-1980s.[12] Paul Kennedy, a prominent voice of that generation, shrouded his pessimism in historical patterns he claimed to find in empires, implying the United States was nearing the end of some sort of natural great-power lifecycle.[13]

One might have expected a bit of modesty from declinists when the Cold War ended, since the relative power of United States dramatically increased, to the point that it became greater than that of any country, ever. Rather than admit that their announcements of waning power were a bit premature, however, declinists tended to dig in their heels. In 1993, Edward Luttwak predicted that the United States was on its way toward becoming a "third world country" by 2020.[14] As late as 1996 Robert Gilpin was proclaiming to be an "unreconstructed declinist."[15] Declinism reappeared in earnest in the first decade of the new century, fueled this time by confidence-shaking events and trends such as the war in Iraq, Chinese economic growth, and the 2008 financial crisis. "America is in unprecedented decline," wrote Robert Pape. Because the relative size of its economy was shrinking, "the unipolar world is indeed coming to an end," which meant the world was entering a "highly dangerous" period.[16] And of course the entire Trump campaign was based on the impression that we stand, as ever, at the end of the American era.

The mere fact that all earlier predictions of decline were wrong does not mean, to paraphrase a prominent declinist, that this time it is not real.[17] Perhaps unipolar systems carry the seeds of their own destruction because they inevitably inspire the rise of rival states or coalitions.[18] Balancing is a central—perhaps *the* central—component of neorealist theory; both offensive and defensive realists assume that states will react to threatening imbalances of power by increasing their own capabilities. Since no structure is more threatening to the average state than unipolarity, many neorealists do not expect the dominance of the United States to continue for very long. Others will rise.

Contrary voices have occasionally emerged. Some have suggested that unipolarity may prove to have greater staying power than is commonly thought, for two reasons. First, declinists may underestimate the contribution of the unipole's character to systemic structure. Not all hegemons create the same balancing impulse; a "benign" hegemony, one that respects international law and promotes an order in the interest of all members, is unlikely to inspire serious countervailing imperatives.[19] This assumption is based upon the redefinition of balancing provided by Stephen Walt, who argued that states balance threat rather than power.[20] If the unipole were generally considered a status-quo state, one trusted to eschew conquest and act in a responsible manner, balancing need not occur, and the unipolar moment could persist.

The second argument for optimism does not rely on the internal characteristics of the United States. William Wohlforth has argued that the structural characteristics of unipolar orders lead more logically to stability than upheaval.[21] The overwhelming capabilities of the lone great power make the prospect of challenge prohibitively daunting. Most potential rising peers are likely to assess balancing's potential costs and choose instead to bandwagon. These barriers to entry make destabilizing, hegemonic war unlikely and suggest that unipolarity could last quite some time. This notion, labeled "power-preponderance theory" by one scholar (an elegant name that unfortunately does not seem to have caught on), is now the dominant academic explanation for why other countries have not shown much urgency to balance U.S. power.[22]

It is too soon to know who is right and how long the moment will last. Predicting the future of unipolarity—or even describing the present—is made especially difficult by the lack of comparable cases.[23] Those states that have in the past dominated their regions still had to worry about extraregional challenges. Rome was without peer in the Mediterranean for half a millennium, but barbarians were always just over the horizon. No European power that followed exerted anything remotely similar to the relative dominance of the United States today. At various times Chinese dynasties controlled their neighborhood, but threats had a nasty tendency to materialize out of the steppes. There simply is no earlier instance of global unipolarity, of systemwide power disparity as dramatic and virtually uncontested, from which we can learn.

A few things can be said with certainty, however. First, the main engine of U.S. decline—the rise of challengers—has not occurred. Whether because of high costs, the essential benevolence of U.S. unipolarity, or some other factor, the world has not witnessed widespread balancing behavior over the last twenty-five years. States have generally tolerated unprecedented disparities in material power without much reaction at all. No new coalitions have formed to counter U.S. capabilities, which would be symptomatic of "external balancing," and few states are building up their militaries, or "internally" balancing the United States.[24] The only major exception to this rule is China, but its commitment to balance is less clear than is sometimes portrayed. Beijing has consistently chosen to devote a very small percentage of its GDP toward defense—at or near 2 percent—a rate that is not growing.[25] Increasing Chinese defense expenditures are a reflection of its growing economy, in other words, but not necessarily an increased imperative to balance the United States. Although the real level of Chinese spending is hotly debated, the Peoples' Republic could certainly devote more to its defense if it felt the need.

Second, perceptions of decline thrive during periods of uncertainty, especially those following foreign-policy disasters. It is no coincidence that Paul Kennedy wrote *Rise and Fall of the Great Powers* in the United States in the 1970s or that Otto Spengler wrote about the decline of the West from the perspective of Germany in the early 1920s.[26] The mixed bag of negative emotions that follow foreign-policy catastrophe—anger, guilt, shame, doubt, insecurity—contributes to an overall sense of pessimism about the future and about foreign policy in general. Disasters always seem to portend even greater ones to come. Status is fueled by perception as much as reality, and when pessimism reigns, decline seems imminent.

Third, the United States is structurally and culturally predisposed to suffer from status insecurity. While all states worry to some degree about their relative power, those at the top tend to worry even more. Psychologists have long known that people are motivated more strongly by the specter of loss than the potential for gain, and no state has more to lose than the unipole.[27] People are naturally insecure about what they value most, and the hypercompetitive United States values its status.[28] As a result, it is predisposed to worry about losing that status and thereby puts more stock in the arguments of declinists than might otherwise be warranted. Michael Cox has observed that "the United States is a very special kind of polity preoccupied by status and consumed by inner doubt."[29] That specialness leads us to fear more than necessary and to obsess over our ranking.

Fourth, proponents of decline tend to confuse concepts. One can argue that unipolarity is coming to an end or that the United States is in hegemonic decline, but the two are not the same. For the former to be true, the *power* of the United States would have to be waning in relation to potential challengers. For the latter, the *influence* of the United States would have to be declining. It is the unipolarity-versus-hegemony distinction once again, and, as usual, the two are not kept separate in much of the writing about systemic durability. Previous iterations of declinism consistently conflated the aggregate power of the United States with its ability to bring about its preferred outcomes. The former is much easier to measure, and definitive statements can be made as a result. Today, the only empirical dimension along which the U.S. advantage may be slipping is in aggregate economic power, which is always expressed in terms of gross domestic product. One measure—the growth in China's GDP—has provided the lion's share of the ammunition for those predicting the end of unipolarity. In nearly all other measures of raw and symbolic power, unipolarity shows little sign of waning.

Hegemony, or, more broadly, the influence that power brings, is much more difficult to measure. As Bruce Russett argued during an earlier discussion of U.S. decline, perceptions of influence are "notoriously difficult to operationalize because by definition they leave no traces in events."[30] Coercion is obvious and leaves a paper trail; influence is subtle and tends to unfold without many obvious signs. This has not stopped observers from making definitive pronouncements, however. The inability to prevail in the various post-9/11 conflicts has fed speculation that U.S. influence is shrinking and unipolarity eroding. The normative implications are different from observer to observer—some lament the perceived erosion, some welcome it—but all such arguments are essentially based on the belief that the ability of Washington to bring about its preferred outcomes is simply not what it used to be.[31]

None of this means that modern declinists are necessarily wrong or that unipolarity is not in its final death throes, only that there are reasons to doubt that the current generation of Chickens Little is any more sagacious than those who came before. Ultimately, the long-term durability of unipolarity remains an open question. One final observation that can be made with confidence is that no matter what the ultimate fate of the system is, U.S. dominance is extremely likely to persist in the short run. Whether the arguments in this book remain relevant for the long term or are overtaken by events much sooner cannot be known. Perhaps it will be in print for decades, perhaps not. But its observations will surely be relevant in the short term, for the foreseeable future, for better or for worse.

## THE EFFECTS OF DECLINE

Why do we fear decline? While concerns for security and prosperity are related to perceptions of relative U.S. power, anxiety over the loss of status goes a bit deeper. With power come perceptions of control, even if in the international system such perceptions do not always match reality. Actors believe that lost power implies lost control, which causes powerful trauma in people across time and culture.[32] "All people need to experience control," wrote Ellen Skinner, who spoke for the conventional wisdom among psychologists. It is "innate and universal, a part of human nature."[33] The collapse of unipolarity would be catastrophic not only for the interests of the United States, in other words, but for its collective psyche.

That such fears are understandable does not make them rational. History is fairly clear on this point: Decline need not result in national catastrophe.[34] Imperial Spain was the closest thing to a world-spanning empire produced by the sixteenth and seventeenth century. Its collapse dealt a serious blow to Spanish glory but not necessarily to its national interests. By the beginning of the eighteenth century, Spain had become a much less significant player in European politics, but its people were relieved of the burden of paying for an empire. The string of bankruptcies that marked the Spanish monarchy stopped, and its young men no longer risked death from Dutch bullets or Peruvian yellow fever. It is hard to argue that the average Castilians were worse off in 1850, by which time Madrid's imperial pretensions had essentially ended, than they were two centuries earlier at the empire's height. By almost any reasonable measure, decline was actually *good* for the vast majority of the Spanish people.[35]

The British experience offers much the same lesson: the people of Great Britain are no worse off for having lost their empire. Their pride may have suffered during the era of imperial decline, but their material, tangible interests were not affected.[36] The cost of sacrificed glory was most acutely borne by elites. The historian Bernard Porter pointed out that the working classes in England, the masses that constitute the "silent majority," were mostly indifferent to the loss of the dominions.[37] As it turns out, the English people were able to adjust rather quickly to the notion of being a normal state rather than an empire.

Not all declines have gone so smoothly for the people who experienced them, of course. Sudden and sharp collapses, whether accompanied by marauding Goths and Vandals or not, are usually unpleasant experiences. The Soviet empire collapsed all at once, as did those of the Habsburgs and Ottomans, which led to instability, economic stagnation, and violence. No such rapid collapse is likely in the United States' future, however. Even the most inveterate pessimists do not envision a sudden reversal of fortunes and end of the unipolar system. All declinists predict a gradual, if inevitable, relative weakening, largely as the result of rising wealth and power elsewhere.[38] The American experience is much more likely to resemble the gradual, graceful decline of Spain or Great Britain than the catastrophic collapse of Rome or the Soviets. And some scholars have even proposed that Chinese leadership would be accompanied by a greater degree of international stability, given Beijing's general disinterest in promoting revolutionary democratic change.[39]

The end of unipolarity will have positive aspects as well. Perception is likely to improve in Washington, for one thing, at least in certain areas. Researchers have found that the kind of overconfident self-assessments that impoverish the decision making of unipolar powers can be diminished if power is reduced.[40] Once their dominance ends, over time the U.S. public might come to perceive the world in a more accurate way and craft better policies to deal with it. Or at least one can hope.

The unipolar order will end slowly, quietly, even imperceptibly, striking a blow to the U.S. ego, perhaps, but not its interest. When modern great powers fade, they tend to do it in ways that leave the people no worse off—and sometimes far better—than they were at the height of empire. To the extent that unipolarity contributes to pathological misperceptions, its end, whenever it arrives, may well improve the strategic thinking in the United States.

Most people devote little time to the finer points of grand strategy, however, and images of decline can create quite negative emotions. Accusations that Washington is allowing the United States to become less great somehow are powerful political tools. Individuals live vicariously through the exploits of their nation. When their country loses, they too are losers; when something good happens, they bask in reflected glory. The benefits of unipolarity are not merely—or even mostly—confined to tangible increases in security. There is little evidence to support the belief, no matter how widely held, that the United States is safer in a world it dominates. A large part of the reason why so many Americans reflexively support their status is emotional and somewhat irrational: They simply enjoy being the best, the greatest, the number-one country in the world. They like to feel like winners.

---

The United States has nothing to fear from decline. In fact, if it weren't for would-be leaders looking to score points against their opponents, it is doubtful the U.S. public would notice if American power waned. The world is remarkably peaceful and stable and is likely to remain so for quite some time. Security is relative and absolute safety an illusion; no matter what various bombastic politicians and misinformed observers may say, Americans are as safe as any people in history. If they would start thinking and acting that way, they would be far better off, and so too would everyone else.

Instead, Americans cling to their fears, making them a central part of the national identity. Those who suggest that lives would improve if the U.S. public embraced threatlessness are dismissed as naïve, as dangerous, as un-American. Donald Trump finds much more success selling apocalyptic visions of national ruin caused by migrating Mexicans, cheating Chinese, and bloodthirsty Muslims. He is the personification of many of the pathologies discussed in these pages, a uniquely American response to misperceived injustices perpetrated by a host of weaker actors. Perhaps his election and disastrous administration will be not the beginning of a long downward slide but a turning point. Perhaps his disgraceful brand of nationalism will force some introspection, some hard thinking about how it all was allowed to happen. Once the emergency is over and the Trumps retire to their various garish

Xanadus, this country will have a chance to ask itself what kind of future it wants, for both itself and the system it still dominates.

Much of the world has confidence in the choices Uncle Sam will make. Whether the American people share that confidence and believe in themselves enough to choose courage over fear, empathy over arrogance, and prudence over belligerence will depend largely on who succeeds President Trump in the White House. Enlightened national leadership is the most effective means by which superpowers can overcome their delusions and pursue more rational, productive, and peaceful futures.

# NOTES

## INTRODUCTION

1. Gregori Arbatov, "It Takes Two to Make a Cold War," *New York Times*, December 8, 1987.

2. Karl Deutsch and J. David Singer, "Multipolar Power Systems and International Stability," *World Politics* 16, no. 3 (April 1964): 390–406; Kenneth N. Waltz, "The Stability of a Bipolar World," *Daedalus* 93, no. 3 (Summer 1964): 881–909; Richard N. Rosecrance, "Bipolarity, Multipolarity, and the Future," *Journal of Conflict Resolution* 10, no. 3 (September 1966): 314–27; Patrick James and Michael Brecher, "Stability and Polarity: New Paths for Inquiry," *Journal of Peace Research* 25, no. 1 (March 1988): 31–42; Ted Hopf, "Polarity, the Offense-Defense Balance, and War," *American Political Science Review* 85, no. 2 (June 1991): 475–93.

3. A phrase generally credited to Charles Krauthammer, "The Unipolar Moment," *Foreign Affairs* 70, no. 1 (1990/1991): 23–33.

4. The choice of terms also often signals the ideological or theoretical predisposition of the analyst. Since polarity tends to be a subject of interest to those with a structural predisposition, most prominent analyses of *unipolarity* are done by neorealists. While *hegemony* is a term favored by critics of U.S. foreign policy, it is also common in more neutral academic debates. *Neoimperialism*, however, is exclusive to Marxist thought. Much less reflexively anti-American sentiment accompanies *primacy*, which is used broadly as a description of either system structure or a specific grand strategy.

5. This is essentially the definition provided by Robert O. Keohane and Joseph S. Nye, *Power and Interdependence: World Politics in Transition* (Boston: Little, Brown, 1977), 44, according to which hegemony is a situation where "one state is powerful enough to maintain essential rules governing interstate relations, and willing to do so."

6. This distinction is explained further in David Wilkinson, "Unipolarity Without Hegemony," *International Studies Review* 1, no. 2 (Summer 1999): 141–72.

7. Some observers might have a tough time imagining unipolarity without hegemony. Not just capability but the willingness to exert power has traditionally been central to many conceptions international status (John Mueller, *Quiet Cataclysm: Reflections on the Recent Transformation of World Politics* [New York: Harper Collins, 1995], 37). The United States had what was by many measures the largest economy in the world by the 1880s and should have been considered a great power, but it was not until it chose to build a proportionately large military and play a greater role in the international issues of the day. A unipolar state that chooses not to develop and then exercise its military potential risks ceding the title, at least in the eyes of those for whom the willingness to make power kinetic is central to the concept. In practice, therefore, it would be difficult to have a consensus unipolar world without some degree of hegemony. But consensus is not a necessary component of empirical reality.

8. Many scholars on the left maintain that the United States essentially operates a neo-imperialist system, controlling the global South through economic means. See Michael Hardt and Antonio Negri, *Empire* (Cambridge, MA: Harvard University Press, 2000).

9. Kenneth N. Waltz, *Theory of International Politics* (Reading, MA: Addison-Wesley, 1979), 131. For a longer discussion, see Benjamin Zala, "Polarity Analysis and Collective Perceptions of Power: The Need for a New Approach," *Journal of Global Security Studies* 2, no. 1 (January 2017): 2–17.

10. The latter figure is estimated in William C. Wohlforth, "Unipolar Stability: The Rules for Power Analysis," *Harvard International Review* 29, no. 1 (Spring 2007): 45.

11. Craig Caffrey, "Russia Announces Its Deepest Defence Budget Cuts Since the 1990s," *Jane's Defence Weekly*, March 16, 2017, http://www.janes.com/article/68766/russia-announces-deepest-defence-budget-cuts-since-1990s.

12. Two-thirds of the world's hard currency reserves remain in dollars. For an explanation of what that means for U.S. power, see Jonathan Kirshner, "Dollar Primacy and American Power: What's at Stake?" *Review of International Political Economy* 15, no. 3 (August 2008), 418–38.

13. Fareed Zakaria, "America is Still Great—but It Needs to Stay Strong," *Washington Post*, May 26, 2016.

14. Robert Jervis, "Unipolarity: A Structural Perspective," *World Politics* 61, no. 1 (January 2009), 188. See also Stephen G. Brooks and William C. Wohlforth, *World Out of Balance: International Relations and the Challenge of American Primacy* (Princeton, NJ: Princeton University Press, 2008).

15. John J. Mearsheimer, *The Tragedy of Great Power Politics* (New York: Norton, 2001), 381.

16. Ian Bremmer, *Every Nation for Itself: What Happens When No One Leads the World* (New York: Portfolio, 2012); Richard N. Haas, "The Age of Nonpolarity: What Will Follow U.S. Dominance," *Foreign Affairs* 87, no. 3 (May–June 2008): 44–56.

17. Simon Reich and Richard Ned Lebow, *Good-Bye Hegemony! Power and Influence in the Global System* (Princeton, NJ: Princeton University Press, 2014).

18. See John Mueller, "The Essential Irrelevance of Nuclear Weapons: Stability in the Postwar World," *International Security* 13, no. 2 (Fall 1988): 55–79.

19. A good discussion of the dominance of the U.S. military, if in dissent, can be found in Christopher A. Preble, *The Power Problem: How American Military Dominance Makes Us Less Safe, Less Prosperous, and Less Free* (Ithaca, NY: Cornell University Press, 2009).

20. Bruce Russett discusses this distinction in "The Mysterious Case of Vanishing Hegemony; or, Is Mark Twain Really Dead?" *International Organization* 39, no. 2 (Spring 1985): 207–31. See also Susan Strange, "The Persistent Myth of Lost Hegemony," *International Organization* 41, no. 4 (Autumn 1987): 551–74; Martha Finnemore, "Legitimacy, Hypocrisy, and the Social Structure of Unipolarity: Why Being a Unipole Isn't All It's Cracked Up to Be," *World Politics* 61, no. 1 (January 2009): 58–85.

21. Reich and Lebow, *Good-Bye Hegemony!*.

22. For early and later discussions, see Herbert C. Kelman, "Social-Psychological Approaches to the Study of International Relations: The Question of Relevance," in *International Behavior: A Social-Psychological Analysis*, ed. Herbert C. Kelman (New York: Holt, Rinehart, and Winston, 1965), 565–607; and the essays in James N. Druckman, Donald Green, James H. Kuklinski, and Arthur Lupia, eds., *Cambridge Handbook of Experimental Political Science* (New York: Cambridge University Press, 2011).

23. Jonathan Mercer, *Reputation in International Politics* (Ithaca, NY: Cornell University Press, 1996), 70.

24. Sydney Verba, "Simulation, Reality, and Theory in International Relations," *World Politics* 16, no. 3 (April 1964): 502.

25. In theory, experiments can also reduce the bias that creeps into other kinds of research. See Rose McDermott, "Experimental Methods in Political Science," *Annual Review of Political Science* 5 (2002): 31–61, esp. 33.

26. See the discussion in Alexander Wendt, "The State as Person in International Theory," *Review of International Studies* 30, no. 2 (April 2004): 289–316, as well as the responses it generated.

## 1. UNIPOLARITY AND THE SYSTEM

1. Although it is hard to imagine that readers of this book would not know this, FARC stands for Revolutionary Armed Forces of Colombia. The handshake was covered by Nicholas Casey, "FARC Rebels in Colombia Reach Cease-Fire Deal with Government," *New York Times*, June 23, 2016.

2. Armed conflict may have been absent for a few months at a time in the early 1920s and late 1930s. The evidence gets sketchier as one goes further back in the historical record, but it is good enough to make clear that there have been no extended periods of hemispheric peace since at least the seventeenth century.

3. Steven Pinker, *The Better Angels of Our Nature: Why Violence Has Declined* (New York: Viking, 2011).

4.  Michael Lind, "The End of Pax Americana?" *Salon*, September 29, 2009, http://www
    .salon.com/2009/09/29/obama_pax_americana/.
5.  Robert Kagan, *The World America Made* (New York: Knopf, 2012), 50.
6.  Nick Miroff, "'Plan Colombia': How Washington Learned to Love Latin American
    Intervention Again," *Washington Post*, September 18, 2016.
7.  John J. Mearsheimer, "Why We Will Soon Miss the Cold War," *Atlantic Monthly* 266,
    no. 2 (August 1990): 35–50.
8.  John J. Mearsheimer, "Back to Future: Instability in Europe After the Cold War,"
    *International Security* 15, no. 1 (Summer 1990): 52.
9.  Mearsheimer, "Back to Future," 6.
10. Christopher Layne, "The Unipolar Illusion: Why New Great Powers Will Rise," *International Security* 17, no. 4 (Spring 1993): 51.
11. Nuno Monteiro, *Theory of Unipolar Politics* (New York: Cambridge University Press,
    2014).
12. Pinker, *The Better Angels of Our Nature*, 295–377. The "Long Peace" is also occasionally used, but that phrase can also refer to the period of great-power peace that followed World War II. See John Lewis Gaddis, "The Long Peace: Elements of Stability
    in the Postwar International System," *International Security* 10, no. 4 (Spring 1986):
    99–142.
13. For up-to-date reviews of the data, see the Human Security Report Project, *Human
    Security Report 2013: The Decline in Global Violence* (Vancouver: Human Security
    Press, 2013); Monty G. Marshall and Benjamin R. Cole, *Global Report 2014: Conflict,
    Governance, and State Fragility* (Vienna, VA: Center for Systemic Peace, 2014); David
    A. Backer, Ravi Bhavnani, and Paul K. Huth, eds., *Peace and Conflict 2016* (New York:
    Routledge, 2016). The most comprehensive review of the New Peace remains Pinker's
    *The Better Angels of Our Nature*, but see also John Mueller, *Retreat from Doomsday:
    The Obsolescence of Major War* (New York: Basic Books, 1989); John Mueller, *The
    Remnants of War* (Ithaca, NY: Cornell University Press, 2004); Robert Jervis, "Theories of War in an Era of Leading Power Peace," *American Political Science Review* 96,
    no. 1 (March 2002): 1–14; Raimo Väyrynen, ed., *The Waning of Major War: Theories
    and Debates* (New York: Routledge, 2006); Christopher J. Fettweis, *Dangerous Times?
    The International Politics of Great Power Peace* (Washington, DC: Georgetown University Press, 2010); Richard Ned Lebow, *Why Nations Fight: Past and Future Motives
    for War* (New York: Cambridge University Press, 2010); Joshua Goldstein, *Winning the
    War on War* (New York: Dutton, 2011); John Horgan, *The End of War* (San Francisco:
    McSweeney's, 2012).
14. Coups: Ivan Perkins, *Vanishing Coup: The Pattern of World History Since 1310* (New
    York: Rowman and Littlefield, 2013); Jonathan M. Powell and Clayton L. Thyne,
    "Global Instances of Coups from 1950 to 2010," *Journal of Peace Research* 48, no. 2
    (March 2011): 249–59. Repression: Victor Asal and Amy Pate, "The Decline of Ethnic
    Political Discrimination 1990–2003," in *Peace and Conflict 2005: A Global Survey of
    Armed Conflicts, Self-Determination Movements, and Democracy*, ed. Ted Robert Gurr
    and Monty G. Marshall (College Park, MD: Center for International Development and

Conflict Management, 2005), 28–38. Chances of dying in battle: Bethany Lacina, Nils Peter Gleditsch, and Bruce Russett, "The Declining Risk of Death in Battle," *International Studies Quarterly* 50, no. 3 (September 2006): 673–80. Border alterations: Mark W. Zacher, "The Territorial Integrity Norm: International Boundaries and the Use of Force," *International Organization* 55, no. 2 (Spring 2001): 215–50. Conquest: Tanisha M. Fazal, *State Death: The Politics and Geography of Conquest, Occupation, and Annexation* (Princeton, NJ: Princeton University Press, 2007). Violence against civilians: Andrew Mack, "Global Political Violence: Explaining the Post–Cold War Decline," Coping with Crisis Working Paper Series, International Peace Academy (March 2007).

15. Nils Petter Gleditsch, "The Liberal Moment Fifteen Years On," *International Studies Quarterly* 52, no. 4 (December 2008): 694; Lotta Harbom, Stina Högbladh, and Peter Wallensteen, "Armed Conflict and Peace Agreements," *Journal of Peace Research* 43, no. 5 (September 2006): 617–31.

16. See data maintained by the World Bank, "Life Expectancy at Birth," http://data .worldbank.org/indicator/SP.DYN.LE00.IN/countries/1W.

17. Bear F. Braumoeller, *Only the Dead: International Order and the Persistence of Conflict in the Modern Age* (working title) (Oxford University Press, forthcoming). Other critics of the data include Anita Gohdes and Megan Price, "First Things First: Assessing Data Quality Before Model Quality," *Journal of Conflict Resolution* 57, no. 6 (December 2013): 1090–1108; Nassim Nicholas Taleb, "The 'Long Peace' Is a Statistical Illusion," unpublished manuscript (Taleb does not subject his work to peer review, believing such a notion to be logically impossible a priori and insulting), May 2015, http://www .fooledbyrandomness.com/longpeace.pdf. For responses, see Bethany Lacina and Nils Petter Gleditsch, "The Waning of War Is Real: A Response to Gohdes and Price," *Journal of Conflict Resolution* 57, no. 6 (December 2013): 1109–27; Steven Pinker, "Fooled by Belligerence," June 2015, http://stevenpinker.com/pinker/files/comments_on_taleb _by_s_pinker.pdf.

18. Johan Galtung, "An Editorial," *Journal of Peace Research* 1, no. 1 (1964): 1–4.

19. The notion that peace is more than merely the absence of war has long roots. In the Middle Ages, many of Europe's Christian scholars believed that true peace could not be achieved as long as evil existed. Their version of "positive peace" was essentially alignment with the teachings of Christ. Jehangir Yezdi Malegam, *The Sleep of the Behemoth: Disputing Peace and Violence in Medieval Europe, 1000–1200* (Ithaca, NY: Cornell University Press, 2013).

20. Gary Goertz, Paul F. Diehl, and Alexandru Balas, *The Puzzle of Peace: The Evolution of Peace in the International System* (New York: Oxford University Press, 2016). Twenty-three indicators of positive peace are measured by the Institute for Economics and Peace; see its *Global Peace Index 2016* (New York and Sydney: Institute for Economics & Peace, June 2016), http://economicsandpeace.org/wp-content/uploads /2016/06/GPI-2016-Report_2.pdf.

21. Joshua S. Goldstein, "World Backsliding on Peace," *Huffington Post*, August 3, 2015, http://www.huffingtonpost.com/joshua-s-goldstein/world-backsliding-on-peace _b_7924964.html.

22. IISS counts around 180,000 battle deaths in 2014, 167,000 in 2015, and 157,000 in 2016. International Institute of Strategic Studies, Armed Conflict Database, https://acd.iiss.org/en.

23. Steven Pinker, "Has the Decline of Violence Reversed Since *The Better Angels of Our Nature* Was Written?" August 2014, unpublished paper, http://stevenpinker.com/has-decline-violence-reversed-better-angels-our-nature-was-written. Perspective is also supplied by Håvard Strand and Halvard Buhaug, "Armed Conflict, 1946–2014," in *Peace and Conflict 2016*, ed. David A. Backer, Ravi Bhavnani, and Paul K. Huth (New York: Routledge, 2016), 19–24.

24. Steven Pinker and Andrew Mack, "The World Is Not Falling Apart," *Slate*, December 22, 2014, http://www.slate.com/articles/news_and_politics/foreigners/2014/12/the_world_is_not_falling_apart_the_trend_lines_reveal_an_increasingly_peaceful.html.

25. Mary Kaldor, *New and Old Wars: Organized Violence in a Global Era* (Stanford, CA: Stanford University Press, 1999).

26. Stathis N. Kalyvas, "'New' and 'Old' Civil Wars: A Valid Distinction?" *World Politics* 54, no. 1 (October 2001): 99–118; Christopher J. L. Murray, Gary King, Alan D. Lopez, et al., "Armed Conflict as a Public Health Problem," *British Medical Journal* 324, no. 7333 (February 9, 2002): 346–49; Errol A. Henderson and J. David Singer, "'New Wars' and Rumors of 'New Wars,'" *International Interactions* 28, no. 2 (April 2002): 165–190; Kelly M. Greenhill, "Counting the Costs: The Politics of Numbers in Armed Conflicts," in *Sex, Drugs, and Body Counts: The Politics of Numbers in Global Crime and Conflict*, ed. Peter Andreas and Kelly M. Greenhill (Ithaca, NY: Cornell University Press, 2010), 127–58; Taylor B. Seybolt, "Significant Numbers: Civilian Casualties and Strategic Peacebuilding," in *Counting Civilian Casualties: An Introduction to Recording and Estimating Nonmilitary Deaths in Conflict*, ed. Taylor B. Seybolt, Jay D. Aronson, and Baruch Fischhoff (New York: Oxford University Press, 2013), 15–28.

27. Erik Melander, Magnus Öberg, and Jonathan Hall, "Are 'New Wars' More Atrocious? Battle Severity, Civilians Killed, and Forced Migration Before and After the End of the Cold War," *European Journal of International Relations* 15, no. 3 (September 2009): 505–36.

28. Mark Kaldor, *New and Old Wars: Organized Violence in a Global Era*, 3rd ed. (Stanford, CA: Stanford University Press, 2012), 202–221.

29. Tanisha M. Fazal, "Dead Wrong? Battle Deaths, Military Medicine, and Exaggerated Reports of War's Demise," *International Security* 39, no. 1 (Summer 2014): 95–125.

30. In their simplest form, beliefs are *ideas that have become internalized and accepted as true*, often without much further analysis. See Christopher J. Fettweis, *The Pathologies of Power: Fear, Honor, Glory, and Hubris in U.S. Foreign Policy* (New York: Cambridge University Press, 2013), 5–10.

31. Robert Jervis, "Understanding Beliefs and Threat Inflation," in *American Foreign Policy and the Politics of Fear: Threat Inflation Since 9/11*, ed. A. Trevor Thrall and Jane K. Cramer (New York: Routledge, 2009), 18.

32. Another quarter (and a fifth of CFR members) consider the dangers to be equivalent. Pew Center for the People and the Press, "America's Place in the World in 2009: An

Investigation of Public and Leadership Opinion About International Affairs," December 2009, http://www.people-press.org/files/legacy-pdf/569.pdf. See also Micah Zenko and Michael A. Cohen, "Clear and Present Safety: The United States Is More Secure Than Washington Thinks," *Foreign Affairs* 91, no. 2 (March/April 2012): 79–93; Christopher A. Preble and John Mueller, eds., *A Dangerous World? Threat Perception and U.S. National Security* (Washington, DC: Cato Institute, 2014).

33. Fettweis, *Dangerous Times?*, 135–53.

34. Bruce M. Russett, "The Calculus of Deterrence," *Journal of Conflict Resolution* 7, no. 2 (June 1963): 98. See also the discussions in Alexander L. George and Richard Smoke, *Deterrence in American Foreign Policy: Theory and Practice* (New York: Columbia University Press, 1974), 516–17; Alexander L. George and Richard Smoke, "Deterrence and Foreign Policy," *World Politics* 41, no. 2 (January 1989): 170–182; Jacek Kugler, "Terror Without Deterrence: Reassessing the Role of Nuclear Weapons," *Journal of Conflict Resolution* 28, no. 2 (September 1984): 470–506.

35. Stephen Van Evera discusses problems with studies of war that choose their cases on the dependent variable (which includes approximately all of them) in *Causes of War: Power and the Roots of Conflict* (Ithaca, NY: Cornell University Press, 1999), 12.

36. Michael Mandelbaum, *The Nuclear Revolution: International Politics Before and After Hiroshima* (Cambridge: Cambridge University Press, 1981); Martin Van Creveld, "The Waning of Major War," in *The Waning of Major War*, ed. Väyrynen, 97–112; Kenneth N. Waltz, "Nuclear Myths and Political Realities," American Political Science Review 84, no. 3 (September 1990): 731–45; Carl Kaysen, "Is War Obsolete? A Review Essay," *International Security* 14, no. 4 (Spring 1990): 42–64; Lawrence Freedman, "Stephen Pinker and the Long Peace: Alliance, Deterrence, and Decline," *Journal of Cold War History* 14, no. 4 (2014): 657–72; Robert A. Rauchhaus, "Evaluating the Nuclear Peace Hypothesis: A Quantitative Approach," *Journal of Conflict Resolution* 53, no. 2 (April 2009): 258–77.

37. To say this idea did not catch on would be something of an understatement. See Waltz's contribution to Scott D. Sagan and Kenneth N. Waltz, *The Spread of Nuclear Weapons: A Debate* (New York: Norton, 1995); Mearsheimer, "Back to the Future."

38. Robert O. Keohane and Joseph S. Nye, *Power and Interdependence: World Politics in Transition* (Boston: Little, Brown, 1977); Robert O. Keohane and Joseph S. Nye, "Power and Interdependence Revisited," *International Organization* 41, no. 4 (Autumn 1987): 725–53. See also Dale C. Copeland, "Economic Interdependence and War: A Theory of Trade Expectations," *International Security* 20, no. 4 (Spring 1996): 5–41; John R. Oneal and Bruce M. Russett, "The Kantian Peace: The Pacific Benefits of Democracy, Interdependence, and International Organizations, 1885–1992," *World Politics* 52, no. 1 (October 1999): 1–37; Edward D. Mansfield and Brian M. Pollins, *Economic Interdependence and International Conflict: New Perspectives on an Enduring Debate* (Ann Arbor: University of Michigan Press, 2003).

39. Stephen G. Brooks, *Producing Security: Multinational Corporations, Globalization, and the Changing Calculus of Conflict* (Princeton, NJ: Princeton University Press, 2005).

40.   Quoted by David S. Fick, *Entrepreneurship in Africa: A Study of Success* (Westport, CT: Greenwood, 2002), 289.

41.   Richard Rosecrance, *The Rise of the Trading State: Commerce and Conquest in the Modern World* (New York: Basic Books, 1986); Richard Rosecrance, *The Rise of the Virtual State: Wealth and Power in the Coming Century* (New York: Basic Books, 1999); Erik Gartzke, "The Capitalist Peace," *American Journal of Political Science* 51, no. 1 (January 2007): 166–91. For a dissenting view, see Kenneth N. Waltz, "Globalization and Governance," *PS: Political Science and Politics* 32, no. 4 (December 1999): 693–700.

42.   He refers to this as the "modernization peace." Azar Gat, *The Causes of War and the Spread of Peace: But Will War Rebound?* (New York: Oxford University Press, 2017).

43.   The modern democratic peace debate began in earnest with Michael W. Doyle, "Liberalism and World Politics," *American Political Science Review* 80, no. 4 (December 1985): 1151–70. A useful review of its first twenty years can be found in the forum involving David Kinsella, Branislav L. Slantchev, Anna Alexandrova, Erik Gartzke, Michael W. Doyle, and Sebastian Rosato in *American Political Science Review* 99, no. 3 (August 2005): 453–72.

44.   For representative works, see Stephen D. Krasner, ed., *International Regimes* (Ithaca, NY: Cornell University Press, 1983); Robert O. Keohane, "International Institutions: Two Approaches," *International Studies Quarterly* 32, no. 4 (December 1988): 379–96; Robert O. Keohane and Lisa L. Martin, "The Promise of Institutional Theory," *International Security* 20, no. 1 (Summer 1995): 39–51; Patrick M. Morgan, "Multilateral Institutions as Restraints on Major War," in *The Waning of Major War: Theories and Debates*, ed. Raimo Väyrynen (New York: Routledge, 2006), 160–84.

45.   Mack, "Global Political Violence"; Goldstein, *Winning the War on War*. For the efficacy of peacekeeping, see the work of Virginia Page Fortna, especially *Does Peacekeeping Work? Shaping Belligerents' Choices After Civil War* (Princeton, NJ: Princeton University Press, 2008); and "Is Peacekeeping 'Winning the War on War'?" *Perspectives on Politics* 11, no. 2 (June 2013): 566–70.

46.   By any reasonable measure, the last decade has been the most peaceful in African history, even when taking into account booming populations and a heavy dose of chronological bias. Paul D. Williams, *War and Conflict in Africa* (Washington: Polity, 2011), chap. 2; Scott Straus, "Wars Do End! Changing Patterns of Political Violence in Sub-Saharan Africa," *African Affairs* 111, no. 443 (March 2012): 179–201; David Burbach and Christopher J. Fettweis, "The Coming Stability? The Decline of Warfare in Africa and the Implications for International Security," *Contemporary Security Policy* 35, no. 3 (Fall 2014): 421–45.

47.   William R. Thompson, "Democracy and Peace: Putting the Cart Before the Horse?" *International Organization* 50, no. 1 (Winter 1996): 141–74; John Mueller, "War Has Almost Ceased to Exist: An Assessment," *Political Science Quarterly* 124, no. 2 (Summer 2009): 297–321; Mark Pietrzyk, *International Order and Individual Liberty: Effects of War and Peace on the Development of Governments* (Lanham, MD: University Press of America, 2002).

48. Pinker, *The Better Angels of Our Nature*, 378–481.

49. Mark L. Haas, "A Geriatric Peace? The Future of U.S. Power in a World of Aging Populations," *International Security* 32, no. 1 (Summer 2007): 112–47; Edward N. Luttwak, "Where Are the Great Powers? At Home with the Kids," *Foreign Affairs* 73, no. 4 (July/August 1994): 23–28.

50. Mueller, *The Remnants of War*; Evan Luard, *War in International Society: A Study in International Sociology* (London: I. B. Tauris, 1986); James Lee Ray, "The Abolition of Slavery and the End of International War," *International Organization* 43, no. 3 (Summer 1989); 405–39; Fettweis, *Dangerous Times?*; Pinker, *The Better Angels of Our Nature*.

51. Charles Kindleberger, *The World in Depression, 1929–1939* (Berkeley: University of California Press, 1974); Robert O. Keohane, *After Hegemony: Cooperation and Discord in the World Political Economy* (Princeton, NJ: Princeton University Press, 1984); David A. Lake, "Leadership, Hegemony, and the International Economy: Naked Emperor or Tattered Monarch with Potential?", *International Studies Quarterly* 37, no. 4 (December 1993): 459–89.

52. Michael Mandelbaum, *The Case for Goliath: How America Acts as the World's Government in the Twenty-First Century* (New York: Public Affairs, 2005), xix.

53. This distinction is similar but not identical to Jonathan Monten's conception of conservative and liberal hegemonies in "Primacy and Grand Strategic Beliefs in U.S. Unilateralism," *Global Governance* 13, no. 1 (January–March 2007): 119–38.

54. See the vast corpus of G. John Ikenberry, most recently *Liberal Leviathan: The Origins, Crisis, and Transformation of the American World Order* (Princeton, NJ: Princeton University Press, 2011); Michael Ignatieff, "The American Empire: The Burden," *New York Times Magazine*, January 5, 2003; Michael Lind, *The American Way of Strategy* (New York: Oxford University Press, 2006); Carla Norrlof, *America's Global Advantage: U.S. Hegemony and International Cooperation* (New York: Cambridge University Press, 2010); Georg Sorenson, *A Liberal World Order in Crisis: Choosing Between Imposition and Restraint* (Ithaca, NY: Cornell University Press, 2011).

55. G. John Ikenberry, "The Future of the Liberal World Order," *Foreign Affairs* 90, no. 3 (May/June 2011): 58.

56. William Kristol and Robert Kagan, "Toward a Neo-Reaganite Foreign Policy," *Foreign Affairs* 75, no. 4 (July/August 1996): 18–33; Niall Ferguson, *Colossus: The Price of America's Empire* (New York: Penguin, 2004); Mandelbaum, *The Case for Goliath*; Mackubin Owens, "The Bush Doctrine: The Foreign Policy of Republican Empire," *Orbis* 53, no. 1 (January 2009): 23–40; Charles Krauthammer, "In Defense of Democratic Realism," *National Interest* 77 (Fall 2004): 15–25; Robert J. Lieber, *The American Era: Power and Strategy for the Twenty-First Century* (New York: Cambridge University Press, 2005); Max Boot, "The Case for American Empire," *The Weekly Standard* 7, no. 5 (October 15, 2001): 27–35; and almost anything by Robert Kagan, including most recently *The World America Made*.

57. Richard N. Haass, *The Reluctant Sheriff: The United States After the Cold War* (New York: Council on Foreign Relations Press, 1997); Colin S. Gray, *The Sheriff: America's Defense of the New World Order* (Lexington: University Press of Kentucky, 2004).

58.  Kagan, *The World America Made*, 134.

59.  Lawrence F. Kaplan and William Kristol, *The War Over Iraq: Saddam's Tyranny and America's Mission* (San Francisco: Encounter Books, 2003), 118.

60.  While all neoconservatives believe that the United States is the primary force for global stability, most also maintain that the world remains a very dangerous place. As a group, they reject the New Peace or claim that it is fated to be brief. For a discussion of both neoconservatism and its exceptionally high perception of threat, see Stefan Halper and Jonathan Clarke, *American Alone: The Neo-Conservatives and the Global Order* (New York: Cambridge University Press, 2004).

61.  Samuel Huntington, "Why International Primacy Matters," *International Security* 17, no. 4 (Spring 1993): 68–83; William C. Wohlforth, "The Stability of a Unipolar World," *International Security* 24, no. 1 (Summer 1999): 5–41; Mandelbaum, *The Case for Goliath*; Sebastian Mallaby, "The Reluctant Imperialist: Terrorism, Failed States, and the Case for American Empire," *Foreign Affairs* 81, no. 2 (March/April 2002): 2–7; Robert Kaplan, "Supremacy by Stealth: Ten Rules for Managing the World," *Atlantic Monthly* 292, no. 1 (July/August 2003): 65–83.

62.  Thomas Hobbes, *Leviathan* (New York: Cambridge University Press, 1996).

63.  For an explanation, see Jean Hampton, *Hobbes and the Social Contract Tradition* (New York: Cambridge University Press, 1986), esp. chap. 3.

64.  Stephen M. Walt, *The Origin of Alliances* (Ithaca, NY: Cornell University Press, 1987), explains the imperative of balancing threat.

65.  Wohlforth ("The Stability of a Unipolar World") in particular has argued that balancing only makes sense when it is possible to do so. Cost prohibits smaller countries from trying to catch up to hegemonic powers that have a major head start, especially when they are not likely to be able to do so anyway.

66.  Bradley A. Thayer, "Humans, Not Angels: Reasons to Doubt the Decline of War Thesis," *International Studies Review* 15, no. 3 (September 2013): 405–11.

67.  Huntington, "Why International Primacy Matters," 83.

68.  Jervis, "Theories of War in an Era of Leading Power Peace," 9; Alexander Wendt, *Social Theory of International Relations* (New York: Cambridge University Press, 1999), 312.

69.  Fettweis, *Dangerous Times?*, 49–53.

70.  John Lewis Gaddis, *Strategies of Containment: A Critical Appraisal of Postwar American National Security Policy* (New York: Oxford University Press, 1982), esp. 30–31.

71.  The belief that behavioral norms, especially advantageous ones, can spread throughout the system is shared by many scholars; see Kenneth N. Waltz's discussion of "sameness" in *Theory of International Politics* (Reading, MA: Addison-Wesley, 1979), 76, 127.

72.  Andrew J. Bacevich makes this case in *America's War for the Middle East: A Military History* (New York: Random House, 2016).

73.  Jane Perlez, "U.S. Did Little to Deter Buildup as Ethiopia and Eritrea Prepared for War," *New York Times*, May 22, 2000.

74.  Michael O'Hanlon, "America's Military, Cut to the Quick," *Washington Post*, August 9, 1998.

75. Kristol and Kagan, "Toward a Neo-Reaganite Foreign Policy," 24.

76. From SIPRI figures, http://first.sipri.org. The upper levels of that range were reached during the peak of the wars in Iraq and Afghanistan and the lower ranges during the mid-1990s as well as after the wars ended.

77. Robert Kagan and William Kristol, "National Interest and Global Responsibility," in *Present Dangers: Crisis and Opportunity in American Foreign and Defense Policy*, ed. Robert Kagan and William Kristol (San Francisco: Encounter, 2000), 4.

78. Brett Stephens, *America in Retreat: The New Isolationism and the Coming Global Disorder* (New York: Sentinel, 2014), xv.

79. The quotation is from G. John Ikenberry, "The End of the Neo-Conservative Moment," *Survival* 46, no. 1 (Spring 2004): 7; the argument is better explained in his "America's Imperial Ambition," *Foreign Affairs* 81, no. 5 (September/October 2002): 44–60.

80. Stephen Brooks, G. John Ikenberry, and William C. Wohlforth, "Don't Come Home, America: The Case Against Retrenchment," *International Security* 37, no. 3 (Winter 2012–13): 7–51.

81. Barry R. Posen and Andrew L. Ross, "Competing Visions for U.S. Grand Strategy," *International Security* 21, no. 3 (Winter 1996/1997): 5–53.

82. For other taxonomies of grand strategy, see Alexander Nacht, "U.S. Foreign Policy Strategies," *Washington Quarterly* 18, no. 3 (Summer 1995): 195–210; Robert J. Art, *A Grand Strategy for America* (Ithaca, NY: Cornell University Press, 2003); Colin Dueck, "Ideas and Alternatives in American Grand Strategy, 2000–2004," *Review of International Studies* 30, no. 4 (October 2004): 511–35. Art identifies and evaluates seven different grand strategies; the rest, four.

83. For the liberal expectation of chaos, in addition to the Ikenberry work cited above, see Thomas M. Nichols, *Eve of Destruction: The Coming Age of Preventive War* (Philadelphia: University of Pennsylvania Press, 2008). Neoconservative tocsins are not hard to find; for a well-known one, see Dick Cheney and Liz Cheney, *Exceptional: Why the World Needs a Powerful America* (New York: Simon and Schuster, 2015).

84. Of the few hegemonic-stability theorists from elsewhere, most hail from the United Kingdom and counsel the United States to follow the lead of the British Empire. See Niall Ferguson, *Empire: The Rise and Demise of the British World Order and the Lessons for Global Power* (New York: Basic Books, 2002); Gray, *The Sheriff.*

85. Ellen Langer, "The Illusion of Control," *Journal of Personality and Social Psychology* 32, no. 2 (August 1975): 311–28.

86. For a review of the first two decades of research, see Paul K. Presson and Victor A. Benassi, "Illusion of Control: A Meta-Analytic Review," *Journal of Social Behavior and Personality* 11, no. 3 (September 1996): 493–510.

87. Richard deCharms, *Personal Causation: The Internal Affective Determinants of Behavior* (New York: Academic Press, 1968), esp. 269.

88. Ellen J. Langer and Jane Roth, "Heads I Win, Tails It's Chance: The Illusion of Control as a Function of the Sequence of Outcomes in a Purely Chance Task," *Journal of Personality and Social Psychology* 32, no. 6 (December 1975): 951–55.

89.   Anthony G. Greenwald, "The Totalitarian Ego: Fabrication and Revision of Personal History," *American Psychologist* 35, no. 7 (July 1980): 603–18.

90.   Nathaneal J. Fast, Deborah H. Gruenfeld, Niro Sivanthan, and Adam D. Galinsky, "Illusory Control: A Generative Force Behind Power's Far-Reaching Effects," *Psychological Science* 20, no. 4 (April 2009): 502–8.

91.   Nathanael J. Fast, Niro Sivanathan, Nicole D. Mayer, and Adam D. Galinsky, "Power and Overconfident Decision-Making," *Organizational Behavior and Human Decision Processes* 117, no. 2 (March 2012): 249–260; Leigh Plunkett Tost, Francesca Gino, and Richard Larrick, "Power, Competitiveness, and Advice Taking: Why the Powerful Don't Listen," *Organizational Behavior and Human Decision Making Processes* 117, no. 1 (January 2012): 53–65.

92.   Richard E. Nisbett, *The Geography of Thought: How Asians and Westerners Think Differently . . . and Why* (New York: Free Press, 2003), 100.

93.   Li-Jun Ji, Kaiping Peng, and Richard E. Nisbett, "Culture, Control, and Perception of Relationships in the Environment," *Journal of Personality and Social Psychology* 78, no. 5 (May 2000): 943–55; John R. Weisz, Fred M. Rothbaum, and Thomas C. Blackburn, "Standing Out and Standing In: The Psychology of Control in America and Japan," *American Psychologist* 39, no. 9 (September 1984): 955–69; Miriam Hernandez and Sheena S. Iyengar, "What Drives Whom? A Cultural Perspective on Human Agency," *Social Cognition* 19, no. 3 (June 2001): 269–294; Hannah Faye Chua, Janxin Leu, and Richard E. Nisbett, "Culture and Divergent Views of Social Events," *Personality and Social Psychology Bulletin* 31, no. 7 (July 2005): 925–934. For an anthropological discussion of the differences in cultural psychology, see Hazel Rose Markus and Shinobu Kitayama, "Culture and the Self: Implications for Cognition, Emotion, and Motivation," *Psychological Review* 98, no. 2 (April 1991): 224–53.

94.   It is also possible, but not as certain, that illusions of control might help explain our national fears, too. Some research has suggested that when actors experience perceptions of control in objectively uncontrollable situations, anxiety and depression result. In one study, for example, adolescents who believed that they could influence the course of their parents' marriages or serious illnesses suffered from higher levels of anxiety and depression than those who felt that outcome was beyond their control. When actors feel that outcomes are a result of their actions, they feel greater pressure to shape those outcomes. These findings are not terribly robust, however; perceptions of control may also have many beneficial outcomes for the psyche. For now, the connection between illusions of control and the anxiety that accompanies responsibility, while plausible, is not (yet?) fully supported by the current state of the literature. See the review in Ellen A. Skinner, *Perceived Control, Motivation, and Coping* (London: Sage, 1995), 134–36.

95.   Barry R. Posen, "Command of the Commons: The Military Foundation of U.S. Hegemony," *International Security* 28, no. 1 (Summer 2003): 5–46.

96.   Minor naval clashes occurred elsewhere, such as during the 1971 Indo-Pakistani and 1973 Yom Kippur Wars. From the sixteenth through the eighteenth centuries, by contrast, naval warfare was essentially constant. The nineteenth century was somewhat

more peaceful at sea, but battles still occurred in twenty-seven of the sixty-five years after Trafalgar. See Barrett Tillman, "Fear and Loathing in the Post-Naval Era," *Proceedings* 135, no. 6 (June 2009): 16–21.

97.   For more on this idea, see Rosecrance, *The Rise of the Trading State.*

98.   You Ji, "Dealing with the Malacca Dilemma: China's Effort to Protect Its Energy Supply," *Strategic Analysis* 31, no. 3 (May 2007): 467–489; Marc Lanteigne, "China's Maritime Security and the 'Malacca Dilemma,'" *Asian Security* 4, no. 2 (May 2008): 143–61.

99.   For a discussion of the Strait of Hormuz and deep skepticism regarding Iran's ability to close it off, see Eugene Gholz and Daryl G. Press, "Protecting 'the Prize': Oil and the U.S. National Interest," *Security Studies* 19, no. 3 (July–September 2010): 453–85.

100.   Kori Schake, "Will Washington Abandon the Order? The False Logic of Retreat," *Foreign Affairs* 96, no. 1 (January/February 2017): 45.

101.   The author is well aware of the continued existence of pirates. Once again, however, the interests of all states align. Coastal policing, rather than expensive blue-water capabilities, is best suited for fights against pirates. And it can be extremely effective, as recent experience off the Horn of Africa indicates.

102.   Robert A. Dahl, "The Concept of Power," *Behavioral Science* 2, no. 3 (July 1957): 201–15.

103.   Robert Jervis, *Perception and Misperception in International Politics* (Princeton, NJ: Princeton University Press, 1976), 343–55. See also Allan Fenigstein, "Self-Consciousness and the Overperception of Self as a Target," *Journal of Personality and Social Psychology* 47, no. 4 (October 1984): 860–70; John R. Chambers and Carsten K. W. De Dreu, "Egocentrism Drives Misunderstandings in Conflict and Negotiation," *Journal of Experimental Social Psychology* 51 (March 2014): 15–26; and the other works cited in this section.

104.   This is related to what has become known as the "availability heuristic." Amos Tversky and Daniel Kahneman, "Availability: A Heuristic for Judging Frequency and Probability," *Cognitive Psychology* 5, no. 2 (April 1973): 207–32. See also Michael Ross and Fiore Sicoly, "Egocentric Biases in Availability and Attribution," *Journal of Personality and Social Psychology* 37, no. 3 (March 1979): 322–36.

105.   The phenomenon was first described by Fritz Heider in *The Psychology of Interpersonal Relations* (New York: Wiley, 1958). Meta-analyses of the research on it since include Robert Arkin, Harris Cooper, and Thomas Kolditz, "A Statistical Review of the Literature Concerning the Self-Serving Attribution Bias in Interpersonal Influence Situations," *Journal of Personality* 48, no. 4 (December 1980): 435–48; Brian Mullen and Catherine A. Riordan, "Self-Serving Attributions for Performance in Naturalistic Settings: A Meta-Analytic Review," *Journal of Applied Social Psychology* 18, no. 1 (January 1988): 3–22; W. Keith Campbell and Constantine Sedikides, "Self-Threat Magnifies the Self-Serving Bias: A Meta-Analytic Integration," *Review of General Psychology* 3, no. 1 (March 1999): 23–43.

106.   Two-hundred sixty-six studies on culture and the self-serving bias were analyzed in Amy H. Mezulis, Lyn Y. Abramson, Janet S. Hyde, and Benjamin L. Hankin, "Is

There a Universal Positivity Bias in Attributions? A Meta-Analytic Review of the Individual, Developmental, and Cultural Differences in the Self-Serving Attributional Bias," *Psychological Bulletin* 130, no. 5 (September 2004): 711–47.

107.  Miron Zuckerman, Michael H. Kernis, Salvatore M. Guarnera, et al., "The Ego-Centric Bias: Seeing Oneself as Cause and Target of Others' Behavior," *Journal of Personality* 51, no. 4 (December 1983): 621–30; Allan Fenigstein, "Self-Consciousness and the Overperception of Self as a Target," *Journal of Personality and Social Psychology* 47, no. 4 (October 1984): 860–70.

108.  Madeleine K. Albright, interview on NBC's *The Today Show*, February 19, 1998, http://secretary.state.gov/www/statements/1998/980219a.html.

109.  Henry Kissinger, the Arthur K. Solomon Lecture, New York University, September 19, 1977, reprinted as "Continuity and Change in American Foreign Policy," *Society* 15, no. 1 (November/December 1977): 98.

110.  See a new English translation of the Russian original book by Vladimir Snegirev and Valery Samunin, published in English as *The Dead End: The Road to Afghanistan*, available at the National Security Archive at George Washington University, National Security Archive Electronic Briefing Book no. 396 (2012), http://www.gwu.edu/~nsarchiv/NSAEBB/NSAEBB396/Full%20Text%20Virus%20A.pdf. See also Aleksandr Antonovich Lyakhovskiy, *Inside the Soviet Invasion of Afghanistan and the Seizure of Kabul, December 1979* (Washington, DC: Woodrow Wilson Center), Cold War International History Project, Working Paper 51, January 2007; Anatoly Dobrynin, *In Confidence* (New York: Random House, 1995), esp. 441.

111.  See Richard Ned Lebow and Janice Gross Stein, "Afghanistan, Carter, and Foreign Policy Change: The Limits of Cognitive Models," in *Diplomacy, Force, and Leadership: Essays in Honor of Alexander L. George*, ed. Dan Caldwell and Timothy J. McKeown (Boulder, CO: Westview, 1993), 95–128; Janice Gross Stein, "Building Politics Into Psychology: The Misperception of Threat," *Political Psychology* 9, no. 2 (June 1988): 245–71.

112.  Carter, quoted by Dobrynin, *In Confidence*, 443.

113.  John Mearsheimer, "Why the Ukraine Crisis Is the West's Fault," *Foreign Affairs* 93, no. 5 (September/October 2014): 77–89.

114.  Ronald Reagan, *An American Life* (New York: Simon and Schuster, 1990), 588.

115.  Robert Kagan, "The Benevolent Empire," *Foreign Policy* 111 (Summer 1998): 32.

116.  Zbigniew Brzezinksi was one of the strongest proponents of this position. See his "A Plan for Europe: How to Expand NATO," *Foreign Affairs* 74, no. 1 (January/February 1995): 26–42.

117.  James M. Goldgeier, *Not Whether but When: The U.S. Decision to Enlarge NATO* (Washington, DC: Brookings Institution Press, 1999), 86–87.

118.  Historians and political scientists had been nearly united in opposition, a phenomenon that John Lewis Gaddis called "uncharacteristic," which was surely an understatement. John Lewis Gaddis, "History, Grand Strategy, and NATO Enlargement," *Survival* 40, no. 1 (Spring 1998): 145–51.

119.  The classic treatment is Edward E. Jones and Richard Nisbett, "The Actor and the Observer: Divergent Perceptions of the Causes of Behavior," in *Attribution:*

*Perceiving the Causes of Behavior*, ed. Edward E. Jones et al. (Morristown, NJ: General Learning Press, 1972), 79–94. See also Bertram F. Malle, "The Actor-Observer Asymmetry in Attribution: A (Surprising) Meta-Analysis," *Psychological Bulletin* 136, no. 6 (November 2006): 895–919.

120.   Janice Gross Stein, "Building Politics Into Psychology: The Misperception of Threat," *Political Psychology* 9, no. 2 (June 1988): 245–71, esp. 255; Richard Nesbitt and Lee Ross, *Human Inference: Strategies and Shortcomings of Social Judgment* (Englewood Cliffs, NJ: Prentice Hall, 1980).

121.   Deborah Welch Larson, *Origins of Containment: A Psychological Explanation* (Princeton, NJ: Princeton University Press, 1985), 350.

122.   John H. Harvey, Ben Harris, and Richard D. Barnes, "Actor-Observer Differences in the Perceptions of Responsibility and Freedom," *Journal of Personality and Social Psychology* 32, no. 1 (July 1975): 22–28.

123.   Lee Ross, David Greene, and Pamela House, "The 'False Consensus Effect': An Ego-Centric Bias in Social Perception and Attribution Processes," *Journal of Experimental Social Psychology* 13, no. 3 (May 1977): 279–301.

124.   See the extensive review in Steven J. Heine, Daniel R. Lehman, Hazel Rose Markus, and Shinobu Kitayama, "Is There a Universal Need for Positive Self-Regard?" *Psychology Review* 106, no. 4 (October 1999): 766–94.

125.   David Sanger, "Witness to Auschwitz Evil, Bush Draws a Lesson," *New York Times*, June 1, 2003. Discussed further in Robert Jervis, "Understanding the Bush Doctrine," *Political Science Quarterly* 118, no. 3 (Fall 2003): 385.

126.   Gallup International, "End of Year Survey 2013," January 2014, http://www.wingia .com/en/services/end_of_year_survey_2013/7/

127.   See the symposium on counterfactual analysis edited by Andrew Bennett, Colin Elman, and John M. Owen in *Security Studies* 24, no. 3 (July 2015): 377–430.

128.   Jervis, *Perception and Misperception in International Politics*, 58–113. Jervis never actually refers to the deterrence "model," but that is how the concept has entered the popular imagination.

129.   The best explanation of this argument remains Rosecrance, *The Rise of the Trading State*. Peter Liberman argues that such changes are illusory in *Does Conquest Pay? The Exploitation of Industrialized Societies* (Princeton, NJ: Princeton University Press, 1996), but his cases are from World War II. Robust counterarguments include Brooks, *Producing Security*; Zacher, "The Territorial Integrity Norm."

130.   Hardly anyone recognizes that this was central to Angell's arguments because hardly anyone has actually read what he wrote. See not only his famous *The Great Illusion: A Study of the Relation of Military Power to National Advantage*, 2nd ed. (London: William Heinemann, 1913), but also *The Fruits of Victory: A Sequel to the Great Illusion*, 2nd ed. (New York: Garland, 1973).

131.   Angell, *The Great Illusion*, 175.

## 2. UNIPOLARITY AND NUCLEAR WEAPONS

1.  "There's nobody that understands the horror of nuclear better than me"—candidate Trump on June 15, 2016. So we can all relax.

2.  Paul Bracken may be most closely associated with the "second nuclear age," but he did not coin the term. See his *Fire in the East: The Rise of Asian Military Power and the Second Nuclear Age* (New York: Harper Collins, 1999), and *The Second Nuclear Age: Strategy, Danger, and the New Power Politics* (New York: Henry Holt, 2012), but also Keith B. Payne, *Deterrence in the Second Nuclear Age* (Lexington: University Press of Kentucky, 1996); Colin S. Gray, *The Second Nuclear Age* (Boulder, CO: Lynn Reinner, 1999); Toshi Yoshihara and James R. Holmes, eds., *Strategy in the Second Nuclear Age: Power, Ambition, and the Ultimate Weapon* (Washington, DC: Georgetown University Press, 2012), 81–98; and those cited later in this chapter.

3.  Bracken, *The Second Nuclear Age*, 1, 105.

4.  Bracken, *Fire in the East*, 95.

5.  Bracken, *Fire in the East*, 96.

6.  Bracken, *The Second Nuclear Age*, 10.

7.  Scott D. Sagan and Kenneth N. Waltz, *The Spread of Nuclear Weapons: A Debate* (New York, Norton, 1995), 1.

8.  John J. Mearsheimer, "Back to Future: Instability in Europe After the Cold War," *International Security* 15, no. 1 (Summer 1990): 37, 39. See also Benjamin Frankel, "The Brooding Shadow: Systemic Incentives and Nuclear Weapons Proliferation," *Security Studies* 2, nos. 3/4 (Spring/Summer 1993): 37–78.

9.  John J. Mearsheimer, "Disorder Restored," in *Rethinking America's Security: Beyond Cold War to New World Order*, ed. Graham Allison and Gregory F. Treverton (New York: Norton, 1992), 225. For specific predictions of proliferation in the Third World, see 234–235.

10. Graham Allison, *Nuclear Terrorism: The Ultimate Preventable Catastrophe* (New York: Henry Holt, 2004), 186.

11. Bracken, *The Second Nuclear Age*, 95. Not everyone foresaw increased proliferation, of course. See Jacques E. C. Hymans, *The Psychology of Nuclear Proliferation: Identity, Emotions, and Foreign Policy* (New York: Cambridge University Press, 2006).

12. Bracken, *The Second Nuclear Age*, 3. See also Fred Charles Iklé, "The Second Coming of the Nuclear Age," *Foreign Affairs* 75, no. 1 (January/February 1996): 119–28.

13. Paul Bracken, *Fire in the East: The Rise of Asian Military Power and the Second Nuclear Age* (New York: Harper Collins, 1999), 113. On the same page, Bracken demonstrates that he is one of those people who believe "penultimate" means "extra ultimate." Bracken's history of ethnocentrism is reviewed by Victor D. Cha in "The Second Nuclear Age: Proliferation Pessimism Versus Sober Optimism in South Asia and East Asia," *Journal of Strategic Studies* 24, no. 4 (December 2001): esp. 100–101.

14. Cha makes the point about overdetermination in "The Second Nuclear Age," 79 and thereafter, and Payne worries about undeterrable actors throughout his *Deterrence in the Second Nuclear Age*, esp. 40–52.

15. See Rebecca Davis Gibbons and Matthew Kroenig, "Reconceptualizing Nuclear Risks: Bringing Deliberate Nuclear Use Back In," *Comparative Strategy* 35, no. 5 (October 2016): 407–22. The authors claim to "marshal empirical evidence" to support the contention that the danger of an intentional use of nuclear weapons is increasing.

16. "Tailored deterrence" made its debut as a concept in the 2006 Quadrennial Defense Review of the U.S. Department of Defense. White House, "Quadrennial Defense Review Report," February 6, 2006, http://archive.defense.gov/pubs/pdfs/QDR 20060203.pdf.

17. This is a rather bizarre line of argument, since North Korea had nuclear weapons for a decade without such bullying. Chris Hill, "Avoiding the Temptation to Do Nothing," *Time*, April 3, 2017.

18. Nuno Monteiro, *Theory of Unipolar Politics* (New York: Cambridge University Press, 2014), 14–15.

19. Bracken, *The Second Nuclear Age*, 160.

20. The terms "nonproliferation" and "counterproliferation" are often conflated. The former aims at preventing proliferation; the latter (an invention of the U.S. Department of Defense in the 1990s) essentially refers to rolling back existing WMD programs. According to Barry Schneider of the USAF Counterproliferation Center, the basic difference is that nonproliferation "features the velvet glove of the diplomat" and counterproliferation "the iron fist of the military." See Barry R. Schneider, "Military Responses to Proliferation Threats," in *Pulling Back from the Nuclear Brink: Reducing and Countering Nuclear Threats*, ed. Barry R. Schneider and William L. Dowdy (London: Frank Cass, 1998), 306.

21. Payne, *Deterrence in the Second Nuclear Age*, 118.

22. Keir A. Lieber and Daryl G. Press, "The End of MAD? The Nuclear Dimension of U.S. Primacy," *International Security* 30, no. 4 (Spring 2006): 7–44.

23. Lieber and Press, "The End of MAD?," 8.

24. Austin Long and Brendan Rittenhouse Green, "Stalking the Secure Second Strike: Intelligence, Counterforce, and Nuclear Strategy," *Journal of Strategic Studies* 38, nos. 1/2 (February 2015): 38–73; Keir A. Lieber and Daryl G. Press, "The New Era of Counterforce: Technological Change and the Future of Deterrence," *International Security* 41, no. 4 (Spring 2017): 9–49.

25. Allison, *Nuclear Terrorism*, 120.

26. Daniel Deudney, "Unipolarity and Nuclear Weapons," in *International Relations Theory and the Consequences of Unipolarity*, ed. G. John Ikenberry, Michael Mastunduno, and William C. Wohlforth (New York: Cambridge University Press, 2011), 308.

27. The clock was at two minutes until midnight between 1952 and 1960 and dipped down to three minutes from 1983 to 1988. Its timeline can be accessed at http://thebulletin .org/timeline.

28. Bracken, *The Second Nuclear Age*, 7.

29. John J. Mearsheimer, "The Case for a Ukrainian Nuclear Deterrent," *Foreign Affairs* 72, no. 3 (Summer 1993): 50–66.

30. Nuclear Energy Institute, "Nuclear Energy Around the World," April 2017, https://www.nei.org/Knowledge-Center/Nuclear-Statistics/World-Statistics.

31. By one estimate, there are nearly fifty "nuclear-capable" countries. See Hymans, *The Psychology of Nuclear Proliferation*, 4; Adam N. Stulberg and Matthew Fuhrmann, eds., *The Nuclear Renaissance and International Security* (Stanford, CA: Stanford University Press, 2013).

32. Those like Bracken (*The Second Nuclear Age*, 93) who insist on claiming that both are new members of the nuclear club should explain how the Pakistanis could go from zero to testing in seventeen days following the surprise Indian test. Nonetheless, he has made this claim repeatedly. There he also says that Israel is "coming out of the closet" with its arsenal and that other countries are considering joining the club.

33. The story is told well by George Perkovich in *India's Nuclear Bomb: The Impact on Global Proliferation* (Berkeley, CA: University of California Press, 1999). The "peaceful nuclear device" is explained on 161–189.

34. The era is reviewed in Strobe Talbott, *Engaging India: Diplomacy, Democracy, and the Bomb* (Washington: Brookings Institution Press, 2004).

35. David E. Sanger, "Secretary of State Rejects Talks with North Korea on Nuclear Program," *New York Times*, March 18, 2017.

36. Ambassador Bolton tweeted out his concern on August 14, 2017. https://twitter.com/AmbJohnBolton; his handle is @AmbJohnBolton.

37. Leon V. Sigal, *Disarming Strangers: Nuclear Diplomacy with North Korea* (Princeton, NJ: Princeton University Press, 1998); Dennis Roy, "North Korea and the 'Madman Theory,'" *Security Dialogue* 25, no. 3 (September 1994): 307–16; David C. Kang, "International Relations Theory and the Second Korean War," *International Studies Quarterly* 47, no. 3 (September 2003): 301–24; Victor D. Cha, "Five Myths About North Korea," *Washington Post*, December 10, 2010; Terrence Roehrig, "North Korea's Nuclear Weapons Program: Motivations, Strategy, and Doctrine," in *Strategy in the Second Nuclear Age*, ed. Yoshihara and Holmes, 81–98; Max Fisher, "North Korea, Far from Crazy, Is All Too Rational," *New York Times*, September 10, 2016.

38. All arms-control agreements expire after a certain period. The Non-Proliferation Treaty has been renegotiated and (so far) renewed every five years, for example, and SALT agreements only lasted eight. The JCPOA has a period of fifteen years, longer than any similar agreement, and was written under the impression that it will be extended.

39. Matthew Kroenig, "Time to Attack Iran: Why a Strike Is the Least Bad Option," *Foreign Affairs* 91, no. 1 (January/February 2012): 86. See also his *A Time to Attack: The Looming Iranian Nuclear Threat* (New York: St. Martin's Press, 2014); Norman Podhoretz, "The Case for Bombing Iran," *Commentary* 123, no. 6 (June 2007): 17–23; Alan J. Kuperman, "There's Only One Way to Stop Iran," *New York Times*, December 24, 2009; Joshua Moravchik, "War with Iran Is Probably Our Best Option," *Washington Post*, March 13, 2015.

40. John R. Bolton, "To Stop Iran's Bomb, Bomb Iran," *New York Times*, March 26, 2015.

41. National Intelligence Council, "Iran: Nuclear Capabilities and Intentions," November 2007, http://www.isisnucleariran.org/assets/pdf/2007_Iran_NIE.pdf.

42. On China's nuclear program, see Jeffrey Lewis, *Paper Tigers: China's Nuclear Posture* (London: International Institute for Strategic Studies, December 2014). For an analysis of Chinese nuclear behavior in the early days of the Trump regime, see Melissa Hanham, "China's Happy to Sit Out the Nuclear Arms Race," *Foreign Policy* blog, January 30, 2017, http://foreignpolicy.com/2017/01/30/chinas-happy-to-sit-out-the-nuclear-arms-race/.

43. Hans M. Kristensen and Robert S. Norris, "Russian Nuclear Forces, 2016," *Bulletin of the Atomic Scientists* 72, no. 3 (April 16, 2016): 125–34.

44. On the taboo, see Nina Tannenwald, *The Nuclear Taboo: The United States and Non-Use of Nuclear Weapons Since 1945* (New York: Cambridge University Press, 2007); on other reasons for nonuse, see Thomas M. Nichols, *No Use: Nuclear Weapons and U.S. National Security* (Philadelphia: University of Pennsylvania Press, 2013).

45. Remarks on *Meet the Press*, March 16, 2003, https://georgewbush-whitehouse.archives.gov/vicepresident/news-speeches/speeches/vp20010916.html.

46. Philosophers and grammarians might point out that it would have been technically impossible for Hussein to "reconstitute" weapons he had not previously constituted.

47. Flynt L. Leverett, "Why Libya Gave Up on the Bomb," *New York Times*, January 23, 2004; Martin S. Indyk, "The War in Iraq Did Not Force Gadaffi's Hand," *Financial Times*, March 9, 2004.

48. William R. Tobey, "A Message from Tripoli: How Libya Came to Give Up Its WMD," *Bulletin of the Atomic Scientists*, December 3, 2014, http://thebulletin.org/message-tripoli-how-libya-gave-its-wmd7834, which is the first of a five-part series on the issue.

49. Jacques E. C. Hymans makes the case that strong state institutions are necessary conditions for nuclear development in *Achieving Nuclear Ambitions: Scientists, Politicians, and Proliferation* (New York: Cambridge University Press 2012). Libya is discussed on 239–248; its crated centrifuges on 242. See also Målfrid Braut-Hegghammer, *Unclear Physics: Why Iraq and Libya Failed to Get the Bomb* (Ithaca, NY: Cornell University Press, 2016).

50. Bruce W. Jentleson and Christopher A. Whytock, "Who 'Won' Libya? The Force-Diplomacy Debate and Its Implications for Theory and Policy," *International Security* 30, no. 3 (Winter 2005/2006): 47–86.

51. A January 2015 report in *Der Spiegel* made waves by suggesting that the Syrian program may have restarted: see Erich Follath, "Evidence Points to Syrian Push for Nuclear Weapons," *Der Spiegel* online, January 9, 2015, http://www.spiegel.de/international/world/evidence-points-to-syria-still-working-on-a-nuclear-weapon-a-1012209.html. Subsequent reports have strongly disagreed. The Nuclear Threat Initiative has concluded that "it is highly unlikely that Syria currently has an active nuclear weapons program": http://www.nti.org/learn/countries/syria/nuclear/.

52. Leonard S. Specter and Avner Cohen, "Israel's Airstrike on Syria's Reactor: Implications for the Nonproliferation Regime," *Arms Control Today* 38, no. 6 (July/August 2007): 15–21.

53.   John Mueller reviews the black market for fissile material in *Atomic Obsession: Nuclear Alarmism from Hiroshima to Al-Qaeda* (New York: Oxford University Press, 2009), 169–172.

54.   Quoted by Jussi M. Hanhimaki, "The (Really) Good War? Cold War Nostalgia and American Foreign Policy," *Cold War History* 14, no. 4 (November 2014): 673–74.

55.   Thom Shanker, "Gates Counters Putin's Words on U.S. Power," *New York Times*, February 11, 2007.

56.   Rex W. Tillerson, "Remarks to U.S. Department of State Employees," May 3, 2017, https://www.state.gov/secretary/remarks/2017/05/270620.htm.

57.   "Notes from the Chairman," *Foreign Affairs* 95, no. 5 (September/October 2016): 2. His long track record of nostalgia is critically addressed throughout the essays in Christopher A. Preble and John Mueller, eds., *A Dangerous World? Threat Perception and U.S. National Security* (Washington, DC: Cato Institute, 2014).

58.   Paul Kennedy makes similar points in "The Good Old Days of the Cold War," *Los Angeles Times*, February 18, 2007.

59.   Televisions occasionally fall on people, and cows kill more Americans than ISIS does. See Andrew Shaver, "You're More Likely to Be Fatally Crushed by Furniture Than Killed by a Terrorist," *Washington Post*, November 23, 2015, https://www.washingtonpost.com/news/monkey-cage/wp/2015/11/23/youre-more-likely-to-be-fatally-crushed-by-furniture-than-killed-by-a-terrorist/; Christopher Ingraham, "Chart: The Animals That Are Most Likely to Kill You This Summer," *Washington Post*, June 16, 2015, https://www.washingtonpost.com/news/wonk/wp/2015/06/16/chart-the-animals-that-are-most-likely-to-kill-you-this-summer/.

60.   Not everyone agrees with (or realizes the basic truth of) this statement, including General Michael Flynn, the disgraced first national security advisor of President Trump. Over and over throughout a book he cowrote with Michael Ledeen (*Field of Fight: How We Can Win the Global War Against Radical Islam and Its Allies* [New York: St. Martin's Press, 2016]), Flynn warns that the United States is losing the war on terror. How exactly the United States could possibly "lose" in any real way is left, shall we say, underexplained.

61.   Richard Pipes, "Why the Soviet Union Thinks It Could Fight and Win a Nuclear War," *Commentary* 64, no. 1 (July 1977): 34.

62.   For Cold War hawks, "mirror imaging" referred to the fallacy of believing that opponents think like we do. For political psychologists, the term refers to the tendency to perceive others as the opposite of oneself, as one would see in mirror. For the former usage, see Raymond L. Garthoff, "On Estimating and Imputing Intentions," *International Security* 2, no. 3 (Winter 1978): 22–33; for the latter, Ralph K. White, "Images in the Context of International Conflict: Soviet Perceptions of the U.S. and the USSR," in *International Behavior: A Social-Psychological Analysis*, ed. Herbert C. Kelman (New York: Holt, Rinehart and Winston, 1965), esp. 255–258.

63.   Quoted by Lawrence S. Wittner, *Resisting the Bomb: A History of the World Nuclear Disarmament Movement, 1954–1970* (Palo Alto, CA: Stanford University Press, 1997), 161–62.

64. Francis J. Gavin, "Same as It Ever Was: Nuclear Alarmism, Proliferation, and the Cold War," *International Security* 34, no. 3 (Winter 2009/2010): 15.

65. William Burr and Jeffrey T. Richelson, "Whether to 'Strangle the Baby in the Cradle': The United States and the Chinese Nuclear Program, 1960–64," *International Security* 25, no. 3 (Winter 2000/2001): 54–99.

66. Michael Mandelbaum, "The Bomb, Dread, and Eternity," *International Security* 5, no. 2, (Autumn 1980): 3–23.

67. Contemporary research on the effect of the Cold War nuclear standoff on the psychology of young people can be found in Lisa A. Goodman, John E. Mack, William R. Beardslee, and Roberta M. Snow, "The Threat of Nuclear War and the Nuclear Arms Race: Adolescent Experience and Perceptions," *Political Psychology* 4, no. 3 (September 1983): 501–530; Eric Chivian, John Robinson, Jonathan R. H. Tudge, et al., "American and Soviet Teenagers' Concerns About Nuclear War and the Future," *New England Journal of Medicine* 319, no. 7 (August 18, 1988): 407–41.

68. For one of the earliest major works, see Frederic C. Bartlett, *Remembering: A Study in Experimental and Social Psychology* (London: Cambridge University Press, 1932). See also Elizabeth Loftus, *Memory* (Reading, MA: Addison Wesley, 1980); Daniel L. Schacter, *Searching for Memory: The Brain, the Mind, and the Past* (New York: Basic Books, 1996).

69. Terence R. Mitchell and Leigh Thompson, "A Theory of Temporal Adjustments of the Evaluation of Events: Rosy Prospection and Rosy Retrospection," in *Advances in Managerial Cognition and Organizational Information-Processing*, ed. Chuck Stubbart, James R. Meindl, and Joseph Francis Allen Porac (Greenwich, CT: JAI, 1994), 5:85–114. See also Anthony G. Greenwald, "The Totalitarian Ego: Fabrication and Revision of Personal History," *American Psychologist* 35, no. 7 (July 1980): 603–18; Timothy D. Wilson, Jay Meyers, and Daniel T. Gilbert, " 'How Happy Was I, Anyway?' A Retrospective Impact Bias," *Social Cognition* 21, no. 6 (December 2003): 421–46.

70. Daniel L. Schacter, *The Seven Sins of Memory: How the Mind Forgets and Remembers* (Boston: Houghton-Mifflin, 2001); Michael C. Anderson, "Active Forgetting: Evidence for Functional Inhibition as a Source of Memory Failure," *Journal of Aggression, Maltreatment, and Trauma* 4, no. 2 (2001): 185–210; Benjamin C. Storm and Tara A. Jobe, "Retrieval-Induced Forgetting Predicts Failure to Recall Negative Autobiographical Memories," *Psychological Science* 23, no. 11 (November 2012): 1356–1363.

71. Robert I. Sutton, "Feelings About a Disneyland Visit: Photographs and Reconstruction of Bygone Emotions," *Journal of Management Inquiry* 1 no. 4 (December 1992): 278–87; Terence R. Mitchell, Leigh Thompson, Erika Peterson, and Randy Cronk, "Temporal Adjustments in the Evaluation of Events: The 'Rosy' View," *Journal of Experimental Social Psychology* 33, no. 4 (July 1997): 421–48; Jenny (Jiyeon) Lee and Gerard T. Kyle, "Recollection Consistency of Festival Consumption Emotions," *Journal of Travel Research* 51, no. 2 (March 2012): 178–90.

72. Leaf Van Boven, Katherine White, and Michael Huber, "Immediacy Bias in Emotion Perception: Current Emotions Seem More Intense Than Previous Emotions,"

*Journal of Experimental Psychology* 138, no. 3 (August 2009): 368–382; Katherine White and Leaf Van Boven, "Immediacy Bias in Social-Emotional Comparisons," *Emotion* 12, no. 4 (August 2012): 737–47.

73. Michaela Huber, Leaf Van Boven, A. Peter McGraw, and Laura Johnson-Graham, "Whom to Help? Immediacy Bias in Judgments and Decisions About Humanitarian Aid," *Organizational Behavior and Human Decision Processes* 115, no. 2 (July 2011): 283–93.

74. That teenager is discussed by Van Boven, White, and Huber, "Immediacy Bias in Emotion Perception," 368.

75. According to one count, forty-one articles discussed CLT between 1998 (when it was first articulated) and 2005, 476 between 2006 and 2010, and more than 1,100 between 2011 and the middle of 2014. Martin M. Weisner, "Using Construal Level Theory to Motivate Accounting Research: A Literature Review," *Behavioral Research in Accounting* 27, no. 1 (Spring 2015): 139.

76. Construal-level theorizing began with Nira Liberman and Yaacov Trope, "The Role of Feasibility and Desirability Considerations in Near and Distant Future Decisions: A Test of Temporal Construal Theory," *Journal of Personality and Social Psychology* 75, no. 1 (July 1998): 5–18. See also Yaacov Trope and Nira Liberman, "Temporal Construal," *Psychological Review* 110, no. 3 (July 2003): 403–21; Stefan T. Trautmann and Gijs van de Kuilen, "Prospect Theory or Construal Level Theory? Diminishing Sensitivity vs. Psychological Distance in Risky Decisions," *Acta Psychologica* 139, no. 1 (January 2012): 254–60.

77. Nira Liberman, Yaacov Trope, and Elena Stephan, "Psychological Distance," in *Social Psychology: Handbook of Basic Principles*, 2nd ed., ed. Arie W. Kruglanski and E. Tory Higgins (New York: Guilford, 2007), 353.

78. Yaacov Trope and Nira Liberman, "Construal-Level Theory of Psychological Distance," *Psychological Review* 117, no. 2 (April 2010), 441. See also Jens Förster, Ronald S. Friedman, and Nira Liberman, "Temporal Construal Effects on Abstract and Concrete Thinking: Consequences for Insight and Creative Cognition," *Journal of Personality and Social Psychology* 87, no. 2 (August 2004): 177–89.

79. Yaacov Trope and Nira Liberman, "Temporal Construal and Time-Dependent Changes in Preference," *Journal of Personality and Social Psychology* 79, no. 6 (December 2000): 876–89. The valence-dependent time-discounting hypothesis has been around for quite some time; see Kurt Lewin, *Field Theory in Social Science: Selected Theoretical Papers* (New York: Harper & Row, 1951).

80. Trope and Liberman, "Temporal Construal," 404.

81. This story is related by Robert M. Gates in *From the Shadows: The Ultimate Insider's Story of Five Presidents and How they Won the Cold War* (New York: Simon & Shuster, 1996), 114.

82. Stanislav Petrov's amazing story is told by David E. Hoffman in "I Had a Funny Feeling in My Gut," *Washington Post*, February 10, 1999. See also his Pulitzer Prize-winning *The Dead Hand: The Untold Story of the Cold War Arms Race and Its Dangerous Legacy* (New York: Anchor, 2009), esp. 6–11.

83. This has been a consistent finding across many strains of psychology literature for decades. See Lawrence A. Pervin, "The Need to Predict and Control Under Conditions of Threat," *Journal of Personality* 31, no. 4 (December 1963); Alan Monat, James R. Averill, and Richard S. Lazarus, "Anticipatory Stress Reactions Under Various Conditions of Uncertainty," *Journal of Personality and Social Psychology* 24, no. 2 (November 1972): 237–253; Jaap M. Koolhaas, Alessandro Bartolomucci, Bauke Buwalda, et al., "Stress Revisited: A Critical Evaluation of the Stress Concept," *Neuroscience and Behavioral Reviews* 35, no. 4 (April 2011): 1291–301; Archy O. de Berker, Robb B. Rutledge, Christoph Mathys, et al., "Computations of Uncertainty Mediate Acute Stress Response in Humans," *Nature Communications* 7, no. 10996 (March 2016): 1–11.

84. Donald Rumsfeld, remarks at DoD News Briefing, February 12, 2002, www .defenselink.mil/transcripts/transcript.aspx?transcriptid=2636.

85. Les Aspin, "The Counterproliferation Initiative," speech at the National Academy of Sciences, Washington, D.C., December 7, 1993. See also Ashley J. Tellis, "No Escape: The Enduring Reality of Nuclear Weapons," in *Asia in the Second Nuclear Age*, ed. Ashley J. Tellis, Abraham M. Denmark, and Travis Tanner (Washington, DC: National Bureau of Asian Research, 2013), 11.

86. A series of op-ed pieces from 2007 to 2011 advocating nuclear disarmament by George Schultz, Henry A. Kissinger, Sam Nunn, and William J. Perry is available under the heading "Toward a World Without Nuclear Weapons," Nuclear Security Project of the Nuclear Threat Initiative, Stanford University, http://www.nti.org /media/pdfs/NSP_op-eds_final_.pdf.

87. In addition to those sources cited in the previous chapter (note 34), this argument is made by John Mueller in "The Essential Irrelevance of Nuclear Weapons: Stability in the Post War World," *International Security* 13, no. 2 (Fall 1988): 55–79.

88. John Mueller, *Quiet Cataclysm: Reflections on the Recent Transformation of World Politics* (New York: Harper Collins, 1995), 14.

89. Mueller, *Quiet Cataclysm*, 8.

## 3. UNIPOLARITY AND PERCEPTION

1. See the essays in Christopher A. Preble and John Mueller, eds., *A Dangerous World? Threat Perception and U.S. National Security* (Washington, DC: Cato Institute, 2014).

2. George F. Kennan, *The Cloud of Danger: Current Realities of American Foreign Policy* (Boston: Little, Brown, 1977); James Chace and Caleb Carr, *America Invulnerable: The Quest for Absolute Security from 1812 to Star Wars* (New York: Summit, 1988); John A. Thompson, "The Exaggeration of American Vulnerability: The Anatomy of a Tradition," *Diplomatic History* 16, no. 1 (Winter 1992): 23–43; Robert H. Johnson, *Improbable Dangers: U.S. Conceptions of Threat in the Cold War and After* (New York: St. Martin's Press, 1994).

3. Another quarter (and a fifth of CFR members) considers the dangers to be equivalent. Pew Center for the People and the Press, "America's Place in the World in 2009:

An Investigation of Public and Leadership Opinion about International Affairs," December 2009, http://www.people-press.org/files/legacy-pdf/569.pdf. See also Micah Zenko and Michael A. Cohen, "Clear and Present Safety: The United States Is More Secure Than Washington Thinks," *Foreign Affairs* 91, no. 2 (March/April 2012): 79–93.

4.  For an elaboration of this point, see Christopher J. Fettweis, *Pathologies of Power: Fear, Honor, Glory, and Hubris in U.S. Foreign Policy* (New York: Cambridge University Press, 2013), esp. chap. 1.

5.  For the early history of the psychological study of power and the observation that the field did not pay the topic much attention before the mid-1990s, see Dacher Keltner, Deborah H Gruenfeld, and Cameron Anderson, "Power, Approach, and Inhibition," *Psychological Review* 110, no. 2 (April 2003): 265–84.

6.  Dacher Keltner, *The Power Paradox: How We Gain and Lose Influence* (New York: Penguin, 2016), 7.

7.  Cameron Anderson and Jennifer L. Berdahl, "The Experience of Power: Examining the Effects of Power on Approach and Inhibition," *Journal of Personality and Social Psychology* 83, no. 6 (December 2002): 1362–77.

8.  This technique appears to have been adapted for this literature by Adam D. Galinsky, Deborah H Gruenfeld, and Joe C. Magee, "From Power to Action," *Journal of Personality and Social Psychology* 85, no. 3 (September 2003): 453–66.

9.  An example of experiments run with mixed measures of power can be found in Cameron Anderson and Adam D. Galinsky, "Power, Optimism, and Risk-Taking," *European Journal of Social Psychology* 36, no. 4 (July/August 2006): 511–36.

10. Henry Adams, *The Education of Henry Adams* (Boston: Massachusetts Historical Society, 2007), 114–15.

11. Deborah H. Gruenfeld, M. Ena Inesi, Joe C. Magee, and Adam D. Galinsky, "Power and the Objectification of Social Targets," *Journal of Personality and Social Psychology* 95, no. 1 (July 2008): 111–27.

12. In psychology, *objectification* has a specific meaning, one with rather obvious implications for international politics: "the notion of viewing others in ways that facilitate using them for personal gain," and a "process of subjugation, whereby the needs, interests, and experiences of those with less power are subordinated to those of the powerful." Dacher Keltner, Deborah Gruenfeld, Adam Galinsky, and Michael W. Kraus, "Paradoxes of Power: Dynamics of the Acquisition, Experience, and Social Regulation of Social Power," in *The Social Psychology of Power*, ed. Ana Guinote and Theresa K. Vescio (New York: Guilford, 2010), 177–208.

13. Empathy is defined a few different ways. This chapter will employ the traditional understanding in political psychology, as described by Ralph White: "a realistic understanding of the thoughts and feelings of others." Ralph K. White, "Empathizing with Rulers of the USSR," *Political Psychology* 4, no. 1 (May 1993): 121.

14. Robert Jervis, "Images and the Gulf War," in *The Political Psychology of the Gulf War: Leaders, Publics, and the Process of Conflict*, ed. Stanley A. Renshon (Pittsburgh: University of Pittsburgh Press, 1993), 176.

15. Research on empathy is closely related to that on attribution, discussed in chapter 1. Begin with Edward Jones and Richard Nisbett, *The Actor and the Observer: Divergent Perceptions of the Causes of Behavior* (Morristown, NJ: General Learning Press, 1971).

16. Adam D. Galinsky, Joe C. Magee, M. Ena Inesi, and Deborah H. Gruenfeld, "Power and Perspectives Not Taken," *Psychological Science* 17, no. 12 (December 2006): 1068–74; Ian H. Robertson, "How Power Affects the Brain," *Psychologist* 26, no. 3 (March 2013): 186–89.

17. Jeremy Hogeveen, Michael Inzlicht, and Sukhvinder S. Obhi, "Power Changes How the Brain Responds to Others," *Journal of Experimental Psychology: General* 143, no. 2 (April 2014): 755–62; Katherine R. Naish and Sukhvinder S. Ohbi, "Self-Selected Conscious Strategies Do Not Modulate Motor Cortical Output During Action Observation," *Journal of Neurophysiology* 114, no. 4 (October 2015): 2278–84.

18. At various times, other acronyms (FON, FONA) are also used. For a tendentious but interesting analysis, see Amitai Etzioni, "Freedom of Navigation Assertions: The United States as the World's Policeman," *Armed Forces and Society* 42, no. 3 (July 2016): 501–17.

19. Galinsky, Gruenfeld, and Magee, "From Power to Action"; Ana Guinote, "Power and Goal Pursuit," *Personality and Social Psychology Bulletin* 33, no. 8 (August 2007): 1076–87.

20. Keltner, *The Power Paradox*, 102–103, 130–35.

21. Serena Chen, Annette Y. Lee-Chai, and John A. Bargh, "Relationship Orientation as a Moderator of the Effects of Social Power," *Journal of Personality and Social Psychology* 80, no. 2 (February 2001): 173–87.

22. Anderson and Galinsky, "Power, Optimism, and Risk-Taking."

23. Steve Yetiv recently claimed that the pathological effects of overconfidence are "one of the most reliable findings in decision-making." *National Security Through a Cockeyed Lens: How Cognitive Bias Impacts U.S. Foreign Policy* (Baltimore, MD: Johns Hopkins University Press, 2013), 50. See also David Dunning, Dale W. Griffin, James D. Milojkovic, and Lee Ross, "The Overconfidence Effect in Social Prediction," *Journal of Personality and Social Psychology* 58, no. 4 (April 1990): 568–81; Robert Vallone, Dale W. Griffin, Sabrina Lin, and Lee Ross, "Overconfident Prediction of Future Actions and Outcomes by Self and Others," *Journal of Personality and Social Psychology* 58, no. 4 (April 1990): 582–92.

24. Scott Plaus, *The Psychology of Judgment and Decision Making* (New York: McGraw-Hill, 1993), 217. See also Don A. Moore and Paul J. Healy, "The Trouble with Overconfidence," *Psychological Review* 115, no. 2 (April 2008): 502–17.

25. Dominic D. P. Johnson, *Overconfidence and War: The Havoc and Glory of Positive Illusions* (Cambridge, MA: Harvard University Press, 2004).

26. Daniel Kahneman and Jonathan Renshon, "Hawkish Biases," in *American Foreign Policy and the Politics of Fear: Threat Inflation Since 9/11*, ed. A. Trevor Thrall and Jane K. Cramer (New York: Routledge, 2009), 82.

27.  Baruch Fischhoff, Paul Slovic, and Sarah Lichtenstein, "Knowing with Certainty: The Appropriateness of Extreme Confidence," *Journal of Experimental Psychology* 3, no. 4 (November 1977): 552–64.

28.  Kenneth Adelman, "Cakewalk in Iraq," *Washington Post*, February 13, 2002. Discerning optimists can perhaps detect a subtle distinction between "cakewalk" and "walk in the park," which is what he predicted six months later. Kenneth Adelman, "Desert Storm II Would Be a Walk in the Park," *London Times*, August 29, 2002.

29.  Dick Cheney, speech to Veterans of Foreign Wars, Nashville, TN, August 26, 2002.

30.  See Rajiv Chandrasekaran, *Imperial Life in the Emerald City: Inside Iraq's Green Zone* (New York: Knopf, 2007), 29–37.

31.  Brantly Womack, "How Size Matters: The United States, China and Asymmetry," *Journal of Strategic Studies* 24, no. 4 (December 2001): 123–50; Brantly Womack, "Asymmetry and Systemic Misperception: China, Vietnam and Cambodia During the 1970s," *Journal of Strategic Studies* 26, no. 2 (June 2003): 92–119; Brantly Womack, *China and Vietnam: The Politics of Asymmetry* (New York: Cambridge University Press, 2006); Brantly Womack, *Asymmetry and International Relationships* (New York: Cambridge University Press, 2016).

32.  See Womack, *Asymmetry and International Relationships*, 51, where he builds upon the work of Albert O. Hirschman, *National Power and the Structure of Foreign Trade* (Berkeley, CA: University of California Press, 1980).

33.  Ann Marie Russell and Susan T. Fiske, "Power and Social Perception," in *The Social Psychology of Power*, ed. Ana Guinote and Theresa K. Vescio (New York: Guilford, 2010), esp. 239–240.

34.  Russell and Fiske, "Power and Social Perception," 232.

35.  Susan T. Fiske, "Controlling Other People: The Impact of Power on Stereotyping," *American Psychologist* 48, no. 6 (June 1993): 621–28.

36.  Insight on heuristics from psychology and political science can be found in Daniel Kahneman, Amos Tversky, and Paul Slovic, eds., *Judgment Under Uncertainty: Heuristics and Biases* (New York: Cambridge University Press, 1982); Nancy Kanwisher, "Cognitive Heuristics and American Security Policy," *Journal of Conflict Resolution* 33, no. 4 (December 1989): 652–55; Thomas Gilovich, Dale Griffin, and Daniel Kahneman, eds., *Heuristics and Biases: The Psychology of Intuitive Judgment* (New York: Cambridge: Cambridge University Press, 2002).

37.  Russell and Fiske, "Power and Social Perception," 234.

38.  The seminal work is David Kipnis, *The Powerholders* (Chicago: University of Chicago Press, 1976).

39.  Ana Guinote and Adele Phillips, "Power Can Increase Stereotyping: Evidence from Managers and Subordinates in the Hotel Industry," *Social Psychology* 41, no. 1 (January 2010): 3–9; Theresa K. Vescio, Sarah J. Gervais, Larisa Heiphetz, and Brittany Bloodhart, "The Stereotypic Behaviors of the Powerful and Their Effect on the Relatively Powerless," in *Handbook of Prejudice, Stereotyping, and Discrimination*, ed. Todd D. Nelson (New York: Psychology Press, 2009), 247–65.

40. Susan T. Fiske and Eric Dépret, "Control, Interdependence, and Power: Understanding Social Cognition in Its Social Context," *European Review of Social Psychology* 7, no. 1 (1996): 31–61.

41. Womack, *Asymmetry and International Relationships*, 40.

42. Comments made multiple times to the author, who served as the admiral's teaching assistant at the Naval Academy from 2001 to 2003.

43. Charles A. Duelfer and Stephen Benedict Dyson, "Chronic Misperception and International Conflict: The U.S.-Iraq Experience," *International Security* 36, no. 1 (Summer 2011): 73–100.

44. Womack, *Asymmetry and International Relationships*, 206–207.

45. Giulio M. Gallarotti, *The Power Curse: Influence and Illusion in World Politics* (Boulder, CO: Lynne Rienner, 2010), 13.

46. Fettweis, *Pathologies of Power*, chap. 4.

47. Dacher Keltner, "Don't Let Power Corrupt You," *Harvard Business Review* 94, no. 10 (October 2016): 112–15.

48. Aaron James, *Assholes: A Theory* (New York: Anchor, 2012).

49. Paul K. Piff, Daniel M. Stancato, Stéphane Côté, et al., "Higher Social Class Predicts Increased Unethical Behavior," *Proceedings of the National Academy of Sciences of the United States of America* 109, no. 11 (March 13, 2012): 4086–91.

50. Keltner, "Don't Let Power Corrupt You," 113.

51. See the reviews in Joseph E. Uscinski and Joseph M. Parent, *American Conspiracy Theories* (New York: Oxford University Press, 2014); Cass R. Sunstein and Adrian Vermeule, "Conspiracy Theories: Causes and Cures," *Journal of Political Philosophy* 17, no. 2 (June 2009): 202–27.

52. Richard Hofstadter, *The Paranoid Style in American Politics and Other Essays* (New York: Knopf, 1965), esp. 39; Jennifer A. Whitson and Adam D. Galinsky, "Lacking Control Increases Illusory Pattern Perception," *Science* 322, no. 5898 (October 3, 2008): 115–17; Daniel Sullivan, Mark J. Landau, and Zachary K. Rothschild, "An Existential Function of Enemyship: Evidence That People Attribute Influence to Personal and Political Enemies to Compensate for Threats to Control," *Journal of Personality and Social Psychology* 98, no. 3 (March 2010): 434–49; Marina Abalakina-Paap, Walter G. Stephan, Traci Craig, and W. Larry Gregory, "Beliefs in Conspiracies," *Political Psychology* 20, no. 3 (September 1999): 637–47.

53. The various nuclear crises on the Korean peninsula are coordinated in Washington, according to at least some of the Chinese leadership, as part of the secret U.S. plan to surround and eventually annihilate the People's Republic. Xie Tao, "US-China Relations: In the Shadow of Conspiracy Theories," *The Diplomat*, February 22, 2016, http://thediplomat.com/2016/02/us-china-relations-in-the-shadow-of-conspiracy-theories/. Plenty of anti-China conspiracy theories exist in the United States, too, which is a sign of the rising power of China. See Michael Pillsbury, *The Hundred-Year Marathon: China's Secret Strategy to Replace America as the Global Superpower* (New York: St. Martin's Press, 2015).

54. See, for example, John M. Carey, "Conspiracy Theories Won't Save the Governing Party in Venezuela," *Washington Post*, December 3, 2015, https://www.washingtonpost

.com/news/monkey-cage/wp/2015/12/03/conspiracy-theories-wont-save-the -governing-party-in-venezuela/.

55. Tim Arango and Ceylan Yeginsu, "Turks Can Agree on One Thing: U.S. Was Behind Failed Coup," *New York Times*, August 2, 2016.

56. Robert Mackey, "Borne by Facebook, Conspiracy Theory That U.S. Created ISIS Spreads Across the Middle East," *New York Times*, August 26, 2014; "The US, IS and the Conspiracy Theory Sweeping Lebanon," *BBC News*, August 12, 2014, http://www .bbc.com/news/world-middle-east-28745990. Hassan Nasrallah, the leader of Hezbollah, claimed in a speech that Trump "has data and documents." See Ben Gittleson, "Hezbollah Leader Echoes Trump That Obama, Clinton Founded ISIS," *ABC News*, August 14, 2016, http://abcnews.go.com/Politics/hezbollah-leader-echoes-trump -obama-clinton-founded-isis/story?id=41374713.

57. Arthur Gladstone, "The Conception of the Enemy," *Journal of Conflict Resolution* 3, no. 2 (June 1959): 132–37; David J. Finlay, Ole R. Holsti, and Richard R. Fagen, *Enemies in Politics* (Chicago: Rand McNally, 1967); Robert Jervis, *Perception and Misperception in International Politics* (Princeton, NJ: Princeton University Press, 1976); Douglas Stuart and Harvey Starr, "The 'Inherent Bad Faith Model' Reconsidered: Dulles, Kennedy, and Kissinger," *Political Psychology* 3, nos. 3/4 (Autumn 1981/Winter 1982): 1–33; Ralph K. White, *Fearful Warriors: A Psychological Profile of U.S.-Soviet Relations* (New York: Free Press, 1984); Richard Herrmann, "Analyzing Soviet Images of the United States: A Psychological Theory and Empirical Study," *Journal of Conflict Resolution* 29, no. 4 (December 1985): 665–97.

58. Kenneth E. Boulding, *The Image* (Ann Arbor: University of Michigan Press, 1956); Kenneth E. Boulding, "National Image and International Systems," *Journal of Conflict Resolution* 3, no. 2 (June 1959): 120–31; Robert Jervis, *The Logic of Images in International Relations* (Princeton, NJ: Princeton University Press, 1970).

59. Ralph K. White, *Nobody Wanted War: Misperception in Vietnam and Other Wars* (Garden City, NY: Doubleday, 1968).

60. This point remains controversial. See, most prominently, Vamik D. Volkan, *The Need to Have Enemies and Allies: From Clinical Practice to International Relationships* (Northvale, NJ: Jason Aronson, 1988); but also Frederick H. Hartmann, *The Conservation of Enemies: A Study in Enmity* (Westport, CT: Greenwood, 1982); Brett Silverstein and Robert R. Holt, "Research on Enemy Images: Present Status and Future Prospects," *Journal of Social Issues* 45, no. 2 (Summer 1989): 159–75; Sam Keen, *Faces of the Enemy: Reflections of a Hostile Imagination* (New York: Harper Collins, 1991); David Barash, *Beloved Enemies: Our Need for Opponents* (Amherst, NY: Prometheus, 1994). For skepticism, see Shoon Kathleen Murray and Jason Meyers, "Do People Need Foreign Enemies? American Leaders' Beliefs After the Soviet Demise," *Journal of Conflict Resolution* 43, no. 5 (October 1999): 555–69.

61. Quoted by Nicholas Thompson, *The Hawk and the Dove: Paul Nitze, George Kennan, and the History of the Cold War* (New York: Henry Holt, 2009), 271.

62. Deborah Welch Larson, *Anatomy of Mistrust: U.S.-Soviet Relations During the Cold War* (Ithaca, NY: Cornell University Press, 1997), 1.

63. Quoted by Brett Silverstein in "Enemy Images: The Psychology of U.S. Attitudes and Cognitions Regarding the Soviet Union," *American Psychologist* 44, no. 6 (June 1989): 904.

64. Robert Jervis, *Perception and Misperception in International Politics* (Princeton, NJ: Princeton University Press, 1976), 314.

65. Richard K. Herrmann and Michael Fischerkeller, "Beyond the Enemy Image and Spiral Model: Cognitive-Strategic Research After the Cold War," *International Organization* 49, no. 3 (Summer 1995): 415–50. This work extends Herrmann's earlier *Perceptions and Behavior in Soviet Foreign Policy* (Pittsburgh: University of Pittsburgh Press, 1985), esp. 30–42.

66. Richard K. Herrmann, James F. Voss, Tonya Y. E. Schooler, and Joseph Ciarrochi, "Images in International Relations: An Experimental Test of Cognitive Schemata," *International Studies Quarterly* 41, no. 3 (September 1997): 403–33; Michele G. Alexander, Marilynn B. Brewer, and Richard K. Herrmann, "Images and Affect: A Functional Analysis of Out-Group Stereotypes," *Journal of Personality and Social Psychology* 77, no. 1 (December 1999): 78–93; Marilynn B. Brewer and Michele G. Alexander, "Intergroup Emotions and Images," in *From Prejudice to Intergroup Emotions: Differentiated Reactions to Social Groups*, ed. Diane M. Mackie and Eliot R. Smith (New York: Psychology Press, 2002), 209–25; Michele G. Alexander, Shana Levin, and P. J. Henry, "Image Theory, Social Identity, and Social Dominance: Structural Characteristics and Individual Motives Underlying International Images," *Political Psychology* 26, no. 1 (February 2005): 27–45; Veronique Eicher, Felicia Pratto, and Peter Wilhelm, "Value Differentiation Between Allies and Enemies: Value Projection in National Images," *Political Psychology* 34, no. 1 (February 2013): 127–44.

67. K. P. O'Reilly, "Perceiving Rogue States: The Use of the 'Rogue State' Concept by U.S. Foreign Policy Elites," *Foreign Policy Analysis* 3, no. 4 (October 2007): 295–315. See also Paul D. Hoyt, "The 'Rogue State' Image in American Foreign Policy," *Global Society* 14, no. 2 (April 2000): 297–310.

68. Keltner, Gruenfeld and Anderson, "Power, Approach, and Inhibition."

69. Karl W. Deutsch discusses a version of this in *The Analysis of International Relations* (Englewood Cliffs, NJ: Prentice-Hall, 1968), 88; see also Fettweis, *The Pathologies of Power*, chap. 1.

70. Jack Snyder, "Imperial Myths and Threat Inflation," in *American Foreign Policy and the Politics of Fear*, ed. Thrall and Cramer, 41.

71. Robert Jervis, "Unipolarity: A Structural Perspective," *World Politics* 61, no. 1 (January 2009): 200.

72. The French foreign minister Hubert Védrine is widely credited with popularizing the term "hyperpower" to describe the United States, but Trump advisor and alpha-male Sebastian Gorka was the most recent to use it. "We were a superpower," said "Dr." Gorka on Fox News in August 2017. "We are now a hyperpower." http://insider .foxnews.com/2017/08/09/sebastian-gorka-says-trumps-message-north-korea-dont -test-white-house.

73. The classic treatment is in Theodor Mommsen, *The History of Rome*, vol. 4, trans. W. Dickson (New York: Dutton, 1911). See also Tenney Frank, *Roman Imperialism* (New York: Macmillan, 1914); Robert M. Errington, *The Dawn of Empire: Rome's Rise to Power* (London: Hamish Hamilton, 1971); Erich S. Gruen, *The Hellenistic World and the Coming of Rome* (Berkeley, CA: University of California Press, 1986); A. Brunt, *Roman Imperial Themes* (Oxford: Clarendon, 1990), esp. 102.

74. Quoted by William V. Harris (a critic of this argument) in *War and Imperialism in Republican Rome, 327–70 B.C.* (Oxford: Clarendon, 1985), 164.

75. Joseph A. Schumpeter, *Imperialism and Social Classes* (Oxford: Basil Blackwell), 65.

76. Quoted by Geoffrey Parker in "The Making of Strategy in Hapsburg Spain: Philip II's 'Bid for Mastery,' 1559–1598," in *The Making of Strategy: Rulers, States, and War*, ed. Williamson Murray, MacGregor Knox, and Alvin Bernstein (New York: Cambridge University Press), 119.

77. J. H. Elliott, "Managing Decline: Olivares and the Grand Strategy of Imperial Spain," in *Grand Strategies in War and Peace*, ed. Paul Kennedy (New Haven, CT: Yale University Press, 1991), 87–104.

78. John S. Galbraith, "The 'Turbulent Frontier' as a Factor in British Expansion," *Comparative Studies in Society and History* 2, no. 2 (January 1960): 168. See also Ronald Robinson and John Gallagher, *Africa and the Victorians: The Official Mind of Imperialism* (London: Page, 1961); Eric Adler, "Late Victorian and Edwardian Views of Rome and the Nature of 'Defensive Imperialism,'" *International Journal of the Classical Tradition* 15, no. 2 (June 2008): 187–216.

79. This is related to the process Jack Snyder discussed in *Myths of Empire: Domestic Politics and International Ambition* (Ithaca, NY: Cornell University Press, 1991).

80. Robert Jervis has argued that although logic dictates that the United States ought to be a status-quo power, it often does not act that way. See his "The Remaking of a Unipolar World," *Washington Quarterly* 29, no. 3 (Summer 2006): 7–19.

81. Patrick E. Tyler, "U.S. Strategy Plan Calls for Insuring No Rivals Develop," *New York Times*, March 8, 1992.

82. Robert Kagan, *Of Paradise and Power: America and Europe in the New World Order* (New York: Knopf, 2003), 34–36.

83. Status as an explanatory factor in state behavior has received a good deal of attention of late. See the essays in T. V. Paul, Deborah Welch Larson, and William C. Wohlforth, eds., *Status in World Politics* (New York: Cambridge University Press, 2014); Jonathan Renshon, "Status Deficits and War," *International Organization* 70, no. 3 (June 2016): 513–50.

84. For a meta-analysis of dozens of studies that draw this conclusion, see John C. Georgesen and Monica J. Harris, "Why's My Boss Always Holding Me Down? A Meta-Analysis of Power on Performance Evaluations," *Personality and Social Psychology Review* 2, no. 3 (August 1998): 184–95.

85. Joris Lammers and Diederik A. Stapel, "Power Increases Dehumanization," *Group Processes and Intergroup Relations* 14, no. 1 (January 2011): 113–26.

86. Amos Tversky and Daniel Kahneman, "Judgment Under Uncertainty: Heuristics and Biases," *Science* 185, no. 4157 (September 27, 1974):1124–31. The pair is profiled by

Michael Lewis in *The Undoing Project: A Friendship That Changed Our Minds* (New York: Norton, 2016).

87. White uses a similar formula for fear (the product of hostility and strength) in *Fearful Warriors*, 336.

88. See Raymond L. Garthoff, "On Estimating and Imputing Intentions," *International Security* 2, no. 3 (Winter 1978): 22–33; Matthew Evangelista, "The 'Soviet Threat': Intentions, Capabilities, and Context," *Diplomatic History* 22, no. 3 (July 1998): 439–49.

89. Benjamin Netanyahu on *Meet the Press*, April 5, 2015, http://www.nbcnews.com/meet-the-press/meet-the-press-transcript-april-5-2015-n336061.

90. Arthur A. Stein discusses the scenarios in which misperception can be expected to lead to conflict in "When Misperception Matters," *World Politics* 34, no. 4 (July 1982): 505–26.

91. Quoted by Jason C. Flanagan, *Imagining the Enemy: American Presidential War Rhetoric from Woodrow Wilson to George W. Bush* (Claremont, CA: Regina, 2009), 186.

92. Hal Brands and David Palkki, "'Conspiring Bastards': Saddam Hussein's Strategic View of the United States," *Diplomatic History* 36, no. 3 (June 2012): 625–59.

93. Duelfer and Dyson, "Chronic Misperception and International Conflict," 88, 91, 98.

## 4. IDENTIFYING THE ENEMY IMAGE

1. Hal R. Arkes, "Costs and Benefits of Judgment Errors: Implications for Debiasing," *Psychological Bulletin* 110, no. 3 (November 1991): 486–98; Scott O. Lilienfeld, Rachel Ammirati, and Kristin Landfield, "Giving Debiasing Away: Can Psychological Research on Correcting Cognitive Errors Promote Human Welfare?" *Perspectives on Psychological Science* 4, no. 4 (July 2009): 390–98; Stephan Lewandowsky, Ullrich K. H. Ecker, Colleen M. Seifert, et al., "Misinformation and Its Correction: Continued Influence and Successful Debiasing," *Psychological Science in the Public Interest* 13, no. 3 (September 2012): 106–31.

2. See the work of Brendan Nyhan and Jason Reifler, especially "When Corrections Fail: The Persistence of Political Misperception," *Journal of Political Behavior* 32, no. 2 (June 2010): 303–30; and "Displacing Misinformation About Events: An Experimental Test of Causal Corrections," *Journal of Experimental Political Science* 2, no. 1 (April 2015): 81–93.

3. Leo Tolstoy, *What Is Art?* (New York: Funk and Wagnalls, 1904), 143.

4. These and other pathological beliefs are reviewed in Christopher J. Fettweis, *The Pathologies of Power: Fear, Honor, Glory, and Hubris in U.S. Foreign Policy* (New York: Cambridge University Press, 2013).

5. Craig A. Anderson, Mark R. Lepper, and Lee Ross, "Perseverance of Social Theories: The Role of Explanation in the Persistence of Discredited Information," *Journal of Personality and Social Psychology* 39, no. 6 (December 1980): 1037–49; Charles G. Lord, Lee Ross, and Mark. R. Lepper, "Biased Assimilation and Attitude Polarization:

The Effects of Prior Theories on Subsequently Considered Evidence," *Journal of Personality and Social Psychology* 37, no. 11 (November 1979): 2098–109; Krystyna Rojahn and Thomas F. Pettigrew, "Memory for Schema-Relevant Information: A Meta-Analytic Resolution," *British Journal of Social Psychology* 31, no. 2 (June 1992): 81–109. See also Dan Reiter, *Crucible of Beliefs: Learning, Alliance, and World Wars* (Ithaca, NY: Cornell University Press, 1996).

6.   See Lewandowsky et al., "Misinformation and Its Correction."

7.   Howard Gardner, *Changing Minds: The Art and Science of Changing Our Own and Other People's Minds* (Boston: Harvard Business School Press, 2006).

8.   Gardner discusses Kuhn in *Changing Minds*, 117.

9.   Mark Peffley and Jon Hurwitz, "International Events and Foreign Policy Beliefs: Public Response to Changing Soviet-U.S. Relations," *American Journal of Political Science* 36, no. 2 (May 1992): 431–61.

10.   Micah Zenko, *Red Team: How to Succeed by Thinking Like the Enemy* (New York: Basic Books, 2015).

11.   Deborah Welch Larson makes a similar point in *Anatomy of Mistrust: U.S.-Soviet Relations During the Cold War* (Ithaca, NY: Cornell University Press, 1997), 5.

12.   Robert Jervis, *Perception and Misperception in International Politics* (Princeton, NJ: Princeton University Press, 1976), 409.

13.   Quoted by Douglas Stuart and Harvey Starr, "The 'Inherent Bad Faith Model' Reconsidered: Dulles, Kennedy, and Kissinger," *Political Psychology* 3, no. 3/4 (Autumn 1981/Winter 1982): 12.

14.   Bernard Lewis, *The End of Modern History in the Middle East* (Stanford, CA: Hoover Institute Press, 2011), 148. See also Norman Podhoretz, *World War IV: The Long Struggle Against Islamofascism* (New York: Doubleday, 2007).

15.   Westmoreland's sentiments are included in the 1974 Oscar-winning documentary *Hearts and Minds* and are followed by harrowing images suggesting that the general might have been wrong. The filmmaker, Peter Davis, said afterward that he offered the general two opportunities to amend his sentiments. See Derrick Z. Jackson, "The Westmoreland Mind-Set," *New York Times*, July 25, 2005.

16.   For a marvelous review of racial prejudice and propaganda in the Pacific theater of World War II, see John W. Dower, *War Without Mercy: Race and Power in the Pacific War* (New York: Pantheon, 1986).

17.   See David Satter, "Russia Needs to Learn the Value of Human Life," *American Interest*, July 25, 2014, http://www.the-american-interest.com/2014/07/25/russia-needs-to-learn-the-value-of-human-life/.

18.   Richard Pipes, "Why the Soviet Union Thinks It Could Fight and Win a Nuclear War," *Commentary* 64, no. 1 (July 1977): 21–34.

19.   Daniel Frei, *Perceived Images: U.S. and Soviet Assumptions and Perceptions in Disarmament* (Totowa, NJ: Rowman & Allanheld, 1986), 144.

20.   For one such believer, see the discussion of Richard Perle in Keith L. Shimko, *Images and Arms Control: Perceptions of the Soviet Union in the Reagan Administration* (Ann Arbor: University of Michigan Press, 1991), 70.

21. Robert Scheer, *With Enough Shovels: Reagan, Bush, and Nuclear War* (New York: Vintage, 1983).

22. Soviet archives paint a picture of a Soviet leadership that thought much the same way about nuclear weapons as its American counterpart. See John Lewis Gaddis, *We Now Know: Rethinking Cold War History* (New York: Oxford University Press, 1997), esp. 221–259; Richard Ned Lebow, "Deterrence: Then and Now," *Journal of Strategic Studies* 28, no. 5 (October 2005): 765–73.

23. Thomas Donnelly, Danielle Pletka, and Maseh Zarif, *Containing and Deterring a Nuclear Iran: Questions for Strategy, Requirements for Military Forces* (Washington, DC: American Enterprise Institute, December 2011); Robert G. Joseph and Keith B. Payne, "On Deterring Iran," *National Review*, June 25, 2012.

24. David G. Coleman, *The Fourteenth Day: JFK and the Aftermath of the Cuban Missile Crisis* (New York: Norton, 2012), 37.

25. Quoted in Derek Leebaert, *The Fifty-Year Wound: The True Price of America's Cold War Victory* (New York: Little, Brown, 2002), 299.

26. John Mearsheimer disagrees, suggesting instead that lying in international politics is actually relatively rare: *Why Leaders Lie: The Truth About Lying in International Politics* (New York: Oxford University Press, 2011). One wonders how the second edition will deal with the Trump era.

27. The term "fundamental attribution error" was coined by Lee Ross in "The Intuitive Psychologist and His Shortcomings: Distortions in the Attribution Process," in *Advances in Experimental Social Psychology*, ed. Leonard Berkowitz (New York: Academic Press, 1977), 10:173–220.

28. Quoted in Frei, *Perceived Images*, 125.

29. Richard Pipes, "How to Cope With the Soviet Threat: A Long-Term Strategy for the West," *Commentary* 78, no. 2 (August 1984), esp. 18.

30. Quoted by Robert Jervis in "The United States and Iran: Perceptions and Policy Traps," in *U.S.-Iran Misperceptions: A Dialogue*, ed. Abbas Maleki and John Tirman (New York: Bloomsbury, 2014), 18.

31. Charles E. Osgood, "Suggestions for Winning the Real War with Communism," *Journal of Conflict Resolution* 3, no. 4 (December 1959): 295–325. See also Jason C. Flanagan, *Imagining the Enemy: American Presidential War Rhetoric from Woodrow Wilson to George W. Bush* (Claremont, CA: Regina, 2009).

32. Ralph K. White, *Fearful Warriors: A Psychological Profile of U.S.-Soviet Relations* (New York: Free Press, 1984), 148.

33. David J. Finlay, Ole R. Holsti, and Richard R. Fagen, *Enemies in Politics* (Chicago: Rand McNally, 1967), 67.

34. Michael Ledeen, *Accomplice to Evil: Iran and the War Against the West* (New York: St. Martin's Press, 2009), 189.

35. Kenneth Adelman, "Cakewalk in Iraq," *Washington Post*, February 13, 2002. See also Eliot A. Cohen, "Iraq Can't Resist Us," *Wall Street Journal*, December 23, 2001.

36. Richard R. Herrmann, "American Perspectives of Soviet Foreign Policy: Reconsidering Three Competing Perspectives," *Political Psychology* 6, no. 3 (September 1985): esp. 378.

37.  Senator John McCain was typical of this sentiment, complaining that the president failed to "unleash America's full moral power to support the Iranian people." Leashed moral power is evidently insufficient to topple enemy regimes. Quoted in "What If the Obama Administration Fully Sided with Iran's Green Movement?" *Washington Post*, June 12, 2010.

38.  Thomas Christensen memorably called China the "high church of realpolitik." "Chinese Realpolitik," *Foreign Affairs* 75, no. 5 (September/October 1995): 37.

39.  See Arnold Wolfers, *Discord and Collaboration: Essays on International Politics* (Baltimore, MD: Johns Hopkins University Press, 1962), 125–26; Randall L. Schweller, "Bandwagoning for Profit: Bringing the Revisionist State Back In," *International Security* 19, no. 1 (Summer 1994): 72–107.

40.  *Intelligence Community Experiment in Competitive Analysis: Soviet Strategic Objectives: An Alternative View*, Report of Team "B," December 1976, 2. On its inaccuracies, see Anne Hessing Cahn, *Killing Détente: The Right Attacks the CIA* (University Park: Pennsylvania State University Press, 1998).

41.  William D. Jackson, "Soviet Images of the U.S. as a Nuclear Adversary, 1969–1979," *World Politics* 33, no. 4 (July 1981): 617–18.

42.  Jervis discusses this in *Perception and Misperception in International Politics*, 310.

43.  Memorandum to President Truman, September 24, 1946, http://projects.ecfs.org /fieldston57/since40/units/unit1/supplements/clifford.html.

44.  Helen Thomas, "Reagan: Air Strike Against Libya Victory Against Terrorism," *UPI*, April 15, 1966, http://100years.upi.com/sta_1986-04-15.html.

45.  Madeleine Albright, *Madam Secretary: A Memoir* (New York: Miramax, 2005), 408.

46.  Truman stated repeatedly to his advisors that "force is the only thing they [Soviets] understand." Quoted in Mark K. Updegrove, *Baptism by Fire: Eight Presidents Who Took Office in Times of Crisis* (New York: St. Martin's, 2008), 166.

47.  George Kennan, "The Charge in the Soviet Union (Kennan) to the Secretary of State," a.k.a. the "Long Telegram," February 22, 1946, http://www2.gwu.edu/~nsarchiv/cold war/documents/episode-1/kennan.htm. He also once wrote that "the endless, fluid pursuit of power is a habit of Russian statesmanship, ingrained not only in the traditions of the Russian State but also in the ideology of the Communist Party." Quoted in Ernest May, *"Lessons" of the Past: The Uses and Misuses of History in American Foreign Policy* (New York: Oxford University Press, 1972), 27.

48.  Finlay, Holsti, and Fagen, *Enemies in Politics*, 84.

49.  Flanagan, *Imagining the Enemy*, 87.

50.  President George W. Bush, "Remarks by the President at Thaddeus McCotter for Congress Dinner," October 14, 2002, http://georgewbush-whitehouse.archives.gov /news/releases/2002/10/print/20021014-3.html.

51.  Flynn and his coauthor throw around the term "alliance" rather loosely. Michael Flynn and Michael Ledeen, *The Field of Fight: How We Can Win the Global War Against Radical Islam and Its Allies* (New York: St. Martin's, 2016).

52.  George Kennan, *At a Century's Ending: Reflections 1982–1995* (New York: Norton, 1996), 87.

53. See Seyed Hossein Mousavian, "Iranian Perceptions of U.S. Policy Toward Iran: Aya-tollah Khamenei's Mind Set," in *U.S.-Iran Misperceptions: A Dialogue*, ed. Abbas Maleki and John Tirman (New York: Bloomsbury, 2014), 37–56; and in the same volume, Kayhan Barzegar, "Iran's Perception of the U.S. Policy Toward the Region," 89–110.

54. Milton Rokeach, *The Open and Closed Mind: Investigations Into the Nature of Belief Systems and Personality Systems* (New York: Basic Books, 1960), 38.

55. General Kelly and General McMaster, Trump's second chief of staff and national security advisor, respectively, were able to fire the author of this memo (a Flynn-era holdover named Rich Higgins), but not before it found its way to the president's desk. See Rosie Gray, "An NSC Staffer Is Forced Out Over a Controversial Memo," *Atlantic*, August 2, 2017, available at https://www.theatlantic.com/politics/archive/2017/08/a-national-security-council-staffer-is-forced-out-over-a-controversial-memo/535725/. Fortunately, since the memo was seven pages long, it is doubtful Trump ever read it.

56. Rokeach, *The Open and Closed Mind*, 56, 403.

57. Jervis, *Perception and Misperception in International Politics*, 319. See also Ann Marie Russell and Susan T. Fiske, "Power and Social Perception," in *The Social Psychology of Power*, ed. Ana Guinote and Theresa K. Vescio (New York: Guilford, 2010), esp. 240.

58. *Intelligence Community Experiment in Competitive Analysis*, 3.

59. In the 1970s, the United States created the Office of Net Assessment in the Pentagon to address its inferiority in long-term planning. See Andrew W. Marshall, *Long-Term Competition with the Soviets: A Framework for Strategic Analysis* (Santa Monica, CA: RAND, April 1972).

60. For some examples of this argument, see Michael Pillsbury, *The Hundred-Year Marathon: China's Secret Strategy to Replace America as the Global Superpower* (New York: Henry Holt, 2015); Kishore Mahbubani, "Smart Power, Chinese Style," *American Interest* 3, no. 4 (March/April 2008): 68–77; Martin Jacques, *When China Rules the World: The End of the Western World and the Birth of a New Global Order*, 2nd ed. (New York: Penguin 2012); Henry Kissinger, *On China* (New York: Penguin, 2012).

61. White House Press Office, "Remarks by the President on Iran Strategy," October 13, 2017, https://www.whitehouse.gov/the-press-office/2017/10/13/remarks-president-trump-iran-strategy.

62. Jervis, *Perception and Misperception in International Politics*, 350.

63. Raymond A. Bauer, "Problems of Perception and the Relations Between the United States and the Soviet Union," *Journal of Conflict Resolution* 5, no. 3 (September 1961): 225.

64. "When it seems that only hostility and duplicity could account for the other's behavior, observers should not immediately assume that any coherent policy lies behind the activities" (Jervis, *Perception and Misperception in International Politics*, 323, 342).

65. At 6:29 pm on July 29, 2017, President Trump tweeted: "I am very disappointed in China. Our foolish past leaders have allowed them to make hundreds of billions of dollars a year in trade, yet. . . . . . they do NOTHING for us with North Korea, just talk. We will no longer allow this to continue. China could easily solve this problem!"

66. There are at least forty-nine references to the "design" of the Kremlin in NSC-68. S. Nelson Drew, ed., *NSC-68: Forging the Strategy of Containment* (Washington, DC: National Defense University, 1996).

67. Richard Pipes, "Militarism and the Soviet State," *Daedalus* 109, no. 4 (Fall 1980): 2.

68. Quoted in Shimko, *Images and Arms Control*, 117.

69. Quoted in Shimko, *Images and Arms Control*, 79.

70. John H. Herz, "Idealist Internationalism and the Security Dilemma," *World Politics* 2, no. 2 (January 1950): 157–80; Robert Jervis, "Cooperation Under the Security Dilemma," *World Politics* 30, no. 2 (January 1978): 167–214.

71. Shimko, *Images and Arms Control*, 69.

72. See Zbigniew Brzezinksi, "A Plan for Europe: How to Expand NATO," *Foreign Affairs* 74, no. 1 (January/February 1995): 26–42.

73. Robert Kagan, "The United States Must Resist a Return to Spheres of Interest in the International System," Brookings Institution blog, February 19, 2015, http://www .brookings.edu/blogs/order-from-chaos/posts/2015/02/19-united-states-must-resist -return-to-spheres-of-interest-international-system-kagan.

74. For an explanation of the spiral model, see Jervis, *Perception and Misperception in International Politics*, 62–78.

75. Bauer, "Problems of Perception."

76. See almost any of the works of Richard Pipes, such as "Can the Soviet Union Reform?" *Foreign Affairs* 63, no. 1 (Fall 1984): 47–61.

77. Bauer, "Problems of Perception."

78. Richard Pipes, "Is Russia Still an Enemy?" *Foreign Affairs* 76, no. 5 (September/ October 1997): 65–78; Zbigniew Brzezinski, "Putin's Choice," *Washington Quarterly* 31, no. 2 (Spring 2008): 95–116; Robert Kagan, *The Return of History and the End of Dreams* (New York: Knopf, 2008).

79. Henry Kissinger, Testimony to the Senate Armed Services Committee, January 30, 2015.

80. Pamela Johnston Conover, Karen A. Mingst, and Lee Sigelman, "Mirror Images in Americans' Perceptions of Nations and Leaders During the Iranian Hostage Crisis," *Journal of Peace Research* 17, no. 4 (1980): 325–37.

81. Leslie H. Gelb and Jeanne-Paloma Zelmati, "Mission Unaccomplished," *Democracy* 13 (Summer 2009): 24.

82. Peffley and Hurwitz, "International Events and Foreign Policy Beliefs."

83. The endowment effect was first described by Richard Thaler in "Toward a Positive Theory of Consumer Choice," *Journal of Economic Behavior and Organization* 1, no. 1 (March 1980): 39–60. See also the review by Keith M. Marzilli Ericson and

Andreas Fuster, "The Endowment Effect," *Annual Review of Economics* 6 (2014): 555–79.

84.  Shoon Kathleen Murray and Jonathan A. Cowden, "The Role of 'Enemy Images' and Ideology in Elite Belief Systems," *International Studies Quarterly* 43, no. 3 (September 1999): 455–81.

85.  See the enormous discussion in John R. Hibbing, Kevin B. Smith, and John R. Alford, "Differences in Negativity Bias Underlie Variations in Political Ideology," *Behavioral and Brain Sciences* 37, no. 3 (June 2014): 297–307. The difference might be physiological. Conservatives appear to have larger amygdalae, the part of the brain that detects danger and produces fear (although it is also possible that conservative amygdalae grow with stimulation). Ryota Kanai, Tom Feilden, Colin Firth, and Geraint Rees, "Political Orientations Are Correlated with Brain Structure in Young Adults," *Current Biology* 21, no. 8 (April 2011): 677–80.

86.  William D. Jackson, "Soviet Images of the U.S. as a Nuclear Adversary, 1969–1979," *World Politics* 33, no. 4 (July 1981): 614–38.

87.  Colin Holbrook, Lucia López-Rodriguez, Daniel M. T. Fessler, et al., "Gulliver's Politics: Conservatives Envision Potential Enemies as Readily Vanquished and Physically Small," forthcoming in *Social Psychological and Personality Science* (2017).

88.  For a discussion of neoconservatism and its exceptionally high perceptions of threat, see Stefan Halper and Jonathan Clarke, *America Alone: The Neo-Conservatives and the Global Order* (New York: Cambridge University Press, 2005).

89.  Some of the more prominent neoconservative works, and those exemplary of the movement's tendency to be in the vanguard of enemy identification, include Robert Kagan and William Kristol, eds., *Present Dangers: Crisis and Opportunity in American Foreign and Defense Policy* (San Francisco: Encounter, 2000); Lawrence F. Kaplan and William Kristol, *The War Over Iraq: Saddam's Tyranny and America's Mission* (San Francisco: Encounter, 2003); Podhoretz, *World War IV*; David Frum and Richard Perle, *An End to Evil: How to Win the War on Terror* (New York: Random House, 2003); Kagan, *The Return of History and the End of Dreams*; Donald Kagan and Frederick W. Kagan, *While America Sleeps: Self-Delusion, Military Weakness, and the Threat to Peace Today* (New York: St. Martin's, 2000).

90.  Pipes, "Why the Soviet Union Thinks It Could Fight and Win a Nuclear War," 27.

91.  These experts are described, if tendentiously, by Wajahat Ali, Eli Clifton, Matthew Duss, Lee Fang, Scott Keyes, and Faiz Shakir in *Fear, Inc.: The Roots of the Islamophobia Network in America* (Washington, DC: Center for American Progress, August 2011), http://www.americanprogress.org/issues/2011/08/pdf/islamophobia.pdf.

92.  Peter Pomerantsev, *Nothing Is True and Everything Is Possible: The Surreal Heart of the New Russia* (New York: Public Affairs, 2014).

93.  The semiofficial *Fars News* of Iran not only compares Israel and the United States to Nazi Germany on a regular basis but has even claimed that the U.S. government has been secretly run by a "shadow government" of space aliens since 1945. Max

Fisher, "Iranian News Agency Says the U.S. Is Secretly Run by Nazi Space Aliens," *Washington Post*, January 13, 2014, http://www.washingtonpost.com/blogs/world-views/wp/2014/01/13/iranian-news-agency-says-the-u-s-is-secretly-run-by-nazi-space-aliens-really/.

94.  To many who remember the era, that count might seem a bit low. William A. Dorman and Steven Livingston, "News and Historical Content: Establishing Phase of the Persian Gulf War Policy Debate," in *Taken by Storm: The Media, Public Opinion, and U.S. Foreign Policy in the Gulf War*, ed. W. Lance Bennet and David L. Paletz (Chicago: University of Chicago Press, 1994), 71.

95.  See Donald Rumsfeld, *Known and Unknown: A Memoir* (New York: Sentinel, 2011), 514; Mark Perry, *How to Lose the War on Terror* (London: Hurst, 2010), 13; Douglas Feith, *War and Decision: Inside the Pentagon at the Dawn of the War on Terrorism* (New York: Harper, 2008), 419, 430. See also Flanagan, *Imagining the Enemy*, 467.

## 5. UNIPOLARITY AND STRATEGY

1.   Daniel J. Hughes, ed., *Moltke on the Art of War* (New York: Ballantine, 1996), 92.

2.   Quoted in Lawrence Freedman, *Strategy: A History* (New York: Oxford University Press, 2013), ix.

3.   Blandness and lack of controversy have been central goals of U.S. government documents since the 1992 Defense Planning Guidance, which asserted a bold path forward for the post–Cold War era. Or it would have, had it ever been released; an early draft of the document was leaked to the press, where it stirred up an unwelcome backlash. It was quickly disavowed and buried.

4.   The concept of the "superempowered individual" was injected into the discussion by Thomas L. Friedman, *The Lexus and the Olive Tree: Understanding Globalization* (New York: Anchor, 2000), 14.

5.   Douglas Jehl, "CIA Nominee Wary of Budget Cuts," *New York Times*, February 3, 1993.

6.   Quoted by Andrew J. Bacevich, *American Empire: The Realities and Consequences of U.S. Diplomacy* (Cambridge, MA: Harvard University Press, 2002), 118.

7.   From a not-for-attribution talk at the Naval War College, 2007.

8.   Daniel Wirls makes a similar point in *Irrational Security: The Politics of Defense from Reagan to Obama* (Baltimore, MD: Johns Hopkins University Press, 2010), 42.

9.   Statistics on terrorism are kept in a number of places. One of the best is the University of Maryland's National Consortium for the Study of Terrorism and Responses to Terrorism, whose databases can be found at http://www.start.umd.edu/. Uri Friedman summarizes much of the recent evidence in "Is Terrorism Getting Worse?", *Atlantic*, July 24, 2016, https://www.theatlantic.com/international/archive/2016/07/terrorism-isis-global-america/490352/. U.S. officialdom is essentially immune to the data. As Ambassador Philip Wilcox, the State Department coordinator for counterterrorism explained, when it comes to measuring terrorism, "we shouldn't place too much emphasis on statistics" (qtd. in Bacevich, *American Empire*, 119).

10. Michael J. Mazarr in "The Rise and Fall of the Failed-State Paradigm: Requiem for a Decade of Distraction," *Foreign Affairs* 93, no.1 (January/February 2014): 113–21.

11. Colin S. Gray, "Clausewitz Rules, OK? The Future Is the Past—with GPS," in *Interregnum: Controversies in World Politics, 1989–1999*, ed. Michael Cox, Ken Booth, and Tim Dunn (New York: Cambridge University Press, 1999), 182; Colin S. Gray, *Weapons Don't Make War: Policy, Strategy, and Military Technology* (Lawrence: University Press of Kansas, 1993), 105.

12. Emily O. Goldman, *Power in Uncertain Times: Strategy in the Fog of Peace* (Stanford, CA: Stanford University Press, 2011), 1.

13. Carl Conetta and Charles Knight, "Inventing Threats," *Bulletin of the Atomic Scientists* 54, no. 2 (March/April 1998): 32–38. See also Benjamin Friedman and Harvey Sapolsky, "You Never Know(ism)," *Breakthroughs* 15, no. 1 (Spring 2006): 3–11.

14. James A. Winnefeld, *The Post–Cold War Sizing Debate: Paradigms, Metaphors, and Disconnects* (Santa Monica, CA: RAND, 1992), 12.

15. Conetta and Knight, "Inventing Threats," 34.

16. Colin Powell, *The National Military Strategy of the United States* (Washington, DC: U.S. Government Printing Office, January 1992), 4.

17. Office of the Secretary of Defense, *The National Defense Strategy of the United States of America* (Washington, DC: U.S. Government Printing Office, March 2005), 2.

18. William S. Cohen, "Quadrennial Defense Review: The Secretary's Message," remarks made on May 19, 1997, http://www.disam.dsca.mil/pubs/INDEXES/Vol%2019_4/Cohen.pdf. See also Conetta and Knight, "Inventing Threats."

19. "DoD News Briefing," February 12, 2002, www.defenselink.mil/transcripts/transcript.aspx?transcriptid=2636.

20. Her Majesty's Government, "A Strong Britain in an Age of Uncertainty: The National Security Strategy," October 2010, https://www.gov.uk/government/uploads/system/uploads/attachment_data/file/61936/national-security-strategy.pdf. The quotations come from 3 and 4. As a point of contrast, the word "uncertainty" does not appear in the European Union Security Strategy, which in many ways does a better job describing the post–Cold War world. See *A Secure Europe in a Better World* (Brussels, December 12, 2003).

21. Williamson Murray, "Thoughts on Grand Strategy," in *The Shaping of Grand Strategy*, ed. Williamson Murray, Richard Hart Sinnreich, and James Lacey (New York: Cambridge University Press, 2011), 32–33.

22. Quoted by Corey Robin in *Fear: The History of a Political Idea* (New York: Oxford University Press), 72.

23. Richard N. Haass, *The Reluctant Sheriff: The United States After the Cold War* (New York: Council on Foreign Relations Press, 1997), 1.

24. Office of the Secretary of Defense, *Sustaining U.S. Global Leadership: Priorities for Twenty-First-Century Defense* (Washington, DC: Government Printing Office, January 2012), 1.

25. Office of the Secretary of Defense, *Quadrennial Defense Review Report* (Washington, DC: Government Printing Office, February 2006), iv.

26. National Intelligence Council, *Joint Vision 2010* (Washington, DC: Government Printing Office, July 1996), 8.

27. Office of the Secretary of Defense, *Quadrennial Defense Review Report.*

28. For a review, see Derek S. Reveron, ed., *Cyberspace and National Security: Threats, Opportunities, and Power in a Virtual World* (Washington, DC: Georgetown University Press, 2012).

29. James R. Clapper, "Worldwide Threat Assessment of the US Intelligence Community," report prepared for the Senate Select Committee on Intelligence, March 12, 2013, http://www.dni.gov/files/documents/Intelligence%20Reports/2013%20ATA %20SFR%20for%20SSCI%2012%20Mar%202013.pdf.

30. For discussion of the effects of technological change on military organizations, see Merritt Roe Smith, ed., *Military Enterprise and Technological Change: Perspectives on the American Experience* (Cambridge, MA: MIT Press, 1985).

31. The literature is quite extensive. Good places to start include Richard K. Betts, *Surprise Attack: Lessons for Defense Planning* (Washington, DC: Brookings Institution Press, 1982); John Lewis Gaddis, *Surprise, Security, and the American Experience* (Cambridge, MA: Harvard University Press, 2004); Charles F. Parker and Eric K. Stern, "Blindsided? September 11 and the Origins of Strategic Surprise," *Political Psychology* 23, no. 3 (September 2002): 601–30.

32. Arnold Wolfers, *Discord and Collaboration: Essays on International Politics* (Baltimore, MD: Johns Hopkins University Press, 1962), 151.

33. Goldman, *Power in Uncertain Times*, 125.

34. See Hew Strachan, "The Lost Meaning of Strategy," *Survival* 47, no. 3 (Autumn 2005): 33–54. For a discussion of the traditional approach, see Thomas C. Schelling, *The Strategy of Conflict* (Cambridge, MA: Harvard University Press, 1960).

35. Arthur F. Lykke Jr., "Toward an Understanding of Military Strategy," in *Military Strategy: Theory and Application* (Carlisle, PA: U.S. Army War College, 1989), 3–8.

36. These questions, and a general discussion of Lykke's influence, can be found in Harry R. Yarger, "Toward a Theory of Strategy: Art Lyyke and the U.S. Army War College Strategy Model," in *Theory of War and Strategy*, 4th ed., ed. J. Boone Bartholomees Jr. (Carlisle, PA: Strategic Studies Institute, 2010), 44–51.

37. Mackubin Thomas Owens, "Strategy and the Strategic Way of Thinking," *Naval War College Review* 60, no. 4 (Autumn 2007): 111. For other prominent, similar descriptions of strategy, see J. Boone Bartholomees Jr., "A Survey of the Theory of Strategy," in *Theory of War and Strategy*, ed. Bartholomees, 13–44; Robert H. Dorff, "A Primer in Strategy Development" in *U.S. Army War College Guide to Strategy*, ed. Joseph R. Cerami and James F. Holcomb Jr. (Carlisle, PA: Strategic Studies Institute, 2001), 11.

38. Derek S. Reveron and James L. Cook, "From National to Theater: Developing Strategy," *Joint Forces Quarterly* 70 (2013): 113.

39. Freedman, *Strategy*, xi. See also the brief discussion on 663n2.

40. Jeffrey W. Meiser, "Ends + Ways + Means = (Bad) Strategy," *Parameters* 46, no. 4 (Winter 2016/2017): 81–91.

41. Donald H. Rumsfeld, "Transforming the Military," *Foreign Affairs* 81, no. 3 (May/June 2002): 24.

42. This debate is reviewed by Winnefeld, *The Post–Cold War Sizing Debate.*

43. Winnefeld, *The Post–Cold War Sizing Debate*, 34. See also Paul K. Davis, ed., *New Challenges for Defense Planning: Rethinking How Much Is Enough* (Santa Monica, CA: RAND, 1994); Paul K. Davis, *Analytic Architecture for Capabilities-Based Planning, Mission-System Analysis, and Transformation* (Santa Monica, CA: RAND, 2002).

44. Davis, *Analytic Architecture*, 1.

45. Davis, *Analytic Architecture*, 2.

46. Marine General Paul Van Riper discussed the exercise in "Wake-Up Call," *Guardian*, September 6, 2002. Details of the exercise are available from U.S. Joint Forces Command, "Millennium Challenge 2002," http://www.jfcom.mil/about/experiments/mco2.htm. The use of Israel as the primary enemy is analyzed in *Nova*'s "Battle Plan Under Fire," May 4, 2004, http://www.pbs.org/wgbh/nova/transcripts/3110_wartech.html.

47. Derek Reveron, *Exporting Security: International Engagement, Security Cooperation, and the Changing Face of the U.S. Military* (Washington, DC: Georgetown University Press, 2010), 2.

48. Powell, *The National Military Strategy of the United States*, 7.

49. For an exemplary discussion, see Andrew F. Krepinevich Jr., "Strategy in a Time of Austerity: Why the Pentagon Should Focus on Assuring Access," *Foreign Affairs* 91, no. 6 (November/December 2012): 58–69.

50. Gen. Norton A. Schwartz and Adm. Jonathan W. Greenert, "Air-Sea Battle: Promoting Stability in an Era of Uncertainty," *American Interest*, February 20, 2012, http://www.the-american-interest.com/articles/2012/2/20/air-sea-battle/; Stephen Biddle and Ivan Oelrich, "Future Warfare in the Western Pacific: Chinese Antiaccess/Area Denial, U.S. AirSea Battle, and Command of the Commons in East Asia," *International Security* 41, no. 1 (Summer 2016): 7–48.

51. Office of the Secretary of Defense, *Sustaining U.S. Global Leadership*, 9. See also Schwartz and Greenert, "Air-Sea Battle."

52. For good discussions of credibility in international affairs, see Robert Jervis and Jack Snyder, eds., *Dominoes and Bandwagons: Strategic Beliefs and Great Power Competition in the Eurasian Rimland* (New York: Oxford University Press, 1991); Jonathan Mercer, *Reputation and International Politics* (Ithaca, NY: Cornell University Press, 1996); Daryl G. Press, *Calculating Credibility: How Leaders Assess Military Threats* (Ithaca, NY: Cornell University Press, 2006).

53. Robert J. McMahon, "Credibility and World Power: Exploring the Psychological Dimension in Postwar American Diplomacy," *Diplomatic History* 15, no. 4 (Fall 1991): 455–71.

54. Lou Cannon and Don Oberdorfer, "Standing Fast: 'Vital Interests' of U.S. at Stake," *Washington Post*, October 25, 1983.

55. Michael Ledeen, "The Lessons of Lebanon," *Commentary* 77, no. 5 (May 1984): 21–22.

56.   For more explanation of these (perhaps counterintuitive) points, see Christopher J. Fettweis, *The Pathologies of Power: Fear, Honor, Glory, and Hubris in U.S. Foreign Policy* (New York: Cambridge University Press, 2013), esp. chap. 2, "Honor."

57.   On the importance of credibility in the post–Cold War world, see Christopher J. Fettweis, "Credibility and the War on Terror," *Political Science Quarterly* 122, no. 4 (Winter 2007/2008): 607–33.

58.   "Fetishizing credibility," according to Walt, "is one of the reasons American diplomacy has achieved relatively little since the end of the Cold War." Stephen M. Walt, "Why Are U.S. Leaders so Obsessed with Credibility?" *Foreign Policy* blog, September 11, 2012, http://walt.foreignpolicy.com/posts/2012/09/11/the_credibility_fetish.

59.   Among those who felt that NATO was doomed were Christopher Layne, "Superpower Disengagement," *Foreign Policy* 77 (Winter 1989/1990): 17–40; John J. Mearsheimer, "Back to the Future: Instability in Europe After the Cold War," *International Security* 15, no. 1 (Summer 1990): 5; Kenneth N. Waltz, "The Emerging Structure of International Politics," *International Security* 18, no. 2 (Fall 1993): 75.

60.   James B. Steinberg and Philip G. Gordon, "NATO Enlargement: Moving Forward; Expanding the Alliance and Completing Europe's Integration," Brookings Policy Brief Series 90, November 2001.

61.   Zbigniew Brzezinski, "NATO—Expand or Die?" *New York Times*, December 28, 1994.

62.   Lord Hastings Ismay, the first secretary general of NATO, is generally credited with being the first to say that the alliance's purpose was to "keep the Russians out, the Americans in, and the Germans down."

63.   Colin Powell, "A Strategy of Partnerships," *Foreign Affairs* 83, no. 1 (January/February 2004): 22–34.

64.   Richard K. Betts, "Institutional Imperialism," *National Interest* 113 (May/June 2011): 86.

65.   The assertion that the credibility of NATO was one of the central motivations for the intervention in Kosovo is uncontroversial. See, for instance, G. Gerard Ong, "Credibility Over Courage: NATO's Misintervention in Kosovo," *Journal of Strategic Studies* 26, no. 1 (2003): 73–108.

66.   Allison Astorino-Courtois, "The Effects of Stakes and Threat on Foreign Policy Decision Making," *Political Psychology* 21, no. 3 (September 2000): 489–510.

67.   John W. Payne, James R. Bettman, and Eric J. Johnson, "Adaptive Strategy Selection in Decision Making," *Journal of Experimental Psychology: Learning, Memory, and Cognition* 14, no. 3 (July 1988): 534–552; Frank R. Kardes, A. V. Muthukrushnan, and Vladimir Pashkevich, "On the Conditions Under Which Experience and Motivation Accentuate Bias in Intuitive Judgment," in *The Routines of Decision Making*, ed. Tilmann Betsch and Susanne Haberstroh (New York: Psychology Press, 2005), 139–56. Further nuance and a good review of the early literature can be found in Jennifer S. Lerner and Philip E. Tetlock, "Accounting for the Effects of Accountability," *Psychological Bulletin* 125, no. 2 (March 1999): 255–75.

68.   Charles W. Ostrom Jr. and Brian L. Job, "The President and the Political Use of Force," *American Political Science Review* 80, no. 2 (June 1986): 541–566; Laurence

Paquette and Thomas Kida, "The Effect of Decision Strategy and Task Complexity on Decision Performance," *Organizational Behavior and Human Decision Processes* 41, no. 1 (February 1988): 128–42; Brett W. Pelham and Efrat Neter, "The Effect of Judgment Depends on the Difficulty of the Judgment," *Journal of Personality and Social Psychology* 68, no. 4 (April 1995): 581–94; Ming-Chien Sung, Johnnie Eric Victor Johnson, and Itiel E. Dror, "Complexity as a Guide to Understanding Decision Bias: A Contribution to the Favorite-Longshot Bias Debate," *Journal of Behavioral Decision Making* 22, no. 3 (July 2009): 318–37; Benedict G. C. Dellaert, Bas Donkers, and Arthur Van Soest, "Complexity Effects in Choice Experiment-Based Models," *Journal of Marketing Research* 49, no. 3 (June 2012): 424–34.

69. Jack Snyder, Robert Y. Shapiro, and Yaeli Bloch-Elkon, "Free Hand Abroad, Divide and Rule at Home," *World Politics* 61, no. 1 (January 2009): 155–87.

70. John Newhouse, "Diplomacy, Inc.: The Influence of Lobbies on U.S. Foreign Policy," *Foreign Affairs* 88, no. 3 (May/June 2009): 73–92.

71. William M. Leogrande, "The Cuba Lobby," *Foreign Policy*, April 26, 2013.

72. Morton H. Halperin, *Bureaucratic Politics and Foreign Policy* (Washington, DC: Brookings Institution Press, 1974).

73. Supporters include Baker Spring, Mackenzie Eaglen, and James Jay Carafano, "4 Percent of GDP Defense Spending: Sustained Spending, Not Economic Stimulus," Heritage Foundation WebMemo 2243, January 26, 2009, http://www.heritage.org /research/reports/2009/01/4-percent-of-gdp-defense-spending-sustained-spending -not-economic-stimulus; Mackubin Thomas Owens, "A Balanced Force Structure to Achieve a Liberal World Order," *Orbis* 50, no. 2 (Spring 2006): 307–25; Martin Feldstein, "The Underfunded Pentagon," *Foreign Affairs* 86, no. 2 (March/April 2007): 134–40. For a critique, see Travis Sharp, "Tying U.S. Defense Spending to GDP: Bad Logic, Bad Policy," *Parameters* 38, no. 3 (Autumn 2008): 5–17.

74. The rule was put into place after a number of psychiatrists expressed opinions about Barry Goldwater's fitness to be president during the 1964 presidential campaign. American Psychiatric Association, *The Principles of Medical Ethics with Annotations Especially Applicable to Psychiatry*, 5th ed. (Arlington, VA: American Psychiatric Association, 2013), 9. The taboo against diagnosing from afar may be weakening; see Bandy Lee, ed., *The Dangerous Case of Donald Trump: Twenty-Seven Psychiatrists and Mental Health Experts Assess a President* (New York: St. Martin's Press, 2017).

75. American Psychiatric Association, *Diagnostic and Statistical Manual of Mental Disorders*, 5th ed. (Arlington, VA: American Psychiatric Association, 2013), 301.81 (F60.81). All quotations are from that section of the manual. Less widely accepted but perhaps even more relevant is the "Hubris Syndrome," which adds to the list, among other indicators, "A tendency to speak in the third person," "Restlessness, recklessness and impulsiveness," and "an unshakable belief that in that court [of history] they will be vindicated." David Owen and Jonathan Davidson, "Hubris Syndrome: An Acquired Personality Disorder? A Study of U.S. Presidents and UK Prime Ministers Over the Last 100 Years," *Brain* 132, no. 5 (May 2009): 1396–1406.

76.   Jerrold M. Post, "Current Concepts of the Narcissistic Personality: Implications for Political Psychology," *Political Psychology* 14, no. 1 (March 1993): 100, 104, 112, 110.

77.   Nikhil Dhawan, Mark E. Kunik, John Oldham, and John Coverdale, "Prevalence and Treatment of Narcissistic Personality Disorder in the Community: A Systematic Review," *Comprehensive Psychiatry* 51, no. 4 (July/August 2010): 333–39. See also Heinz Kohut, *The Analysis of the Self: A Systemic Approach to the Psychoanalytic Treatment of Narcissistic Personality Disorders* (Chicago: University of Chicago Press, 2009).

78.   Post, "Current Concepts of the Narcissistic Personality," 99.

79.   Quoted by Samuel F. Wells Jr., "Sounding the Tocsin: NSC 68 and the Soviet Threat," *International Security* 4, no. 2 (Autumn 1979): 128.

## 6. UNIPOLARITY AND GRAND STRATEGY

1.   Brian Knowlton, "Gates Calls European Mood a Danger to Peace," *New York Times*, February 23, 2010.

2.   Jeffrey Goldberg, "The Obama Doctrine," *Atlantic* 317, no. 3 (April 2016): 78.

3.   Robert Kagan, *Of Paradise and Power: America and Europe in the New World Order* (New York: Knopf, 2003), 3. See also Gary Schmitt, "The Demilitarization of Europe," *Wall Street Journal*, October 6, 2010.

4.   Even those Europeans who discuss the subject focus more on what Uncle Sam is doing far more than they focus on other states. Niall Ferguson, *Colossus: The Price of America's Empire* (New York: Penguin, 2004); Colin S. Gray, *The Sheriff: America's Defense of the New World Order* (Lexington: University Press of Kentucky, 2004).

5.   Robert Jervis, "U.S. Grand Strategy: Mission Impossible," *Naval War College Review* 51, no. 3 (Summer 1998): 118–33; Steven A. Yetiv, *The Absence of Grand Strategy: The United States in the Persian Gulf, 1972–2005* (Baltimore, MD: Johns Hopkins University Press, 2008); David Sylvan and Stephen Majeski, *U.S. Foreign Policy in Perspective: Clients, Enemies, and Empire* (New York: Routledge, 2009); Walter A. McDougall, "Can the United States Do Grand Strategy?" *Orbis* 54, no. 2 (Spring 2010): 165–84.

6.   Eric A. Nordlinger, *Isolationism Reconfigured: American Foreign Policy for a New Century* (Princeton, NJ: Princeton University Press, 1995), 4. See also Eugene Gholz, Daryl G. Press, and Harvey M. Sapolsky, "Come Home America: The Strategy of Restraint in the Face of Temptation," *International Security* 21, no. 4 (Spring 1997): 5–48; Christopher A. Preble, *The Power Problem: How American Military Dominance Makes Us Less Safe, Less Prosperous, and Less Free* (Ithaca, NY: Cornell University Press, 2009); Barry Posen, *Restraint: A New Foundation for U.S. Grand Strategy* (Ithaca, NY: Cornell University Press, 2014).

7.   2015 nominal GDP figures and population for the European Union come from the CIA World Fact Book, https://www.cia.gov/library/publications/the-world-factbook/geos/ee.html; GDP for the United States is from the Bureau of Economic Analysis, U.S. Department of Commerce, http://www.bea.gov/national/index.htm#gdp; population figures are from http://www.census.gov/popclock/.

8.  Ryan Browne, "NATO Members to Increase Defense Spending," *CNN*, June 29, 2017, http://www.cnn.com/2017/06/29/politics/nato-members-increase-defense-spending/index.html. The increases should not be overstated—Germany, for instance, has pledged to raise its spending from 1.2% of its GDP to 1.22%.

9.  Michael Mandelbaum, "Foreign Policy as Social Work," *Foreign Affairs* 75, no. 1 (January/February 2006): 16–32.

10. Quoted by James J. Sheehan, *Where Have All the Soldiers Gone? The Transformation of Modern Europe* (New York: Houghton-Mifflin, 2008), xvi.

11. There are many such lists, and they tend to arrive at roughly the same conclusions. The list cited here, which has thirty-eight European countries in its top fifty, is an aggregate of economic, social, and cultural globalization. "KOF Index of Globalization 2016," March 4, 2016, http://globalization.kof.ethz.ch/.

12. Sheehan, *Where Have All the Soldiers Gone?*, xvi.

13. Kagan, *Of Paradise and Power*, 32.

14. *A Secure Europe in a Better World* (Brussels, December 12, 2003).

15. White House, *The National Security Strategy of the United States of America* (Washington DC, March 2006). The 2010 *National Security Strategy* released by the Obama administration is not as stark in its language but clearly senses danger in the world.

16. See Nordlinger, *Isolationism Reconfigured*, 269–70.

17. Richard K. Betts, "A Disciplined Defense: How to Regain Strategic Solvency," *Foreign Affairs* 86, no. 6 (November/December 2007): 67–80.

18. Chapter 1 contains a discussion of the basic options and cites some useful taxonomies.

19. Sometimes the value of that position is questioned, though. See Robert Jervis, "International Primacy: Is the Game Worth the Candle?" *International Security* 17, no. 4 (Spring 1993): 52–67.

20. Peter Wyden, *Bay of Pigs: The Untold Story* (New York: Simon and Schuster, 1979), 8.

21. Richard E. Neustadt and Ernest R. May, *Thinking in Time: The Uses of History for Policymakers* (New York: Free Press, 1986), 1.

22. Gregory A. Raymond, "Necessity in Foreign Policy," *Political Science Quarterly* 113, no. 4 (Winter 1998/1999): 673–88.

23. Raymond, "Necessity in Foreign Policy," 684–85.

24. John Mueller, "Embracing Threatlessness: U.S. Military Spending, Newt Gingrich, and the Costa Rica Option," in *The Case for Restraint in U.S. Foreign Policy*, ed. A. Trevor Thrall and Benjamin H. Friedman, forthcoming.

25. Barry R. Posen, "The Case for Restraint," *American Interest* 3, no. 2 (November/December 2007): 13.

## UNIPOLARITY AND ITS CONCLUSION

1.  Zbigniew Brzezinski, "After America," *Foreign Policy* 191 (January/February 2012): 1–4. Candidates for new imperial powers included China, Turkey, Russia, and Brazil. See also Robert Kagan, *The World America Made* (New York: Knopf, 2012).

2.  All these and more can be found in Niall Ferguson, "A World Without Power," *Foreign Policy* 143 (July/August 2004): 32–39. The most frightening page is 39.

3.  Robert Kagan, "Backing Into World War III," *Foreign Policy*, February 6, 2017, http://foreignpolicy.com/2017/02/06/backing-into-world-war-iii-russia-china-trump-obama/.

4.  Immanuel Wallerstein, "Consequences of U.S. Decline," web commentary 364, November 1, 2013, http://iwallerstein.com/consequences-decline/. See also his *The Decline of American Power: The U.S. in a Chaotic World* (New York: New Press, 2003); Noam Chomsky, "American Decline: Causes and Consequences," *Al-Akhbar*, August 24, 2011, https://chomsky.info/20110824/.

5.  Among the better-known, incorrect prophets of doom at the moment of the previous systemic realignment were John J. Mearsheimer, "Back to Future: Instability in Europe After the Cold War," *International Security* 15, no. 1 (Summer 1990): 5–56; Kenneth N. Waltz, "The Emerging Structure of International Politics," *International Security* 18, no. 2 (Fall 1993): 44–79; Samuel Huntington, "The Clash of Civilizations?" *Foreign Affairs* 72, no. 3 (Summer 1993): 22–49; and Robert D. Kaplan, "The Coming Anarchy," *Atlantic Monthly* 273, no. 2 (February 1994): 44–76.

6.  The theory was first described by A. F. K. Organski in his textbook *World Politics* (New York: Knopf, 1958), 338–76. See also Ronald L. Tammen, Jacek Kugler, Douglas Lemke, et al., *Power Transitions: Strategies for the Twenty-First Century* (New York: Chatham House, 2000).

7.  Thucydides, *History of the Peloponnesian War* (New York: Penguin, 1972), 49.

8.  By far the most prominent is Graham Allison, *Destined for War: Can America and China Escape Thucydides's Trap?* (New York: Houghton Mifflin Harcourt, 2017).

9.  For a wonderful review, see Josef Joffe, *The Myth of America's Decline: Politics, Economics, and a Half-Century of False Prophecies* (New York: Norton, 2014).

10.  Arthur Herman, *The Idea of Decline in Western History* (New York: Free Press, 1997).

11.  Henry A. Kissinger, *The Necessity for Choice: Prospects of American Foreign Policy* (Garden City, NY: Anchor, 1962), 1.

12.  Samuel Huntington discusses the previous waves of Cold War declinism in "The U.S.: Decline or Renewal?" *Foreign Affairs* 67, no. 2 (Winter 1988): 94–95.

13.  Paul Kennedy, *The Rise and Fall of the Great Powers: Economic Change and Military Conflict from 1500 to 2000* (New York: Random House, 1987). See also Walter Russell Mead, *Mortal Splendor: The American Empire in Transition* (Boston: Houghton Mifflin, 1988); David Calleo, *Beyond American Hegemony: The Future of the Western Alliance* (New York: Basic Books, 1987); Robert W. Tucker, "America in Decline: The Foreign Policy of 'Maturity,'" *Foreign Affairs* 58, no. 3 (1979): 449–84; Robert Keohane, *After Hegemony: Cooperation and Discord in the World Political Economy* (Princeton, NJ: Princeton University Press, 1984).

14.  Edward N. Luttwak, *The Endangered American Dream: How to Stop the United States from Becoming a Third World Country and How to Win the Geo-Economic Struggle for Industrial Supremacy* (New York: Simon and Schuster, 1993), 118. Luttwak did not

recognize the impossibility of becoming a "third world" country once the "second world" had disappeared.

15.  Robert Gilpin, "No One Loves a Political Realist," *Security Studies* 5, no. 3 (Spring 1996): 5. There were some exceptions: Kennedy, for instance, wrote in 1999 that "in virtually all dimensions of power . . . the United States seems at present in a relatively more favorable position in the world than at any time since the 1940s." Paul Kennedy, "The Next American Century?" *World Policy Journal* 16, no. 1 (Spring 1999): 56.

16.  Robert A. Pape, "Empire Falls," *National Interest* 99 (January/February 2009): 21–34. See also Fareed Zakaria, *The Post-American World* (New York: Norton, 2008); Charles Kupchan, *The End of the American Era: U.S. Foreign Policy and the Geopolitics of the Twenty-First Century* (New York: Knopf, 2002); T. R. Reid, *The United States of Europe: The New Superpower and the End of American Supremacy* (New York: Penguin, 2004); Gideon Rachman, "Think Again: American Decline," *Foreign Policy* 184 (January/February 2011): 59–63; Christopher Layne, "This Time It's Real: The End of Unipolarity and the *Pax Americana*," *International Studies Quarterly* 56, no. 1 (March 2012): 202–13; Zbigniew Brzezinski, *Strategic Vision: America and the Crisis of Global Power* (New York: Basic Books, 2012).

17.  Layne, "This Time It's Real."

18.  The most prominent and consistent advocates of this view have been Christopher Layne and Charles Kupchan. From the former, see "The Unipolar Illusion: Why New Great Powers Will Rise," *International Security* 17, no. 4 (Spring 1993): 5–51; "The Unipolar Illusion Revisited: The Coming End of the United States' Unipolar Moment," *International Security* 31, no. 2 (Fall 2006): 7–41; "The Waning of U.S. Hegemony—Myth or Reality?" *International Security* 34, no. 1 (Summer 2009): 147–72; and "This Time It's Real." From the latter, see "After Pax Americana: Benign Power, Regional Integration, and the Sources of a Stable Multipolarity," *International Security* 23, no. 2 (Fall 1998): 40–79; "Life After Pax Americana," *World Policy Journal* 16, no. 3 (Fall 1999): 20–27; *The End of the American Era: U.S. Foreign Policy and the Geopolitics of the Twenty-First Century* (New York: Knopf, 2002); and "The Decline of the West: Why America Must Prepare for the End of Dominance," *Atlantic*, March 20, 2012.

19.  Robert Kagan, "The Benevolent Empire," *Foreign Policy* 111 (Summer 1998): 24–35; John M. Owen IV, "Transnational Liberalism and U.S. Primacy," *International Security* 26, no. 3 (Winter 2001/2002): 117–52.

20.  Stephen M. Walt, *The Origin of Alliances* (Ithaca, NY: Cornell University Press, 1987).

21.  William C. Wohlforth, "The Stability of Unipolar World," *International Security* 24, no. 1 (Summer 1999): 5–41. See also Nuno P. Monteiro, *Theory of Unipolar Politics* (New York: Cambridge University Press, 2014).

22.  Campbell Craig, "American Power Preponderance and the Nuclear Revolution," *Review of International Studies* 35, no. 1 (January 2009): 27–44.

23.  One effort to identify applicable precedents is David Wilkinson, "Unipolarity Without Hegemony," *International Studies Review* 1, no. 2 (Summer 1999): 141–72.

24. The distinction between internal and external balancing is discussed by Kenneth N. Waltz, *Theory of International Politics* (Reading, MA: Addison-Wesley, 1979), 118.

25. Estimating the exact amount China spends on its military, as well as the size of its economy, is not as straightforward as it is with others. The Stockholm International Peace Research Institute does its best in its Military Expenditure Database, https://www.sipri.org/databases/milex.

26. Oswald Spengler, *The Decline of the West* (New York: Knopf, 1926–1928).

27. This is the central observation of "prospect theory." See Daniel Kahneman and Amos Tversky, "Prospect Theory: An Analysis of Decision Under Risk," *Econometrica* 47, no. 2 (March 1979): 263–91.

28. The term "hypercompetitive" was coined by the psychoanalyst Karen Horney in "Culture and Neurosis," *American Sociological Review* 1, no. 2 (April 1936): 221. See also Christopher J. Fettweis, *The Pathologies of Power: Fear, Honor, Glory, and Hubris in U.S. Foreign Policy* (New York: Cambridge University Press, 2013), chap. 3.

29. Michael Cox, "Is the United States in Decline—Again? An Essay," *International Affairs* 83, no. 4 (July 2007): 644.

30. Bruce Russett, "The Mysterious Case of Vanishing Hegemony; Or, Is Mark Twain Really Dead?" *International Organization* 39, no. 2 (Spring 1985): 229.

31. Perhaps the most prominent and consistent critic of U.S. foreign policy who delights in the possibility of eroding unipolarity—and indeed appears to be trying to wish it into existence—is Immanuel Wallerstein. See his "The Eagle Has Crash Landed," *Foreign Policy* 131 (July/August 2002): 60–68; *Decline of American Power*; and "Precipitate Decline: The Advent of Multipolarity," *Harvard International Review* 29, no. 1 (Spring 2007): 50–55.

32. Ellen A. Skinner, *Perceived Control, Motivation, and Coping* (London: Sage, 1995), esp. 3.

33. For the classic, definitive statement on this, see Robert W. White, "Motivation Reconsidered: The Concept of Competence," *Psychological Review* 66, no. 5 (September 1959): 297–333. That quotation and a review of the literature can be found in Skinner, *Perceived Control, Motivation, and Coping*, 8.

34. Paul K. MacDonald and Joseph A. Parent, "Graceful Decline: The Surprising Success of Great Power Retrenchment," *International Security* 35, no. 4 (Spring 2011): 7–44.

35. William S. Maltby, *The Rise and Decline of the Spanish Empire* (New York: Palgrave Macmillan, 2008), 191–192.

36. George L. Bernstein, *The Myth of Decline: The Rise of Britain Since 1945* (London: Pimlico, 2004).

37. Bernard Porter, *The Lion's Share: A Short History of British Imperialism 1850–1995* (New York: Longman, 1996), 290–292, 346–347. See also Bernstein, *The Myth of Decline*, 9–10.

38. Fareed Zakaria added to the title of his book to emphasize this point in its second printing: *The Post-American World and the Rise of the Rest* (New York: Penguin, 2009).

39.  Ryan D. Griffiths, "States, Nations, and Territorial Stability: Why Chinese Hegemony Would Be Better for International Order," *Security Studies* 25, no. 3 (July 2016): 519–45.

40.  Dale W. Griffin, David Dunning, and Lee Ross, "The Role of Construal Processes in Overconfident Predictions About the Self and Others," *Journal of Personality and Social Psychology* 59, no. 6 (December 1990): 1128–39.

# BIBLIOGRAPHY

Abalakina-Paap, Marina, Walter G. Stephan, Traci Craig, and W. Larry Gregory. "Beliefs in Conspiracies." *Political Psychology* 20, no. 3 (September 1999): 637–47.

Adams, Henry. *The Education of Henry Adams*. Boston: Massachusetts Historical Society, 2007.

Adelman, Kenneth. "Cakewalk in Iraq." *Washington Post*, February 13, 2002.

——. "Desert Storm II Would Be a Walk in the Park." *London Times*, August 29, 2002.

Adler, Eric. "Late Victorian and Edwardian Views of Rome and the Nature of 'Defensive Imperialism.'" *International Journal of the Classical Tradition* 15, no. 2 (June 2008): 187–216.

Albright, Madeleine. *Madam Secretary: A Memoir*. New York: Miramax, 2005.

Alexander, Michele G., Marilynn B. Brewer, and Richard K. Herrmann. "Images and Affect: A Functional Analysis of Out-Group Stereotypes." *Journal of Personality and Social Psychology* 77, no. 1 (December 1999): 78–93.

Alexander, Michele G., Shana Levin, and P. J. Henry. "Image Theory, Social Identity, and Social Dominance: Structural Characteristics and Individual Motives Underlying International Images." *Political Psychology* 26, no. 1 (February 2005): 27–45.

Ali, Wajahat, Eli Clifton, Matthew Duss, Lee Fang, Scott Keyes, and Faiz Shakir. *Fear, Inc.: The Roots of the Islamophobia Network in America*. Washington, DC: Center for American Progress, 2011. http://www.americanprogress.org/issues/2011/08/pdf/islamophobia .pdf.

Allin, Dana H. *Cold War Illusions: America, Europe and Soviet Power, 1969–1989*. New York: St. Martin's Press, 1994.

Allison, Graham. *Destined for War: Can America and China Escape Thucydides's Trap?* New York: Houghton Mifflin Harcourt, 2017.

——. *Nuclear Terrorism: The Ultimate Preventable Catastrophe*. New York: Henry Holt, 2004.

American Psychiatric Association. 2013. *The Principles of Medical Ethics with Annotations Especially Applicable to Psychiatry.* 5th ed. Arlington, VA: American Psychiatric Association.

Anderson, Cameron, and Adam D. Galinsky. 2006. "Power, Optimism, and Risk-Taking." *European Journal of Social Psychology* 36, no. 4 (July/August): 511–36.

Anderson, Cameron, and Jennifer L. Berdahl. "The Experience of Power: Examining the Effects of Power on Approach and Inhibition." *Journal of Personality and Social Psychology* 83, no. 6 (December 2002): 1362–1377.

Anderson, Craig A., Mark R. Lepper, and Lee Ross. "Perseverance of Social Theories: The Role of Explanation in the Persistence of Discredited Information." *Journal of Personality and Social Psychology* 39, no. 6 (December 1980): 1037–49.

Anderson, Michael C. "Active Forgetting: Evidence for Functional Inhibition as a Source of Memory Failure." *Journal of Aggression, Maltreatment, and Trauma* 4, no. 2 (2001): 185–210.

Angell, Norman. *The Fruits of Victory: A Sequel to the Great Illusion.* 2nd ed. New York: Garland, 1973.

——. *The Great Illusion: A Study of the Relation of Military Power to National Advantage.* 2nd ed. London: William Heinemann, 1913.

Arango, Tim, and Ceylan Yeginsu. "Turks Can Agree on One Thing: U.S. Was Behind Failed Coup." *New York Times,* August 2, 2016.

Arbatov, Gregori. "It Takes Two to Make a Cold War." *New York Times,* December 8, 1987.

Arkes, Hal R. "Costs and Benefits of Judgment Errors: Implications for Debiasing." *Psychological Bulletin* 110, no. 3 (November 1991): 486–98.

Arkin, Robert, Harris Cooper, and Thomas Kolditz. "A Statistical Review of the Literature Concerning the Self-Serving Attribution Bias in Interpersonal Influence Situations." *Journal of Personality* 48, no. 4 (December 1980): 435–48.

Art, Robert J. *A Grand Strategy for America.* Ithaca, NY: Cornell University Press, 2003.

Asal, Victor, and Amy Pate. "The Decline of Ethnic Political Discrimination, 1990–2003." In *Peace and Conflict 2005: A Global Survey of Armed Conflicts, Self-Determination Movements, and Democracy,* ed. Ted Robert Gurr and Monty G. Marshall, 28–38. College Park, MD: Center for International Development and Conflict Management, 2005.

Aspin, Les. "The Counterproliferation Initiative." Speech at the National Academy of Sciences, Washington, D.C., December 7, 1993.

Astorino-Courtois, Allison. "The Effects of Stakes and Threat on Foreign Policy Decision Making." *Political Psychology* 21, no. 3 (September 2001): 489–510.

Bacevich, Andrew J. *America's War for the Middle East: A Military History.* New York: Random House, 2016.

——. *American Empire: The Realities and Consequences of U.S. Diplomacy.* Cambridge, MA: Harvard University Press, 2002.

Backer, David A., Ravi Bhavnani, and Paul K. Huth, eds. *Peace and Conflict 2016.* New York: Routledge, 2016.

Barash, David. *Beloved Enemies: Our Need for Opponents.* Amherst, NY: Prometheus, 1994.

Bartholomees, J. Boone, Jr. "A Survey of the Theory of Strategy." In *Theory of War and Strategy*, ed. J. Boone Bartholomees Jr., 4th ed., 13–44. Carlisle, PA: Strategic Studies Institute, 2010.

Bartlett, Frederic C. *Remembering: A Study in Experimental and Social Psychology*. London: Cambridge University Press, 1932.

Barzegar, Kayhan. "Iran's Perception of the U.S. Policy Toward the Region." In *U.S.-Iran Misperceptions: A Dialogue*, ed. Abbas Maleki and John Tirman, 37–56. New York: Bloomsbury, 2014.

Bauer, Raymond A. "Problems of Perception and the Relations Between the United States and the Soviet Union." *Journal of Conflict Resolution* 5, no. 3 (September 1961): 223–29.

Bernstein, George L. *The Myth of Decline: The Rise of Britain Since 1945*. London: Pimlico, 2004.

Betts, Richard K. "A Disciplined Defense: How to Regain Strategic Solvency." *Foreign Affairs* 86, no. 6 (November/December 2007): 67–80.

——. "Institutional Imperialism." *National Interest* 113 (May/June 2011): 85–96.

——. *Surprise Attack: Lessons for Defense Planning*. Washington, DC: Brookings Institution Press, 1982.

Biddle, Stephen, and Ivan Oelrich. "Future Warfare in the Western Pacific: Chinese Anti-access/Area Denial, U.S. AirSea Battle, and Command of the Commons in East Asia." *International Security* 41, no. 1 (Summer 2016): 7–48.

Bolton, John R. "To Stop Iran's Bomb, Bomb Iran." *New York Times*, March 26, 2015.

Boot, Max. "The Case for American Empire." *Weekly Standard* 7, no. 5 (October 15, 2001): 27–35.

Boulding, Kenneth E. *The Image*. Ann Arbor: University of Michigan Press, 1956.

——. "National Image and International Systems." *Journal of Conflict Resolution* 3, no. 2 (June 1959): 120–31.

Bracken, Paul. *Fire in the East: The Rise of Asian Military Power and the Second Nuclear Age*. New York: Harper Collins, 1999.

——. *The Second Nuclear Age: Strategy, Danger, and the New Power Politics*. New York: Henry Holt, 2012.

Brands, Hal, and David Palkki. "'Conspiring Bastards': Saddam Hussein's Strategic View of the United States." *Diplomatic History* 36, no. 3 (June 2012): 625–59.

Braumoeller, Bear F. *Only the Dead: International Order and the Persistence of Conflict in the Modern Age*. New York: Oxford University Press, in press.

Braut-Hegghammer, Målfrid. *Unclear Physics: Why Iraq and Libya Failed to Get the Bomb*. Ithaca, NY: Cornell University Press, 2016.

Bremmer, Ian. *Every Nation for Itself: What Happens When No One Leads the World*. New York: Portfolio, 2012.

Brewer, Marilynn B., and Michele G. Alexander. "Intergroup Emotions and Images." In *From Prejudice to Intergroup Emotions: Differentiated Reactions to Social Groups*, ed. Diane M. Mackie and Eliot R. Smith, 209–25. New York: Psychology Press, 2002.

Brooks, Stephen G. *Producing Security: Multinational Corporations, Globalization, and the Changing Calculus of Conflict*. Princeton, NJ: Princeton University Press, 2005.

Brooks, Stephen G., John Ikenberry, and William C. Wohlforth. "Don't Come Home, America: The Case Against Retrenchment." International Security 37, no. 3 (Winter 2012–2013): 7–51.

Brooks, Stephen G., and William C. Wohlforth. *World Out of Balance: International Relations and the Challenge of American Primacy*. Princeton, NJ: Princeton University Press, 2008.

Brunt, P. A. *Roman Imperial Themes*. Oxford: Clarendon, 1990.

Brzezinski, Zbigniew. "After America." *Foreign Policy* 191 (January/February 2012): 1–4.

——. "NATO—Expand or Die?" *New York Times*, December 28, 1994.

——. "A Plan for Europe: How to Expand NATO." *Foreign Affairs* 74, no. 1 (January/February 1995): 26–42.

——. *Strategic Vision: America and the Crisis of Global Power*. New York: Basic Books, 2012.

——. "Putin's Choice." *Washington Quarterly* 31, no. 2 (Spring 2008): 95–116.

Burbach, David, and Christopher J. Fettweis. "The Coming Stability? The Decline of Warfare in Africa and the Implications for International Security." *Contemporary Security Policy* 35, no. 3 (Fall 2014): 421–445.

Burr, William, and Jeffrey T. Richelson. "Whether to 'Strangle the Baby in the Cradle': The United States and the Chinese Nuclear Program, 1960–64." *International Security* 25, no. 3 (Winter 2000–2001): 54–99.

Caffrey, Craig. "Russia Announces Its Deepest Defence Budget Cuts Since the 1990s." *Jane's Defence Weekly*, March 16, 2017. http://www.janes.com/article/68766/russia-announces -deepest-defence-budget-cuts-since-1990s.

Cahn, Anne Hessing. *Killing Détente: The Right Attacks the CIA*. University Park: Pennsylvania State University Press, 1998.

Calleo, David. *Beyond American Hegemony: The Future of the Western Alliance*. New York: Basic Books, 1987.

Campbell, W. Keith, and Constantine Sedikides. "Self-Threat Magnifies the Self-Serving Bias: A Meta-Analytic Integration." *Review of General Psychology* 3, no. 1 (March 1999): 23–43.

Cannon, Lou, and Don Oberdorfer. "Standing Fast: 'Vital Interests' of U.S. at Stake." *Washington Post*, October 25, 1983.

Carey, John M. "Conspiracy Theories Won't Save the Governing Party in Venezuela." *Washington Post*, December 3, 2015. https://www.washingtonpost.com/news/monkey-cage /wp/2015/12/03/conspiracy-theories-wont-save-the-governing-party-in-venezuela/.

Casey, Nicholas. "FARC Rebels in Colombia Reach Cease-Fire Deal with Government." *New York Times*, June 23, 2016.

Cha, Victor D. "Five Myths About North Korea." *Washington Post*, December 10, 2010.

——. "The Second Nuclear Age: Proliferation Pessimism Versus Sober Optimism in South Asia and East Asia." *Journal of Strategic Studies* 24, no. 4 (December 2001): 79–120.

Chace, James, and Caleb Carr. *America Invulnerable: The Quest for Absolute Security from 1812 to Star Wars*. New York: Summit Books, 1988.

Chambers, John R., and Carsten K. W. De Dreu. "Egocentrism Drives Misunderstandings in Conflict and Negotiation." *Journal of Experimental Social Psychology* 51 (March 2014): 15–26.

Chandrasekaran, Rajiv. *Imperial Life in the Emerald City: Inside Iraq's Green Zone*. New York: Knopf, 2007.

Chen, Serena, Annette Y. Lee-Chai, and John A. Bargh. "Relationship Orientation as a Moderator of the Effects of Social Power." *Journal of Personality and Social Psychology* 80, no. 2 (February 2001): 173–87.

Cheney, Dick, and Liz Cheney. *Exceptional: Why the World Needs a Powerful America*. New York: Simon and Schuster, 2015.

Chivian, Eric, John P. Robinson, Jonathan R. H. Tudge, et al. "American and Soviet Teenagers' Concerns About Nuclear War and the Future." *New England Journal of Medicine* 319, no. 7 (August 18, 1988): 407–41.

Chomsky, Noam. "American Decline: Causes and Consequences." *Al-Akhbar*, August 24, 2011. https://chomsky.info/20110824/.

Christensen, Thomas. "Chinese Realpolitik." *Foreign Affairs* 75, no. 5 (September/October 1995): 37–52.

Chua, Hannah Faye, Janxin Leu, and Richard E. Nisbett. "Culture and Divergent Views of Social Events." *Personality and Social Psychology Bulletin* 31, no. 7 (July 2005): 925–34.

Clapper, James R. "Worldwide Threat Assessment of the U.S. Intelligence Community." Report prepared for the Senate Select Committee on Intelligence, March 12, 2013. http://www.dni.gov/files/documents/Intelligence%20Reports/2013%20ATA%20SFR%20for%20SSCI%2012%20Mar%202013.pdf.

Cohen, Eliot A. "Iraq Can't Resist Us." *Wall Street Journal*, December 23, 2001.

Cohen, William S. "Quadrennial Defense Review: The Secretary's Message." May 19, 1997. http://www.disam.dsca.mil/pubs/INDEXES/Vol%2019_4/Cohen.pdf.

Coleman, David G. *The Fourteenth Day: JFK and the Aftermath of the Cuban Missile Crisis*. New York: Norton, 2012.

Conetta, Carl and Charles Knight. "Inventing Threats." *Bulletin of the Atomic Scientists* 54, no. 2 (March/April 1998): 32–38.

Conover, Pamela Johnston, Karen A. Mingst, and Lee Sigelman. "Mirror Images in Americans' Perceptions of Nations and Leaders During the Iranian Hostage Crisis." *Journal of Peace Research* 17, no. 4 (1980): 325–37.

Copeland, Dale C. "Economic Interdependence and War: A Theory of Trade Expectations." *International Security* 20, no. 4 (Spring 1996): 5–41.

Cox, Michael. "Is the United States in Decline—Again? An Essay." *International Affairs* 83, no. 4 (July 2007): 643–53.

Craig, Campbell. "American Power Preponderance and the Nuclear Revolution." *Review of International Studies* 35, no. 1 (January 2009): 27–44.

Dahl, Robert A. "The Concept of Power." *Behavioral Science* 2, no. 3 (July 1957): 201–15.

Davis, Paul K. *Analytic Architecture for Capabilities-Based Planning, Mission-System Analysis, and Transformation*. Santa Monica, CA: RAND, 2002.

——, ed. *New Challenges for Defense Planning: Rethinking How Much Is Enough*. Santa Monica, CA: RAND, 1994.

de Berker, Archy O., Robb B. Rutledge, Christoph Mathys, et al. "Computations of Uncertainty Mediate Acute Stress Response in Humans." *Nature Communications* 7, no. 10996 (March 2016): 1–11.

deCharms, Richard. *Personal Causation: The Internal Affective Determinants of Behavior.* New York: Academic Press, 1968.

Dellaert, Benedict G. C., Bas Donkers, and Arthur Van Soest. "Complexity Effects in Choice Experiment-Based Models." *Journal of Marketing Research* 49, no. 3 (June 2012): 424–34.

Desch, Michael C. "America's Liberal Illiberalism: The Ideological Origins of Overreaction in U.S. Foreign Policy." *International Security* 32, no. 3 (Winter 2007/2008): 7–43.

Deudney, Daniel. "Unipolarity and Nuclear Weapons." In *International Relations Theory and the Consequences of Unipolarity*, ed. G. John Ikenberry, Michael Mastunduno and William C. Wohlforth, 282–316. New York: Cambridge University Press, 2011.

Deutsch, Karl W. *The Analysis of International Relations.* Englewood Cliffs, NJ: Prentice-Hall, 1968.

Deutsch, Karl W., and J. David Singer. "Multipolar Power Systems and International Stability." *World Politics* 16, no. 3 (April 1964): 390–406.

Dhawan, Nikhil, Mark E. Kunik, John Oldham, and John Coverdale. "Prevalence and Treatment of Narcissistic Personality Disorder in the Community: A Systematic Review." *Comprehensive Psychiatry* 51, no. 4 (July/August 2010): 333–39.

Dobrynin, Anatoly. *In Confidence.* New York: Random House, 1995.

Donnelly, Thomas, Danielle Pletka, and Maseh Zarif. *Containing and Deterring a Nuclear Iran: Questions for Strategy, Requirements for Military Forces.* Washington, DC: American Enterprise Institute, December 2011.

Dorff, Robert H. "A Primer in Strategy Development." In *U.S. Army War College Guide Strategy*, ed. Joseph R. Cerami and James F. Holcomb Jr., 11–18. Carlisle, PA: Strategic Studies Institute, 2001.

Dorman, William A., and Steven Livingston. "News and Historical Content: Establishing Phase of the Persian Gulf War Policy Debate." In *Taken by Storm: The Media, Public Opinion, and U.S. Foreign Policy in the Gulf War*, ed. W. Lance Bennet and David L. Paletz, 63–81. Chicago: University of Chicago Press, 1994.

Dower, John W. *War Without Mercy: Race and Power in the Pacific War.* New York: Pantheon, 1986.

Doyle, Michael W. "Liberalism and World Politics." *American Political Science Review* 80, no. 4 (December 1985): 1151–70.

Drew, S. Nelson, ed. *NSC-68: Forging the Strategy of Containment.* Washington, DC: National Defense University, 1996.

Druckman, James N., Donald P. Green, James H. Kuklinski, and Arthur Lupia, eds. *Cambridge Handbook of Experimental Political Science.* New York: Cambridge University Press, 2011.

Dueck, Colin. "Ideas and Alternatives in American Grand Strategy, 2000–2004." *Review of International Studies* 30, no. 4 (October 2004): 511–35.

Duelfer, Charles A., and Stephen Benedict Dyson. "Chronic Misperception and International Conflict: The U.S.-Iraq Experience." *International Security* 36, no. 1 (2011): 73–100.

Dunning, David, Dale W. Griffin, Jams D. Milojkovic, and Lee Ross. "The Overconfidence Effect in Social Prediction." *Journal of Personality and Social Psychology* 58, no. 4 (April 1990): 568–81.

Eicher, Veronique, Felicia Pratto, and Peter Wilhelm. "Value Differentiation Between Allies and Enemies: Value Projection in National Images." *Political Psychology* 34, no. 1 (February 2013): 127–44.

Elliott, J. H. "Managing Decline: Olivares and the Grand Strategy of Imperial Spain." In *Grand Strategies in War and Peace*, ed. Paul Kennedy, 87–104. New Haven, CT: Yale University Press, 1991.

Ericson, Keith, M. Marzilli, and Andreas Fuster. "The Endowment Effect." Annual Review of Economics 6 (2014): 555–79.

Errington, Robert M. *The Dawn of Empire: Rome's Rise to Power*. London: Hamish Hamilton, 1971.

Etzioni, Amitai. "Freedom of Navigation Assertions: The United States as the World's Policeman." *Armed Forces and Society* 42, no. 3 (July 2016): 501–17.

European Union. *A Secure Europe in a Better World*. Brussels, December 12, 2003.

Evangelista, Matthew. "The 'Soviet Threat': Intentions, Capabilities, and Context." *Diplomatic History* 22, no. 3 (July 1998): 439–49.

Fast, Nathaneal J., Deborah H. Gruenfeld, Niro Sivanthan, and Adam D. Galinsky. "Illusory Control: A Generative Force Behind Power's Far-Reaching Effects." *Psychological Science* 20, no. 4 (April 2009): 502–508.

Fast, Nathaneal J., Niro Sivanathan, Nicole D. Mayer, and Adam D. Galinsky. "Power and Overconfident Decision-Making." *Organizational Behavior and Human Decision Processes* 117, no. 2 (March 2012): 249–60.

Fazal, Tanisha M. "Dead Wrong? Battle Deaths, Military Medicine, and Exaggerated Reports of War's Demise." *International Security* 39, no. 1 (Summer 2014): 95–125.

——. *State Death: The Politics and Geography of Conquest, Occupation, and Annexation*. Princeton, NJ: Princeton University Press, 2007.

Feith, Douglas. *War and Decision: Inside the Pentagon at the Dawn of the War on Terrorism*. New York: Harper, 2008.

Feldstein, Martin. "The Underfunded Pentagon." *Foreign Affairs* 86, no. 2 (March/April 2007): 134–40.

Fenigstein, Allan. "Self-Consciousness and the Overperception of Self as a Target." *Journal of Personality and Social Psychology* 47, no. 4 (October 1984): 860–70.

Ferguson, Niall. *Colossus: The Price of America's Empire*. New York: Penguin, 2004.

——. *Empire: The Rise and Demise of the British World Order and the Lessons for Global Power*. New York: Basic Books, 2002.

——. 2004. "A World Without Power." *Foreign Policy* 143 (July/August): 32–39.

Fettweis, Christopher J. "Credibility and the War on Terror." *Political Science Quarterly* 122, no. 4 (Winter 2007/2008): 607–33.

——. 2010. *Dangerous Times? The International Politics of Great Power Peace*. Washington, DC: Georgetown University Press, 2010.

——. *Pathologies of Power: Fear, Honor, Glory, and Hubris in U.S. Foreign Policy*. New York: Cambridge University Press, 2013.

Fick, David S. *Entrepreneurship in Africa: A Study of Success*. Westport, CT: Greenwood, 2002.

Finlay, David J., Ole R. Holsti, and Richard R. Fagen. *Enemies in Politics*. Chicago: Rand McNally, 1967.

Finnemore, Martha. "Legitimacy, Hypocrisy, and the Social Structure of Unipolarity: Why Being a Unipole Isn't All It's Cracked Up to Be." *World Politics* 61, no. 1 (January 2009): 58–85.

Fisher, Max. "Iranian News Agency Says the U.S. Is Secretly Run by Nazi Space Aliens." *Washington Post*, January 13, 2014.

——. "North Korea, Far from Crazy, Is All Too Rational." *New York Times*, September 10, 2016.

Fischhoff, Baruch, Paul Slovic, and Sarah Lichtenstein. "Knowing with Certainty: The Appropriateness of Extreme Confidence." *Journal of Experimental Psychology* 3, no. 4 (November 1977): 552–64.

Fiske, Susan T. "Controlling Other People: The Impact of Power on Stereotyping." *American Psychologist* 48, no. 6 (June 1993): 621–28.

Fiske, Susan T., and Eric Dépret. "Control, Interdependence, and Power: Understanding Social Cognition in Its Social Context." *European Review of Social Psychology* 7, no. 1 (1996): 31–61.

FitzGerald, Frances. *Way Out There in the Blue: Reagan, Star Wars, and the End of the Cold War*. New York: Simon & Schuster, 2000.

Flanagan, Jason C. *Imagining the Enemy: American Presidential War Rhetoric from Woodrow Wilson to George W. Bush*. Claremont, CA: Regina, 2009.

Flynn, Michael, and Michael Ledeen. *Field of Fight: How We Can Win the Global War Against Radical Islam and Its Allies*. New York: St. Martin's, 2016.

Follath, Erich. "Evidence Points to Syrian Push for Nuclear Weapons." *Der Spiegel* online, January 9, 2015. http://www.spiegel.de/international/world/evidence-points-to-syria -still-working-on-a-nuclear-weapon-a-1012209.html.

Förster, Jens, Ronald S. Friedman, and Nira Liberman. "Temporal Construal Effects on Abstract and Concrete Thinking: Consequences for Insight and Creative Cognition." *Journal of Personality and Social Psychology* 87, no. 2 (August 2004): 177–89.

Fortna, Virginia Page. *Does Peacekeeping Work? Shaping Belligerents' Choices After Civil War*. Princeton, NJ: Princeton University Press, 2008.

——. "Is Peacekeeping 'Winning the War on War'?" *Perspectives on Politics* 11, no. 2 (June 2013): 566–70.

Frank, Tenney. *Roman Imperialism*. New York: Macmillan, 1914.

Frankel, Benjamin. "The Brooding Shadow: Systemic Incentives and Nuclear Weapons Proliferation." *Security Studies* 2, nos. 3/4 (Spring/Summer 1993): 37–78.

Freedman, Lawrence. "Stephen Pinker and the Long Peace: Alliance, Deterrence, and Decline." *Journal of Cold War History* 14, no. 4 (2014): 657–72.

——. *Strategy: A History*. New York: Oxford University Press, 2013.

Frei, Daniel. *Perceived Images: U.S. and Soviet Assumptions and Perceptions in Disarmament*. Totowa, NJ: Rowman & Allanheld, 1986.

Friedman, Benjamin, and Harvey Sapolsky. "You Never Know(ism)." *Breakthroughs* 15, no. 1 (Spring 2006): 3–11.

Friedman, Thomas L. *The Lexus and the Olive Tree: Understanding Globalization.* New York: Anchor, 2000.

Friedman, Uri. "Is Terrorism Getting Worse?" *Atlantic*, July 24, 2016. https://www .theatlantic.com/international/archive/2016/07/terrorism-isis-global-america/490352/.

Frum, David, and Richard Perle. *An End to Evil: How to Win the War on Terror.* New York: Random House, 2003.

Fukuyama, Francis. *The End of History and the Last Man.* New York: Free Press, 1992.

Gaddis, John Lewis. "History, Grand Strategy, and NATO Enlargement." *Survival* 40, no. 1 (Spring 1998): 145–51.

——. "The Long Peace: Elements of Stability in the Postwar International System." *International Security* 10, no. 4 (Spring 1986): 99–142.

——. *Strategies of Containment: A Critical Appraisal of Postwar American National Security Policy.* New York: Oxford University Press, 1982.

——. *Surprise, Security, and the American Experience.* Cambridge, MA: Harvard University Press, 2004.

——. *We Now Know: Rethinking Cold War History.* New York: Oxford University Press, 1997.

Galbraith, John S. "The 'Turbulent Frontier' as a Factor in British Expansion." *Comparative Studies in Society and History* 2, no. 2 (January 1960): 150–68.

Galinsky, Adam D., Deborah H. Gruenfeld, and Joe C. Magee. "From Power to Action." *Journal of Personality and Social Psychology* 85, no. 3 (September 2003): 453–66.

Galinsky, Adam D., Joe C. Magee, M. Ena Inesi, and Deborah H Gruenfeld. "Power and Perspectives Not Taken." *Psychological Science* 17, no. 12 (December 2006): 1068–74.

Gallarotti, Giulio M. *The Power Curse: Influence and Illusion in World Politics.* Boulder, CO: Lynne Rienner, 2010.

Galtung, Johan. "An Editorial." *Journal of Peace Research* 1, no. 1 (1964): 1–4.

Gardner, Howard. *Changing Minds: The Art and Science of Changing Our Own and Other People's Minds.* Boston: Harvard Business School Press, 2006.

Garthoff, Raymond L. "On Estimating and Imputing Intentions." *International Security* 2, no. 3 (Winter 1978): 22–33.

Gartzke, Erik. "The Capitalist Peace." *American Journal of Political Science* 51, no. 1 (January 2007): 166–91.

Gat, Azar. *The Causes of War and the Spread of Peace: But Will War Rebound?* New York: Oxford University Press, 2017.

Gates, Robert M. *From the Shadows: The Ultimate Insider's Story of Five Presidents and How They Won the Cold War.* New York: Simon & Schuster, 1996.

Gavin, Francis J. "Same as It Ever Was: Nuclear Alarmism, Proliferation, and the Cold War." *International Security* 34, no. 3 (Winter 2009/2010): 7–37.

Gelb, Leslie H., and Jeanne-Paloma Zelmati. "Mission Unaccomplished." *Democracy* 13 (Summer 2009): 10–24.

George, Alexander L., and Richard Smoke. "Deterrence and Foreign Policy." *World Politics* 41, no. 2 (January 1989): 170–82.

——. *Deterrence in American Foreign Policy: Theory and Practice.* New York: Columbia University Press, 1974.

Georgesen, John C., and Monica J. Harris. "Why's My Boss Always Holding Me Down? A Meta-Analysis of Power on Performance Evaluations." *Personality and Social Psychology Review* 2, no. 3 (August 1998): 184–95.

Gholz, Eugene, and Daryl G. Press. "Protecting 'the Prize': Oil and the U.S. National Interest." *Security Studies* 19, no. 3 (July–September 2010): 453–85.

Gholz, Eugene, Daryl G. Press, and Harvey M. Sapolsky. "Come Home America: The Strategy of Restraint in the Face of Temptation." *International Security* 21, no. 4 (1997): 5–48.

Gibbons, Rebecca Davis, and Matthew Kroenig. "Reconceptualizing Nuclear Risks: Bringing Deliberate Nuclear Use Back In." *Comparative Strategy* 35, no. 5 (October 2016): 407–22.

Gilovich, Thomas, Dale Griffin, and Daniel Kahneman, eds. *Heuristics and Biases: The Psychology of Intuitive Judgment.* New York: Cambridge: Cambridge University Press, 2002.

Gilpin, Robert. "No One Loves a Political Realist." *Security Studies* 5, no. 3 (1996): 3–26.

Gittleson, Ben. "Hezbollah Leader Echoes Trump That Obama, Clinton Founded ISIS." *ABC News,* August 14, 2016. http://abcnews.go.com/Politics/hezbollah-leader-echoes-trump -obama-clinton-founded-isis/story?id=41374713.

Gladstone, Arthur. "The Conception of the Enemy." *Journal of Conflict Resolution* 3, no. 2 (June 1959): 132–37.

Gleditsch, Nils Petter. "The Liberal Moment Fifteen Years On." *International Studies Quarterly* 52, no. 4 (December 2008): 691–712.

Goertz, Gary, Paul F. Diehl, and Alexandru Balas. *The Puzzle of Peace: The Evolution of Peace in the International System.* New York: Oxford University Press, 2016.

Gohdes, Anita, and Megan Price. "First Things First: Assessing Data Quality Before Model Quality." *Journal of Conflict Resolution* 57, no. 6 (December 2013): 1090–1108.

Goldberg, Jeffrey. "The Obama Doctrine." *Atlantic* 317, no. 3 (April 2016): 70–90.

Goldgeier, James M. *Not Whether But When: The U.S. Decision to Enlarge NATO.* Washington, DC: Brookings Institution Press, 1999.

Goldman, Emily O. *Power in Uncertain Times: Strategy in the Fog of Peace.* Stanford, CA: Stanford University Press, 2011.

Goldstein, Joshua S. *Winning the War on War.* New York: Dutton, 2011.

——. "World Backsliding on Peace." *Huffington Post,* August 3, 2015. http://www .huffingtonpost.com/joshua-s-goldstein/world-backsliding-on-peace_b_7924964.html.

Goodman, Lisa A., John E. Mack, William R. Beardslee, and Roberta M. Snow. "The Threat of Nuclear War and the Nuclear Arms Race: Adolescent Experience and Perceptions." *Political Psychology* 4, no. 3 (September 1983): 501–30.

Gray, Colin S. "Clausewitz Rules, OK? The Future Is the Past—with GPS." In *Interregnum: Controversies in World Politics, 1989–1999,* ed. Michael Cox, Ken Booth, and Tim Dunn, 171–82. New York: Cambridge University Press, 1999.

——. *The Second Nuclear Age.* Boulder, CO: Lynn Reinner, 1999.

——. *The Sheriff: America's Defense of the New World Order.* Lexington: University Press of Kentucky, 2004.

——. *Weapons Don't Make War: Policy, Strategy, and Military Technology.* Lawrence: University Press of Kansas, 1993.

Greenhill, Kelly M. "Counting the Costs: The Politics of Numbers in Armed Conflicts." In *Sex, Drugs, and Body Counts: The Politics of Numbers in Global Crime and Conflict*, ed. Peter Andreas and Kelly M. Greenhill, 127–58. Ithaca, NY: Cornell University Press, 2010.

Greenwald, Anthony G. "The Totalitarian Ego: Fabrication and Revision of Personal History." *American Psychologist* 35, no. 7 (July 1980): 603–18.

Griffin, Dale W., David Dunning, and Lee Ross. "The Role of Construal Processes in Overconfident Predictions About the Self and Others." *Journal of Personality and Social Psychology* 59, no. 6 (December 1990): 1128–39.

Griffiths, Ryan D. "States, Nations, and Territorial Stability: Why Chinese Hegemony Would Be Better for International Order." *Security Studies* 25, no. 3 (July 2016): 519–45.

Gruen, Erich S. *The Hellenistic World and the Coming of Rome*. Berkeley: University of California Press, 1986.

Gruenfeld, Deborah H., M. Ena Inesi, Joe C. Magee, and Adam D. Galinsky. "Power and the Objectification of Social Targets." *Journal of Personality and Social Psychology* 95, no. 1 (July 2008): 111–27.

Guinote, Ana. "Power and Goal Pursuit." *Personality and Social Psychology Bulletin* 33, no. 8 (August 2007): 1076–87.

Guinote, Ana, and Adele Phillips. "Power Can Increase Stereotyping: Evidence from Managers and Subordinates in the Hotel Industry." *Social Psychology* 41, no. 1 (January 2010): 3–9.

Haas, Mark L. "A Geriatric Peace? The Future of U.S. Power in a World of Aging Populations." *International Security* 32, no. 1 (Summer 2007): 112–47.

Haass, Richard N. "The Age of Nonpolarity: What Will Follow U.S. Dominance." *Foreign Affairs* 87, no. 3 (May/June 2008): 44–56.

——. *The Reluctant Sheriff: The United States After the Cold War*. New York: Council on Foreign Relations Press, 1997.

Halper, Stefan, and Jonathan Clarke. *America Alone: The Neo-Conservatives and the Global Order*. New York: Cambridge University Press, 2005.

Halperin, Morton H. *Bureaucratic Politics and Foreign Policy*. Washington, DC: Brookings Institution Press, 1974.

Hampton, Jean. *Hobbes and the Social Contract Tradition*. New York: Cambridge University Press, 1986.

Hanham, Melissa. "China's Happy to Sit Out the Nuclear Arms Race." *Foreign Policy* blog, January 30, 2017. http://foreignpolicy.com/2017/01/30/chinas-happy-to-sit-out-the-nuclear -arms-race/.

Hanhimaki, Jussi M. "The (Really) Good War? Cold War Nostalgia and American Foreign Policy." *Cold War History* 14, no. 4 (November 2014): 673–83.

Harbom, Lotta, Stina Högbladh, and Peter Wallensteen. "Armed Conflict and Peace Agreements." *Journal of Peace Research* 43, no. 5 (September 2006): 617–31.

Hardt, Michael, and Antonio Negri. *Empire*. Cambridge, MA: Harvard University Press, 2000.

Harr, William V. *War and Imperialism in Republican Rome, 327–70 B.C.* Oxford: Clarendon, 1985.

Hartmann, Frederick H. *The Conservation of Enemies: A Study in Enmity.* Westport, CT: Greenwood, 1982.

Harvey, John H., Ben Harris, and Richard D. Barnes. "Actor-Observer Differences in the Perceptions of Responsibility and Freedom." *Journal of Personality and Social Psychology* 32, no. 1 (July 1975): 22–28.

Heider, Fritz. *The Psychology of Interpersonal Relations.* New York: Wiley, 1958.

Heine, Steven J., Daniel R. Lehman, Hazel Rose Markus, and Shinobu Kitayama. "Is There a Universal Need for Positive Self-Regard?" *Psychology Review* 106, no. 4 (October 1999): 766–94.

Henderson, Errol A., and J. David Singer. "'New Wars' and Rumors of 'New Wars.'" *International Interactions* 28, no. 2 (April 2002): 165–90.

Herman, Arthur. *The Idea of Decline in Western History.* New York: Free Press, 1997.

Hernandez, Miriam, and Sheena S. Iyengar. "What Drives Whom? A Cultural Perspective on Human Agency." *Social Cognition* 19, no. 3 (June 2001): 269–94.

Herrmann, Richard K. "American Perspectives of Soviet Foreign Policy: Reconsidering Three Competing Perspectives." *Political Psychology* 6, no. 3 (September 1985): 375–411.

——. "Analyzing Soviet Images of the United States: A Psychological Theory and Empirical Study." *Journal of Conflict Resolution* 29, no. 4 (December 1985): 665–97.

——. *Perceptions and Behavior in Soviet Foreign Policy.* Pittsburgh: University of Pittsburgh Press, 1985.

Herrmann, Richard K., James F. Voss, Tonya Y. E. Schooler, and Joseph Ciarrochi. "Images in International Relations: An Experimental Test of Cognitive Schemata." *International Studies Quarterly* 41, no. 3 (September 1997): 403–33.

Herrmann, Richard K., and Michael P. Fischerkeller. "Beyond the Enemy Image and Spiral Model: Cognitive-Strategic Research After the Cold War." *International Organization* 49, no. 3 (Summer 1995): 415–50.

Herz, John H. "Idealist Internationalism and the Security Dilemma." *World Politics* 2, no. 2 (January 1950): 157–80.

Hibbing, John R., Kevin B. Smith, and John R. Alford. "Differences in Negativity Bias Underlie Variations in Political Ideology." *Behavioral and Brain Sciences* 37, no. 3 (June 2014): 297–307.

Hill, Chris. "Avoiding the Temptation to Do Nothing." *Time,* April 3, 2017.

Hirschman, Albert O. *National Power and the Structure of Foreign Trade.* Berkeley: University of California Press, 1980.

Hobbes, Thomas. *Leviathan.* New York: Cambridge University Press, 1996.

Hoffman, David E. "I Had a Funny Feeling in My Gut." *Washington Post,* February 10, 1999.

——. *The Dead Hand: The Untold Story of the Cold War Arms Race and Its Dangerous Legacy.* New York: Anchor, 2009.

Hofstadter, Richard. *The Paranoid Style in American Politics and Other Essays.* New York: Knopf, 1965.

Hogeveen, Jeremy, Michael Inzlicht, and Sukhvinder S. Obhi. "Power Changes How the Brain Responds to Others." *Journal of Experimental Psychology: General* 143, no. 2 (April 2014): 755–62.

Holbrook, Colin, Lucia López-Rodriguez, Daniel M. T. Fessler, et al. "Gulliver's Politics: Conservatives Envision Potential Enemies as Readily Vanquished and Physically Small." *Social Psychological and Personality Science* (2017).

Hopf, Ted. "Polarity, the Offense-Defense Balance, and War." *American Political Science Review* 85, no. 2 (June 1991): 475–93.

Horgan, John. *The End of War*. San Francisco, CA: McSweeney's, 2012.

Horney, Karen. "Culture and Neurosis." *American Sociological Review* 1, no. 2 (April 1936): 221–30.

Howorth, Jolyon, and Anand Menon. "Still Not Pushing Back: Why the European Union Is Not Balancing the United States." *Journal of Conflict Resolution* 53, no. 5 (October 2009): 727–44.

Hoyt, Paul D. "The 'Rogue State' Image in American Foreign Policy." *Global Society* 14, no. 2 (April 2000): 297–310.

Huber, Michaela, Leaf Van Boven, A. Peter McGraw, and Laura Johnson-Graham. "Whom to Help? Immediacy Bias in Judgments and Decisions About Humanitarian Aid." *Organizational Behavior and Human Decision Processes* 115, no. 2 (July 2011): 283–93.

Hughes, Daniel J., ed. *Moltke on the Art of War*. New York: Ballantine, 1996.

Human Security Report Project. *Human Security Report 2013: The Decline in Global Violence*. Vancouver: Human Security Press, 2013.

Huntington, Samuel P. "The Clash of Civilizations?" *Foreign Affairs* 72, no. 3 (Summer 1993): 22–49.

——. "The U.S.: Decline or Renewal?" *Foreign Affairs* 67, no. 2 (Winter 1988): 76–96.

——. "Why International Primacy Matters." *International Security* 17, no. 4 (Spring 1993): 68–83.

Hymans, Jacques E. C. *Achieving Nuclear Ambitions: Scientists, Politicians, and Proliferation*. New York: Cambridge University Press, 2012.

——. *The Psychology of Nuclear Proliferation: Identity, Emotions, and Foreign Policy*. New York: Cambridge University Press, 2006.

Ignatieff, Michael. "The American Empire: The Burden." *New York Times Magazine*, January 5, 2003.

Ikenberry, G. John., ed. *America Unrivaled: The Future of the Balance of Power*. Ithaca, NY: Cornell University Press, 2002.

——. "America's Imperial Ambition." *Foreign Affairs* 81, no. 5 (September/October 2002): 44–60.

——. "The End of the Neo-Conservative Moment." *Survival* 46, no. 1 (Spring 2004): 7–22.

——. "The Future of the Liberal World Order." *Foreign Affairs* 90, no. 3 (May/June 2011): 56–68.

——. *Liberal Leviathan: The Origins, Crisis, and Transformation of the American World Order*. Princeton, NJ: Princeton University Press, 2011.

Ikenberry, G. John, Michael Mastunduno, and William C. Wohlforth, eds. *International Relations Theory and the Consequences of Unipolarity*. New York: Cambridge University Press, 2011.

Iklé, Fred Charles. "The Second Coming of the Nuclear Age." *Foreign Affairs* 75, no. 1 (January/February 1996): 119–28.

Indyk, Martin S. "The War in Iraq Did Not Force Gadaffi's Hand." *Financial Times*, March 9, 2004.

Ingraham, Christopher. "Chart: The Animals That Are Most Likely to Kill You This Summer." *Washington Post*, June 16, 2015.

Institute for Economics and Peace. *Global Peace Index 2016*. New York: Institute for Economics and Peace (June 2016). http://economicsandpeace.org/wp-content/uploads/2016/06/GPI-2016-Report_2.pdf.

International Institute of Strategic Studies. *The Military Balance 2016*. London: IISS, 2016.

International Monetary Fund. *World Economic Outlook Database*. 2016. http://www.imf.org/external/pubs/ft/weo/2016/01/weodata/index.aspx.

Jackson, Derrick Z. "The Westmoreland Mind-Set." *New York Times*, July 25, 2005.

Jackson, William D. "Soviet Images of the U.S. as a Nuclear Adversary, 1969–1979." *World Politics* 33, no. 4 (July 1981): 614–38.

Jacques, Martin. *When China Rules the World: The End of the Western World and the Birth of a New Global Order*, 2nd ed. New York: Penguin, 2012.

James, Aaron. *Assholes: A Theory*. New York: Anchor, 2012.

James, Patrick, and Michael Brecher. "Stability and Polarity: New Paths for Inquiry." *Journal of Peace Research* 25, no. 1 (March 1988): 31–42.

Jehl, Douglas. "CIA Nominee Wary of Budget Cuts." *New York Times*, February 3, 1993.

Jentleson, Bruce W., and Christopher A. Whytock. "Who 'Won' Libya? The Force-Diplomacy Debate and Its Implications for Theory and Policy." *International Security* 30, no. 3 (Winter 2005/2006): 47–86.

Jervis, Robert. "Cooperation Under the Security Dilemma." *World Politics* 30, no. 2 (January 1978): 167–214.

——. "Images and the Gulf War." In *The Political Psychology of the Gulf War: Leaders, Publics, and the Process of Conflict*, ed. S. A. Renshon, 173–79. Pittsburgh: University of Pittsburgh Press, 1993.

——. "International Primacy: Is the Game Worth the Candle?" *International Security* 17, no. 4 (Spring 1993): 52–67.

——. *The Logic of Images in International Relations*. Princeton, NJ: Princeton University Press, 1970.

——. *Perception and Misperception in International Politics*. Princeton, NJ: Princeton University Press, 1976.

——. "The Remaking of a Unipolar World." *Washington Quarterly* 29, no. 3 (Summer 2006): 7–19.

——. "Theories of War in an Era of Leading Power Peace." *American Political Science Review* 96, no. 1 (March 2002): 1–14.

——. "Understanding Beliefs and Threat Inflation." In *American Foreign Policy and the Politics of Fear: Threat Inflation Since 9/11*, ed. A. Trevor Thrall and Jane K. Cramer, 16–39. New York: Routledge, 2009.

——. "Understanding the Bush Doctrine." *Political Science Quarterly* 118, no. 3 (Fall 2003): 365–88.

——. "Unipolarity: A Structural Perspective." *World Politics* 61, no. 1 (January 2009): 188–213.

——. "The United States and Iran: Perceptions and Policy Traps." In *U.S.-Iran Misperceptions: A Dialogue*, ed. Abbas Maleki and John Tirman, 15–36. New York: Bloomsbury, 2014.

——. "U.S. Grand Strategy: Mission Impossible." *Naval War College Review* 51, no. 3 (Summer 1998): 118–133.

Jervis, Robert, and Jack Snyder, eds. *Dominoes and Bandwagons: Strategic Beliefs and Great Power Competition in the Eurasian Rimland*. New York: Oxford University Press, 1991.

Ji, Li-Jun, Kaiping Peng, and Richard E. Nisbett. "Culture, Control, and Perception of Relationships in the Environment." *Journal of Personality and Social Psychology* 78, no. 5 (May 2000): 943–55.

Ji, You. "Dealing with the Malacca Dilemma: China's Effort to Protect Its Energy Supply." *Strategic Analysis* 31, no. 3 (May 2007): 467–89.

Joffe, Josef. *The Myth of America's Decline: Politics, Economics, and a Half-Century of False Prophecies*. New York: Norton, 2014.

Johnson, Dominic D. P. *Overconfidence and War: The Havoc and Glory of Positive Illusions*. Cambridge, MA: Harvard University Press, 2014.

Johnson, Robert H. *Improbable Dangers: U.S. Conceptions of Threat in the Cold War and After*. New York: St. Martin's Press, 1994.

Jones, Edward E., and Richard Nisbett. *The Actor and the Observer: Divergent Perceptions of the Causes of Behavior*. Morristown, NJ: General Learning Press, 1971.

——. "The Actor and the Observer: Divergent Perceptions of the Causes of Behavior." In *Attribution: Perceiving the Causes of Behavior*, ed. Edward E. Jones et al., 79–94. Morristown, NJ: General Learning Press, 1972.

Joseph, Robert G., and Keith B. Payne. "On Deterring Iran." *National Review*, June 25, 2012.

Kagan, Donald, and Frederick W. Kagan. *While America Sleeps: Self-Delusion, Military Weakness, and the Threat to Peace Today*. New York: St. Martin's Press, 2000.

Kagan, Robert. "Backing Into World War III." *Foreign Policy*, February 6, 2017. http://foreignpolicy.com/2017/02/06/backing-into-world-war-iii-russia-china-trump-obama/.

——. "The Benevolent Empire." *Foreign Policy* 111 (Summer 1988): 24–35.

——. *Of Paradise and Power: America and Europe in the New World Order*. New York: Knopf, 2003.

——. *The Return of History and the End of Dreams*. New York: Knopf, 2008.

——. "The United States Must Resist a Return to Spheres of Interest in the International System." Brookings Institution blog, February 19, 2015. http://www.brookings.edu/blogs/order-from-chaos/posts/2015/02/19-united-states-must-resist-return-to-spheres-of-interest-international-system-kagan.

——. *The World America Made*. New York: Knopf, 2012.

Kagan, Robert, and William Kristol. "National Interest and Global Responsibility." In *Present Dangers: Crisis and Opportunity in American Foreign and Defense Policy*, ed. Robert Kagan and William Kristol, 3–24. San Francisco: Encounter, 2000.

Kahneman, Daniel, and Amos Tversky. "Prospect Theory: An Analysis of Decision Under Risk." *Econometrica* 47, no. 2 (March 1979): 263–91.

Kahneman, Daniel, Amos Tversky, and Paul Slovic, eds. *Judgment Under Uncertainty: Heuristics and Biases*. New York: Cambridge University Press, 1982.

Kahneman, Daniel, and Jonathan Renshon. "Hawkish Biases." In *American Foreign Policy and the Politics of Fear: Threat Inflation Since 9/11*, ed. A. Trevor Thrall and Jane K. Cramer, 79–96. New York: Routledge, 2009.

Kaldor, Mary. *New and Old Wars: Organized Violence in a Global Era*. Stanford, CA: Stanford University Press, 1999; 3rd ed., 2012.

Kalyvas, Stathis N. "'New' and 'Old' Civil Wars: A Valid Distinction?" *World Politics* 54, no. 1 (October 2001): 99–118.

Kanai, Ryota, Tom Feilden, Colin Firth, and Geraint Rees. "Political Orientations Are Correlated with Brain Structure in Young Adults." *Current Biology* 21, no. 8 (April 2001): 677–80.

Kang, David C. "International Relations Theory and the Second Korean War." *International Studies Quarterly* 47, no. 3 (September 2003): 301–324.

Kanwisher, Nancy. "Cognitive Heuristics and American Security Policy." *Journal of Conflict Resolution* 33, no. 4 (December 1989): 652–55.

Kaplan, Lawrence F., and William Kristol. *The War Over Iraq: Saddam's Tyranny and America's Mission*. San Francisco: Encounter, 2003.

Kaplan, Robert D. "The Coming Anarchy." *Atlantic Monthly* 273, no. 2 (February 1994): 44–76.

——. "Supremacy by Stealth: Ten Rules for Managing the World." *Atlantic Monthly* 292, no. 1 (July/August 2003): 65–83.

Kardes, Frank R., A. V. Muthukrushnan, and Vladimir Pashkevich. "On the Conditions Under Which Experience and Motivation Accentuate Bias in Intuitive Judgment." In *The Routines of Decision-Making*, ed. Tilmann Betsch and Susanne Haberstroh, 139–56. New York: Psychology Press, 2005.

Kaysen, Carl. "Is War Obsolete? A Review Essay." *International Security* 14, no. 4 (Spring 1990): 42–64.

Keen, Sam. *Faces of the Enemy: Reflections of a Hostile Imagination*. New York: Harper Collins, 1991.

Kelman, Herbert C. "Social-Psychological Approaches to the Study of International Relations: The Question of Relevance." In *International Behavior: A Social-Psychological Analysis*, Herbert C. Kelman, 565–607. New York: Holt, Rinehart, and Winston, 1965.

Keltner, Dacher. "Don't Let Power Corrupt You." *Harvard Business Review* 94, no. 10 (October 2016): 112–15.

——. *The Power Paradox: How We Gain and Lose Influence*. New York: Penguin, 2016.

Keltner, Dacher, Deborah H. Gruenfeld, Adam Galinsky, and Michael W. Kraus. "Paradoxes of Power: Dynamics of the Acquisition, Experience, and Social Regulation of Social Power." In *The Social Psychology of Power*, ed. Ana Guinote and Theresa K. Vescio, 177–208. New York: Guilford, 2010.

Keltner, Dacher, Deborah H. Gruenfeld, and Cameron Anderson. "Power, Approach, and Inhibition," *Psychological Review* 110, no. 2 (April 2003): 265–84.

Kennan, George F. *At a Century's Ending: Reflections 1982–1995*. New York: Norton, 1996.

——. "The Charge in the Soviet Union (Kennan) to the Secretary of State." February 22, 1946. http://www2.gwu.edu/~nsarchiv/coldwar/documents/episode-1/kennan.htm.

——. *The Cloud of Danger: Current Realities of American Foreign Policy*. Boston: Little, Brown, 1977.

Kennedy, Paul. "The Good Old Days of the Cold War." *Los Angeles Times*, February 18, 2007.

——. "The Next American Century?" *World Policy Journal* 16, no. 1 (Spring 1999): 52–58.

——. *The Rise and Fall of the Great Powers: Economic Change and Military Conflict from 1500 to 2000*. New York: Random House, 1987.

Keohane, Robert O. *After Hegemony: Cooperation and Discord in the World Political Economy*. Princeton, NJ: Princeton University Press, 1984.

——. "International Institutions: Two Approaches." *International Studies Quarterly* 32, no. 4 (December 1988): 379–96.

Keohane, Robert O., and Joseph S. Nye. *Power and Interdependence: World Politics in Transition*. Boston: Little, Brown, 1977.

——. "Power and Interdependence Revisited." *International Organization* 41, no. 4 (Autumn 1987): 725–53.

Keohane, Robert O., and Lisa L. Martin. "The Promise of Institutional Theory." *International Security* 20, no. 1 (Summer 1995): 39–51.

Kindleberger, Charles. *The World in Depression, 1929–1939*. Berkeley: University of California Press, 1974.

Kipnis, David. *The Powerholders*. Chicago: University of Chicago Press, 1976.

Kirshner, Jonathan. "Dollar Primacy and American Power: What's at Stake?" *Review of International Political Economy* 15, no. 3 (August 2008): 418–38.

Kissinger, Henry A. "Continuity and Change in American Foreign Policy." *Society* 15, no. 1 (November/December 1977): 97–103.

——. *The Necessity for Choice: Prospects of American Foreign Policy*. Garden City, NY: Anchor, 1962.

——. *On China*. New York: Penguin, 2012.

Knowlton, Brian. "Gates Calls European Mood a Danger to Peace." *New York Times*, February 23, 2010.

Kohut, Heinz. *The Analysis of the Self: A Systemic Approach to the Psychoanalytic Treatment of Narcissistic Personality Disorders*. Chicago: University of Chicago Press, 2009.

Koolhaas, Jaap M., Alessandro Bartolomucci, Bauke Buwalda, et al. "Stress Revisited: A Critical Evaluation of the Stress Concept." *Neuroscience and Behavioral Reviews* 35, no. 4 (April 2011): 1291–1301.

Krasner, Stephen D., ed. *International Regimes*. Ithaca, NY: Cornell University Press, 1983.

Krauthammer, Charles. "In Defense of Democratic Realism." *National Interest* 77 (Fall 2004): 15–25.

——. "The Unipolar Moment." *Foreign Affairs* 70, no. 1 (1990/1991): 23–33.

Krepinevich, Andrew F., Jr. "Strategy in a Time of Austerity: Why the Pentagon Should Focus on Assuring Access." *Foreign Affairs* 91, no. 6 (November/December 2012): 58–69.

Kristensen, Hans M., and Robert S. Norris. "Russian Nuclear Forces, 2016." *Bulletin of the Atomic Scientists* 72, no. 3 (April 16, 2016): 125–34.

Kristol, William, and Robert Kagan. "Toward a Neo-Reaganite Foreign Policy." *Foreign Affairs* 75, no. 4 (July/August 1996): 18–33.

Kroenig, Matthew. *A Time to Attack: The Looming Iranian Nuclear Threat.* New York: St. Martin's, 2014.

——. "Time to Attack Iran: Why a Strike Is the Least Bad Option." *Foreign Affairs* 91, no. 1 (January/February 2012): 76–86.

Kugler, Jacek. "Terror Without Deterrence: Reassessing the Role of Nuclear Weapons." *Journal of Conflict Resolution* 28, no. 2 (September 1984): 470–506.

Kupchan, Charles. "After Pax Americana: Benign Power, Regional Integration, and the Sources of a Stable Multipolarity." *International Security* 23, no. 2 (Fall 1988): 40–79.

——. "The Decline of the West: Why America Must Prepare for the End of Dominance." *Atlantic*, March 20, 2012.

——. *The End of the American Era: U.S. Foreign Policy and the Geopolitics of the Twenty-First Century.* New York: Knopf, 2002.

——. "Life After Pax Americana." *World Policy Journal* 16, no. 3 (Fall 1999): 20–27.

Kuperman, Alan J. "There's Only One Way to Stop Iran." *New York Times*, December 24, 2009.

Lacina, Bethany, and Nils Petter Gleditsch. "The Waning of War Is Real: A Response to Gohdes and Price." *Journal of Conflict Resolution* 57, no. 6 (December 2013): 1109–27.

Lacina, Bethany, Nils Peter Gleditsch, and Bruce Russett. "The Declining Risk of Death in Battle." *International Studies Quarterly* 50, no. 3 (September 2006): 673–80.

Lake, David A. "Leadership, Hegemony, and the International Economy: Naked Emperor or Tattered Monarch with Potential?" *International Studies Quarterly* 37, no. 4 (December 1993): 459–489.

Lammers, Joris, and Diederik A. Stapel. "Power Increases Dehumanization." *Group Processes and Intergroup Relations* 14, no. 1 (January 2011): 113–26.

Langer, Ellen J. "The Illusion of Control." *Journal of Personality and Social Psychology* 32, no. 2 (August 1975): 311–28.

Langer, Ellen J., and Jane Roth. "Heads I Win, Tails It's Chance: The Illusion of Control as a Function of the Sequence of Outcomes in a Purely Chance Task." *Journal of Personality and Social Psychology* 32, no. 6 (December 1975): 951–55.

Lanteigne, Marc. "China's Maritime Security and the 'Malacca Dilemma.'" *Asian Security* 4, no. 2 (May 2008): 143–61.

Larson, Deborah Welch. *Anatomy of Mistrust: U.S.-Soviet Relations During the Cold War.* Ithaca, NY: Cornell University Press, 1997.

——. *Origins of Containment: A Psychological Explanation.* Princeton, NJ: Princeton University Press, 1985.

Layne, Christopher. "Superpower Disengagement." *Foreign Policy* 77 (Winter 1989/1990): 17–40.

——. "This Time It's Real: The End of Unipolarity and the *Pax Americana*." *International Studies Quarterly* 56, no. 1 (March 2012): 202–13.

——. "The Unipolar Illusion: Why New Great Powers Will Rise." *International Security* 17, no. 4 (Spring 1993): 5–51.

——. "The Unipolar Illusion Revisited: The Coming End of the United States' Unipolar Moment." *International Security* 31, no. 2 (Fall 2006): 7–41.

——. "The Waning of U.S. Hegemony—Myth or Reality?" *International Security* 34, no. 1 (Summer 2009): 147–72.

Lebow, Richard Ned. "Deterrence: Then and Now." *Journal of Strategic Studies* 28, no. 5 (October 2005): 765–73.

——. *Why Nations Fight: Past and Future Motives for War.* New York: Cambridge University Press, 2010.

Lebow, Richard Ned, and Janice Gross Stein. "Afghanistan, Carter and Foreign Policy Change: The Limits of Cognitive Models." In *Diplomacy, Force, and Leadership: Essays in Honor of Alexander L. George*, ed. Dan Caldwell and Timothy J. McKeown, 95–128. Boulder, CO: Westview, 1993.

Ledeen, Michael. *Accomplice to Evil: Iran and the War Against the West.* New York: St. Martin's, 2009.

——. "The Lessons of Lebanon." *Commentary* 77, no. 5 (May 1984): 15–22.

Lee, Jenny (Jiyeon), and Gerard T. Kyle. "Recollection Consistency of Festival Consumption Emotions." *Journal of Travel Research* 51, no. 2 (March 2012): 178–90.

Leebaert, Derek. *The Fifty-Year Wound: The True Price of America's Cold War Victory.* New York: Little, Brown, 2002.

Leogrande, William M. "The Cuba Lobby." *Foreign Policy*, April 26, 2013.

Lerner, Jennifer S., and Philip E. Tetlock. "Accounting for the Effects of Accountability." *Psychological Bulletin* 125, no. 2 (March 1999): 255–75.

Leverett, Flynt L. "Why Libya Gave Up on the Bomb." *New York Times*, January 23, 2004.

Lewandowsky, Stephan, Ullrich K. H. Ecker, Colleen M. Seifert, et al. "Misinformation and Its Correction: Continued Influence and Successful Debiasing." *Psychological Science in the Public Interest* 13, no. 3 (September 2012): 106–31.

Lewin, Kurt. *Field Theory in Social Science: Selected Theoretical Papers.* New York: Harper & Row, 1951.

Lewis, Bernard. *The End of Modern History in the Middle East.* Stanford, CA: Hoover Institute Press, 2011.

Lewis, Jeffrey. *Paper Tigers: China's Nuclear Posture.* London: International Institute for Strategic Studies, 2014.

Lewis, Michael. *The Undoing Project: A Friendship That Changed Our Minds.* New York: Norton, 2016.

Liberman, Nira, and Yaacov Trope. "The Role of Feasibility and Desirability Considerations in Near and Distant Future Decisions: A Test of Temporal Construal Theory." *Journal of Personality and Social Psychology* 75, no. 1 (July 1998): 5–18.

Liberman, Nira, Yaacov Trope, and Elena Stephan. "Psychological Distance." In *Social Psychology: Handbook of Basic Principles*, 2nd ed., ed. Arie W. Kruglanski and E. Tory Higgins, 353–83. New York: Guilford, 2007.

Liberman, Peter. *Does Conquest Pay? The Exploitation of Industrialized Societies.* Princeton, NJ: Princeton University Press, 1996.

Lieber, Keir A., and Daryl G. Press. "The End of MAD? The Nuclear Dimension of U.S. Primacy." *International Security* 30, no. 4 (Spring 2006): 7–44.

——. "The New Era of Counterforce: Technological Change and the Future of Deterrence." *International Security* 41, no. 4 (Spring 2017): 9–49.

Lieber, Robert J. *The American Era: Power and Strategy for the Twenty-First Century.* New York: Cambridge University Press, 2005.

Lilienfeld, Scott O., Rachel Ammirati, and Kristin Landfield. "Giving Debiasing Away: Can Psychological Research on Correcting Cognitive Errors Promote Human Welfare?" *Perspectives on Psychological Science* 4, no. 4 (July 2009): 390–98.

Lind, Michael. *The American Way of Strategy.* New York: Oxford University Press, 2006.

——. "The End of Pax Americana?" *Salon*, September 29, 2009. http://www.salon.com/2009/09/29/obama_pax_americana/.

Loftus, Elizabeth. *Memory.* Reading, MA: Addison Wesley, 1980.

Long, Austin, and Brendan Rittenhouse Green. "Stalking the Secure Second Strike: Intelligence, Counterforce, and Nuclear Strategy." *Journal of Strategic Studies* 38, no. 1–2 (February 2015): 38–73.

Lord, Charles G., Lee Ross, and Mark R. Lepper. "Biased Assimilation and Attitude Polarization: The Effects of Prior Theories on Subsequently Considered Evidence." *Journal of Personality and Social Psychology* 37, no. 11 (November 1979): 2098–2109.

Luard, Evan. *War in International Society: A Study in International Sociology.* London: I. B. Tauris, 1986.

Luttwak, Edward N. *The Endangered American Dream: How to Stop the United States from Becoming a Third World Country and How to Win the Geo-Economic Struggle for Industrial Supremacy.* New York: Simon and Schuster, 1993.

——. "Where Are the Great Powers? At Home with the Kids." *Foreign Affairs* 73, no. 4 (July/August 1994): 23–28.

Lyakhovskiy, Aleksandr Antonovich. *Inside the Soviet Invasion of Afghanistan and the Seizure of Kabul, December 1979,* Cold War International History Project Working Paper 51. Washington, DC: Woodrow Wilson Center, 2007.

Lykke, Arthur F., Jr. "Toward an Understanding of Military Strategy." In *Military Strategy: Theory and Application*, 3–8. Carlisle, PA: U.S. Army War College, 1989.

Mack, Andrew. "Global Political Violence: Explaining the Post–Cold War Decline," Coping with Crisis Working Paper Series, International Peace Academy, March 2007.

MacDonald, Paul K., and Joseph A. Parent. "Graceful Decline: The Surprising Success of Great Power Retrenchment." *International Security* 35, no. 4 (Spring 2011): 7–44.

Mackey, Robert. "Borne by Facebook, Conspiracy Theory That U.S. Created ISIS Spreads Across the Middle East." *New York Times*, August 26. 2014.

Mahbubani, Kishore. "Smart Power, Chinese Style." *American Interest* 3, no. 4 (March/April 2008): 68–77.

Malegam, Jehangir Yezdi. *The Sleep of the Behemoth: Disputing Peace and Violence in Medieval Europe, 1000–1200*. Ithaca, NY: Cornell University Press, 2013.

Mallaby, Sebastian. "The Reluctant Imperialist: Terrorism, Failed States, and the Case for American Empire." *Foreign Affairs* 81, no. 2 (March/April 2002): 2–7.

Malle, Bertram F. "The Actor-Observer Asymmetry in Attribution: A (Surprising) Meta-Analysis." *Psychological Bulletin* 136, no. 6 (November 2006): 895–919.

Maltby, William S. *The Rise and Decline of the Spanish Empire*. New York: Palgrave Macmillan, 2008.

Mandelbaum, Michael. "The Bomb, Dread, and Eternity." *International Security* 5, no. 2, (Autumn 1980): 3–23.

——. *The Case for Goliath: How America Acts as the World's Government in the Twenty-First Century*. New York: Public Affairs, 2005.

——. "Foreign Policy as Social Work." *Foreign Affairs* 75, no. 1 (January/February 2006): 16–32.

——. *The Nuclear Revolution: International Politics Before and After Hiroshima*. Cambridge: Cambridge University Press, 1981.

Mansfield, Edward D., and Brian M. Pollins. *Economic Interdependence and International Conflict: New Perspectives on an Enduring Debate*. Ann Arbor: University of Michigan Press, 2003.

Markus, Hazel Rose, and Shinobu Kitayama. "Culture and the Self: Implications for Cognition, Emotion, and Motivation." *Psychological Review* 98, no. 2 (April 1991): 224–53.

Marshall, Andrew W. *Long-Term Competition with the Soviets: A Framework for Strategic Analysis*. Santa Monica, CA: RAND, 1972.

Marshall, Monty G., and Benjamin R. Cole. *Global Report 2014: Conflict, Governance, and State Fragility*. Vienna, VA: Center for Systemic Peace, 2014.

May, Ernest. *"Lessons" of the Past: The Uses and Misuses of History in American Foreign Policy*. New York: Oxford University Press, 1972.

Mazarr, Michael J. "The Rise and Fall of the Failed-State Paradigm: Requiem for a Decade of Distraction." *Foreign Affairs* 93, no. 1 (January/February 2014): 113–21.

McDermott, Rose. "Experimental Methods in Political Science." *Annual Review of Political Science* 5 (2002): 31–61.

McDougall, Walter A. "Can the United States Do Grand Strategy?" *Orbis* 54, no. 2 (Spring 2001): 165–184.

McMahon, Robert J. "Credibility and World Power: Exploring the Psychological Dimension in Postwar American Diplomacy." *Diplomatic History* 15, no. 4 (Fall 1991): 455–71.

Mead, Walter Russell. *Mortal Splendor: The American Empire in Transition*. Boston: Houghton Mifflin, 1988.

——. *Power, Terror, Peace, and War: America's Grand Strategy in a World at Risk*. New York: Knopf, 2004.

Mearsheimer, John J. "Back to Future: Instability in Europe After the Cold War." *International Security* 15, no. 1 (Summer 1990): 5–56.

——. "The Case for a Ukrainian Nuclear Deterrent." *Foreign Affairs* 72, no. 3 (Summer 1993): 50–66.

——. "Disorder Restored." In *Rethinking America's Security: Beyond Cold War to New World Order*, ed. Graham Allison and Gregory F. Treverton, 213–37. New York: Norton, 1992.

——. *The Tragedy of Great Power Politics.* New York: Norton, 2001.

——. *Why Leaders Lie: The Truth About Lying in International Politics.* New York: Oxford University Press, 2011.

——. "Why the Ukraine Crisis Is the West's Fault." *Foreign Affairs* 93, no. 5 (September/October 2014): 77–89.

——. "Why We Will Soon Miss the Cold War." *Atlantic Monthly* 266, no. 2 (August 1990): 35–50.

Meiser, Jeffrey W. "Ends + Ways + Means = (Bad) Strategy." *Parameters* 46, no. 4 (Winter 2016/2017): 81–91.

Melander, Erik, Magnus Öberg, and Jonathan Hall. "Are 'New Wars' More Atrocious? Battle Severity, Civilians Killed, and Forced Migration Before and After the End of the Cold War." *European Journal of International Relations* 15, no. 3 (September 2009): 505–36.

Mercer, Jonathan. *Reputation in International Politics.* Ithaca, NY: Cornell University Press, 1996.

Mezulis, Amy H., Lyn Y. Abramson, Janet S. Hyde, and Benjamin L. Hankin. "Is There a Universal Positivity Bias in Attributions? A Meta-Analytic Review of the Individual, Developmental, and Cultural Differences in the Self-Serving Attributional Bias." *Psychological Bulletin* 130, no. 5 (September 2004): 711–47.

Miroff, Nick. "'Plan Colombia': How Washington Learned to Love Latin American Intervention Again." *Washington Post*, September 18, 2016.

Mitchell, Terence R., and Leigh Thompson. "A Theory of Temporal Adjustments of the Evaluation of Events: Rosy Prospection and Rosy Retrospection." In *Advances in Managerial Cognition and Organizational Information-Processing*, ed. Chuck Stubbart et al., 5:85–114. Greenwich, CT: JAI, 1994.

Mitchell, Terence R., Leigh Thompson, Erika Peterson, and Randy Cronk. "Temporal Adjustments in the Evaluation of Events: The 'Rosy' View." *Journal of Experimental Social Psychology* 33, no. 4 (July 1997): 421–48.

Mommsen, Theodor. *The History of Rome.* New York: Dutton, 1911.

Monat, Alan, James R. Averill, and Richard S. Lazarus. "Anticipatory Stress Reactions Under Various Conditions of Uncertainty." *Journal of Personality and Social Psychology* 24, no. 2 (November 1972): 237–53.

Monteiro, Nuno P. *Theory of Unipolar Politics.* New York: Cambridge University Press, 2014.

Monten, Jonathan. "Primacy and Grand Strategic Beliefs in U.S. Unilateralism." *Global Governance* 13, no. 1 (January–March 2007): 119–38.

Moore, Don A., and Paul J. Healy. "The Trouble with Overconfidence." *Psychological Review* 115, no. 2 (April 2008): 502–17.

Moravchik, Joshua. "War with Iran Is Probably Our Best Option." *Washington Post*, March 13, 2015.

Morgan, Patrick M. "Multilateral Institutions as Restraints on Major War." In *The Waning of Major War: Theories and Debates*, ed. Raimo Väyrynen, 160–84. New York: Routledge, 2006.

Mousavian, Seyed Hossein. "Iranian Perceptions of U.S. Policy Toward Iran: Ayatollah Khamenei's Mind Set." In *U.S.-Iran Misperceptions: A Dialogue*, ed. Abbas Maleki and John Tirman, 37–56. New York: Bloomsbury, 2014.

Mueller, John. *Atomic Obsession: Nuclear Alarmism from Hiroshima to Al-Qaeda*. New York: Oxford University Press, 2009.

——. "Embracing Threatlessness: U.S. Military Spending, Newt Gingrich, and the Costa Rica Option." In *The Case for Restraint in U.S. Foreign Policy*, ed. A. Trevor Thrall and Benjamin H. Friedman. Washington, DC: Cato Institute Press, forthcoming.

——. "The Essential Irrelevance of Nuclear Weapons: Stability in the Post War World." *International Security* 13, no. 2 (Fall 1988): 55–79.

——. *Quiet Cataclysm: Reflections on the Recent Transformation of World Politics*. New York: Harper Collins, 1995.

——. *The Remnants of War*. Ithaca, NY: Cornell University Press, 2004.

——. *Retreat from Doomsday: The Obsolescence of Major War*. New York: Basic Books, 1989.

——. "War Has Almost Ceased to Exist: An Assessment." *Political Science Quarterly* 124, no. 2 (Summer 2009): 297–321.

Mullen, Brian, and Catherine A. Riordan. "Self-Serving Attributions for Performance in Naturalistic Settings: A Meta-Analytic Review." *Journal of Applied Social Psychology* 18, no. 1 (January 1988): 3–22.

Murray, Christopher J. L., Gary King, Alan D. Lopez, et al. "Armed Conflict as a Public Health Problem." *British Medical Journal* 324, no. 7333 (February 9, 2002): 346–49.

Murray, Shoon Kathleen, and Jason Meyers. "Do People Need Foreign Enemies? American Leaders' Beliefs After the Soviet Demise." *Journal of Conflict Resolution* 43, no. 5 (October 1999): 555–69.

Murray, Shoon Kathleen, and Jonathan A. Cowden. "The Role of 'Enemy Images' and Ideology in Elite Belief Systems." *International Studies Quarterly* 43, no. 3 (September 1999): 455–81.

Murray, Williamson. "Thoughts on Grand Strategy." In *The Shaping of Grand Strategy*, ed. Williamson Murray et al., 1–33. New York: Cambridge University Press, 2011.

Nacht, Alexander. "U.S. Foreign Policy Strategies." *Washington Quarterly* 18, no. 3 (Summer 1995): 195–210.

Naish, Katherine R., and Sukhvinder S. Ohbi. "Self-Selected Conscious Strategies Do Not Modulate Motor Cortical Output During Action Observation." *Journal of Neurophysiology* 114, no. 4 (October 2015): 2278–84.

National Intelligence Council. *Joint Vision 2010*. Washington, DC: Government Printing Office, 1996.

Neustadt, Richard E., and Ernest R. May. *Thinking in Time: The Uses of History for Policymakers*. New York: Free Press, 1986.

Newhouse, John. "Diplomacy, Inc.: The Influence of Lobbies on U.S. Foreign Policy." *Foreign Affairs* 88, no. 3 (May/June 2009): 73–92.

Nichols, Thomas M. *Eve of Destruction: The Coming Age of Preventive War.* Philadelphia: University of Pennsylvania Press, 2008.

——. *No Use: Nuclear Weapons and U.S. National Security.* Philadelphia: University of Pennsylvania Press, 2013.

Nisbett, Richard E. *The Geography of Thought: How Asians and Westerners Think Differently . . . and Why.* New York: Free Press, 2003.

Nisbett, Richard E., and Lee Ross. *Human Inference: Strategies and Shortcomings of Social Judgment.* Englewood Cliffs, NJ: Prentice Hall, 1980.

Nordlinger, Eric A. *Isolationism Reconfigured: American Foreign Policy for a New Century.* Princeton, NJ: Princeton University Press, 1995.

Norris, Robert, and Hans M. Kristensen. "Global Nuclear Inventories, 1945–2010." *Bulletin of the Atomic Scientists* 66, no. 4 (July 2010): 77–83.

Norrlof, Carla. *America's Global Advantage: U.S. Hegemony and International Cooperation.* New York: Cambridge University Press, 2010.

Nyhan, Brendan, and Jason Reifler. "Displacing Misinformation About Events: An Experimental Test of Causal Corrections." *Journal of Experimental Political Science* 2, no. 1 (April 2015): 81–93.

——. "When Corrections Fail: The Persistence of Political Misperceptions." *Political Behavior* 32, no. 2 (June 2010): 303–30.

Office of the Secretary of Defense. *The National Defense Strategy of the United States of America.* Washington, DC: U.S. Government Printing Office, 2005.

——. *Quadrennial Defense Review Report.* Washington, DC: Government Printing Office, 2006.

——. *Sustaining U.S. Global Leadership: Priorities for Twenty-First-Century Defense.* Washington, DC: Government Printing Office, 2012.

O'Hanlon, Michael. "America's Military, Cut to the Quick." *Washington Post*, August 9, 1998.

Oneal, John R., and Bruce M. Russett. "The Kantian Peace: The Pacific Benefits of Democracy, Interdependence, and International Organizations, 1885–1992." *World Politics* 52, no. 1 (October 1999): 1–37.

Ong, G. Gerard. "Credibility Over Courage: NATO's Misintervention in Kosovo." *Journal of Strategic Studies* 26, no. 1 (2003): 73–108.

O'Reilly, K. P. "Perceiving Rogue States: The Use of the 'Rogue State' Concept by U.S. Foreign Policy Elites." *Foreign Policy Analysis* 3, no. 4 (October 2007): 295–315.

Organski, A. F. K. *World Politics.* New York: Knopf, 1958.

Osgood, Charles E. "Suggestions for Winning the Real War with Communism." *Journal of Conflict Resolution* 3, no. 4 (December 1959): 295–325.

Ostrom, Charles W., Jr., and Brian L. Job. "The President and the Political Use of Force." *American Political Science Review* 80, no. 2 (June 1986): 541–66.

Owen, David, and Jonathan Davidson. "Hubris Syndrome: An Acquired Personality Disorder? A Study of U.S. Presidents and UK Prime Ministers Over the Last 100 Years." *Brain* 132, no. 5 (May 2009): 1396–1406.

Owen, John M., IV. "Transnational Liberalism and U.S. Primacy." *International Security* 26, no. 3 (Winter 2001/2002): 117–52.

Owens, Mackubin Thomas. "A Balanced Force Structure to Achieve a Liberal World Order." *Orbis* 50, no. 2 (Spring 2006): 307–325.

——. "The Bush Doctrine: The Foreign Policy of Republican Empire." *Orbis* 53, no. 1 (January 2009): 23–40.

——. "Strategy and the Strategic Way of Thinking." *Naval War College Review* 60, no. 4 (Autumn 2007): 111–24.

Pape, Robert A. "Empire Falls." *National Interest* 99 (January-February 2009): 21–34.

Paquette, Laurence, and Thomas Kida. "The Effect of Decision Strategy and Task Complexity on Decision Performance." *Organizational Behavior and Human Decision Processes* 41, no. 1 (February 1988): 128–42.

Parker, Charles F., and Eric K. Stern. "Blindsided? September 11 and the Origins of Strategic Surprise." *Political Psychology* 23, no. 3 (September 2002): 601–30.

Parker, Geoffrey. "The Making of Strategy in Hapsburg Spain: Philip II's 'Bid for Mastery,' 1559–1598." In *The Making of Strategy: Rulers, States, and War*, ed. Williamson Murray et al., 115–50. New York: Cambridge University Press, 1996.

Paul, T. V., Deborah Welch Larson, and William C. Wohlforth, eds. *Status in World Politics*. New York: Cambridge University Press, 2014.

Payne, John W., James R. Bettman, and Eric J. Johnson. "Adaptive Strategy Selection in Decision Making." *Journal of Experimental Psychology: Learning, Memory, and Cognition* 14, no. 3 (July 1988): 534–52.

Payne, Keith B. *Deterrence in the Second Nuclear Age*. Lexington: University Press of Kentucky, 1996.

Peffley, Mark, and Jon Hurwitz. "International Events and Foreign Policy Beliefs: Public Response to Changing Soviet-U.S. Relations." *American Journal of Political Science* 36, no. 2 (May 1992): 431–61.

Pelham, Brett W., and Efrat Neter. "The Effect of Judgment Depends on the Difficulty of the Judgment." *Journal of Personality and Social Psychology* 68, no. 4 (April 1995): 581–94.

Perkins, Ivan. *Vanishing Coup: The Pattern of World History Since 1310*. New York: Rowman and Littlefield, 2013.

Perkovich, George. *India's Nuclear Bomb: The Impact on Global Proliferation*. Berkeley: University of California Press, 1999.

Perlez, Jane. "U.S. Did Little to Deter Buildup as Ethiopia and Eritrea Prepared for War." *New York Times*, May 22, 2000.

Perry, Mark. *How to Lose the War on Terror*. London: Hurst, 2010.

Pervin, Lawrence A. "The Need to Predict and Control Under Conditions of Threat." *Journal of Personality* 31, no. 4 (December 1963): 570–87.

Pew Center for the People and the Press. "America's Place in the World in 2009: An Investigation of Public and Leadership Opinion About International Affairs." December 2009. http://www.people-press.org/files/legacy-pdf/569.pdf.

Pietrzyk, Mark. *International Order and Individual Liberty: Effects of War and Peace on the Development of Governments*. Lanham, MD: University Press of America, 2002.

Piff, Paul K., Daniel M. Stancato, Stéphane Côté, et al. "Higher Social Class Predicts Increased Unethical Behavior." *Proceedings of the National Academy of Sciences of the United States of America* 109, no. 11 (March 13, 2012): 4086–91.

Pillsbury, Michael, *The Hundred-Year Marathon: China's Secret Strategy to Replace America as the Global Superpower*. New York: St. Martin's, 2015.

Pinker, Steven. *The Better Angels of Our Nature: Why Violence Has Declined*. New York: Viking, 2011.

——. "Fooled by Belligerence." June 2015. http://stevenpinker.com/pinker/files/comments _on_taleb_by_s_pinker.pdf.

——. "Has the Decline of Violence Reversed Since *The Better Angels of Our Nature* Was Written?" August 2014. http://stevenpinker.com/has-decline-violence-reversed-better -angels-our-nature-was-written.

Pinker, Steven, and Andrew Mack. "The World Is Not Falling Apart." *Slate*, December 22, 2014. http://www.slate.com/articles/news_and_politics/foreigners/2014/12/the_world _is_not_falling_apart_the_trend_lines_reveal_an_increasingly_peaceful.html.

Pipes, Richard. "Can the Soviet Union Reform?" *Foreign Affairs* 63, no. 1 (Fall 1984): 47–61.

——. "How to Cope with the Soviet Threat: A Long-Term Strategy for the West." *Commentary* 78, no. 2 (August 1984): 13–30.

——. "Militarism and the Soviet State." *Daedalus* 109, no. 4 (Fall 1980): 1–12.

——. "Is Russia Still an Enemy?" *Foreign Affairs* 76, no. 5 (September/October 1997): 65–78.

——. "Why the Soviet Union Thinks It Could Fight and Win a Nuclear War." *Commentary* 64, no. 1 (July 1977): 21–34.

Plaus, Scott. *The Psychology of Judgment and Decision Making*. New York: McGraw-Hill, 1993.

Podhoretz, Norman. "The Case for Bombing Iran." *Commentary* 123, no. 6 (June 2007): 17–23.

——. *World War IV: The Long Struggle Against Islamofascism*. New York: Doubleday, 2007.

Pomerantsev, Peter. *Nothing Is True and Everything Is Possible: The Surreal Heart of the New Russia*. New York: Public Affairs, 2014.

Porter, Bernard. *The Lion's Share: A Short History of British Imperialism 1850–1995*. New York: Longman, 1996.

Posen, Barry R. "The Case for Restraint." *American Interest* 3, no. 2 (November/December 2007): 6–17.

——. "Command of the Commons: The Military Foundation of U.S. Hegemony." *International Security* 28, no. 1 (Summer 2003): 5–46.

——. *Restraint: A New Foundation for U.S. Grand Strategy*. Ithaca, NY: Cornell University Press, 2014.

Posen, Barry R., and Andrew L. Ross. "Competing Visions for U.S. Grand Strategy." *International Security* 21, no. 3 (Winter 1996/1997): 5–53.

Post, Jerrold M. "Current Concepts of the Narcissistic Personality: Implications for Political Psychology." *Political Psychology* 14, no. 1 (March 1993): 99–121.

Powell, Colin. *The National Military Strategy of the United States*. Washington, DC: U.S. Government Printing Office, 1992.

——. "A Strategy of Partnerships." *Foreign Affairs* 83, no. 1 (January/February 2004): 22–34.

Powell, Jonathan M., and Clayton L. Thyne. "Global Instances of Coups from 1950 to 2010." *Journal of Peace Research* 48, no. 2 (March 2011): 249–59.

Preble, Christopher A. *The Power Problem: How American Military Dominance Makes Us Less Safe, Less Prosperous, and Less Free.* Ithaca, NY: Cornell University Press, 2009.

Preble, Christopher A., and John Mueller, eds. *A Dangerous World? Threat Perception and U.S. National Security.* Washington, DC: Cato Institute, 2014.

Press, Daryl G. *Calculating Credibility: How Leaders Assess Military Threats.* Ithaca, NY: Cornell University Press, 2006.

Presson, Paul K., and Victor A. Benassi. "Illusion of Control: A Meta-Analytic Review." *Journal of Social Behavior & Personality* 11, no. 3 (September 1996): 493–510.

Rachman, Gideon. "Think Again: American Decline." *Foreign Policy* 184 (January/February 2011): 59–63.

Rauchhaus, Robert A. "Evaluating the Nuclear Peace Hypothesis: A Quantitative Approach." *Journal of Conflict Resolution* 53, no. 2 (April 2009): 258–77.

Ray, James Lee. "The Abolition of Slavery and the End of International War." *International Organization* 43, no. 3 (Summer 1989): 405–39.

Raymond, Gregory A. "Necessity in Foreign Policy." *Political Science Quarterly* 113, no. 4 (Winter 1998/1999): 673–88.

Reagan, Ronald W. *An American Life.* New York: Simon and Schuster, 1990.

Reich, Simon, and Richard Ned Lebow. *Good-Bye Hegemony! Power and Influence in the Global System.* Princeton, NJ: Princeton University Press, 2014.

Reid, T. R. *The United States of Europe: The New Superpower and the End of American Supremacy.* New York: Penguin, 2004.

Reiter, Dan. *Crucible of Beliefs: Learning, Alliance, and World Wars.* Ithaca, NY: Cornell University Press, 1996.

Renshon, Jonathan. "Status Deficits and War." *International Organization* 70, no. 3 (June 2016): 513–50.

Renshon, Jonathan, Allan Dafoe, and Paul Huth. "Reputation and Status as Motives for War." *Annual Review of Political Science* 17 (2014): 371–93.

Reveron, Derek S., ed. *Cyberspace and National Security: Threats, Opportunities, and Power in a Virtual World.* Washington, DC: Georgetown University Press, 2012.

——. *Exporting Security: International Engagement, Security Cooperation and the Changing Face of the U.S. Military.* Washington, DC: Georgetown University Press, 2010.

Reveron, Derek S., and James L. Cook. "From National to Theater: Developing Strategy." *Joint Forces Quarterly*, no. 70 (2013): 113–20.

Robertson, Ian H. "How Power Affects the Brain." *Psychologist* 26, no. 3 (March 2013): 186–89.

Robin, Corey. *Fear: The History of a Political Idea.* New York: Oxford University Press, 2004.

Robinson, Ronald, and John Gallagher. *Africa and the Victorians: The Official Mind of Imperialism.* London: Page, 1961.

Roehrig, Terrence. "North Korea's Nuclear Weapons Program: Motivations, Strategy, and Doctrine." In *Strategy in the Second Nuclear Age: Power, Ambition, and the Ultimate Weapon*, ed. Toshi Yoshihara and James R. Holmes, 81–98. Washington, DC: Georgetown University Press, 2012.

Rokeach, Milton. *The Open and Closed Mind: Investigations Into the Nature of Belief Systems and Personality Systems.* New York: Basic Books, 1960.

Rojahn, Krystyna, and Thomas F. Pettigrew. "Memory for Schema-Relevant Information: A Meta-Analytic Resolution." *British Journal of Social Psychology* 31, no. 2 (June 1992): 81–109.

Rosecrance, Richard. "Bipolarity, Multipolarity, and the Future." *Journal of Conflict Resolution* 10, no. 3 (September 1966): 314–27.

——. *The Rise of the Trading State: Commerce and Conquest in the Modern World.* New York: Basic Books, 1986.

——. *The Rise of the Virtual State: Wealth and Power in the Coming Century.* New York: Basic Books, 1999.

Ross, Lee. "The Intuitive Psychologist and His Shortcomings: Distortions in the Attribution Process." In *Advances in Experimental Social Psychology*, ed. Leonard Berkowitz, 10:173–220. New York: Academic Press, 1977.

Ross, Lee, David Greene, and Pamela House. "The 'False Consensus Effect': An Ego-Centric Bias in Social Perception and Attribution Processes." *Journal of Experimental Social Psychology* 13, no. 3 (May 1977): 279–301.

Ross, Michael, and Fiore Sicoly. "Egocentric Biases in Availability and Attribution." *Journal of Personality and Social Psychology* 37, no. 3 (March 1979): 322–36.

Roy, Dennis. "North Korea and the 'Madman Theory.'" *Security Dialogue* 25, no. 3 (September 1994): 307–16.

Rumsfeld, Donald H. *Known and Unknown: A Memoir.* New York: Sentinel, 2011.

——. Remarks at DoD news briefing, February 12, 2002. http://www.defenselink.mil/transcripts/transcript.aspx?transcriptid=2636.

——. "Transforming the Military." *Foreign Affairs* 81, no. 3 (May/June 2002): 20–32.

Russell, Ann Marie, and Susan T. Fiske. "Power and Social Perception." In *The Social Psychology of Power*, ed. Ana Guinote and Theresa K. Vescio, 231–250. New York: Guilford, 2010.

Russett, Bruce M. "The Calculus of Deterrence." *Journal of Conflict Resolution* 7, no. 2 (June 1963): 97–109.

——. "The Mysterious Case of Vanishing Hegemony; Or, Is Mark Twain Really Dead?" *International Organization* 39, no. 2 (Spring 1985): 207–231.

Sagan, Scott D., and Kenneth N. Waltz. *The Spread of Nuclear Weapons: A Debate.* New York: Norton, 1995.

Sanger, David E. "Secretary of State Rejects Talks with North Korea on Nuclear Program." *New York Times*, March 18, 2017.

——. "Witness to Auschwitz Evil, Bush Draws a Lesson." *New York Times*, June 1, 2003.

Satter, David. "Russia Needs to Learn the Value of Human Life." *American Interest*, July 25, 2014. http://www.the-american-interest.com/2014/07/25/russia-needs-to-learn-the-value-of-human-life/.

Schacter, Daniel L. *Searching for Memory: The Brain, the Mind, and the Past.* New York: Basic Books, 1996.

——. *The Seven Sins of Memory: How the Mind Forgets and Remembers.* Boston: Houghton Mifflin, 2001.

Schake, Kori. "Will Washington Abandon the Order? The False Logic of Retreat." *Foreign Affairs* 96, no. 1 (January/February 2017): 41–46.

Scheer, Robert. *With Enough Shovels: Reagan, Bush, and Nuclear War.* New York: Vintage, 1983.

Schelling, Thomas C. *The Strategy of Conflict.* Cambridge, MA: Harvard University Press, 1960.

Schmitt, Gary. "The Demilitarization of Europe." *Wall Street Journal,* October 6, 2010.

Schneider, Barry R. "Military Responses to Proliferation Threats." In *Pulling Back from the Nuclear Brink: Reducing and Countering Nuclear Threats,* ed. Barry R. Schneider and William L. Dowdy, 294–306. London: Frank Cass, 1998.

Schumpeter, Joseph A. *Imperialism and Social Classes.* Oxford: Basil Blackwell, 1951.

Schwartz, Norton A., and Jonathan W. Greenert. "Air-Sea Battle: Promoting Stability in an Era of Uncertainty." *American Interest,* February 20, 2012. http://www.the-american -interest.com/articles/2012/2/20/air-sea-battle/.

Schweller, Randall L. "Bandwagoning for Profit: Bringing the Revisionist State Back In." *International Security* 19, no. 1 (Summer 1994): 72–107.

——. *Unanswered Threats: Political Constraints on the Balance of Power.* Princeton, NJ: Princeton University Press, 2008.

Seybolt, Taylor B. "Significant Numbers: Civilian Casualties and Strategic Peacebuilding." In *Counting Civilian Casualties: An Introduction to Recording and Estimating Nonmilitary Deaths in Conflict,* ed. Taylor B. Seybolt et al., 15–28. New York: Oxford University Press, 2013.

Shanker, Thom. "Gates Counters Putin's Words on U.S. Power." *New York Times,* February 11, 2007.

Sharp, Travis. "Tying U.S. Defense Spending to GDP: Bad Logic, Bad Policy." *Parameters* 38, no. 3 (Autumn 2008): 5–17.

Shaver, Andrew. "You're More Likely to Be Fatally Crushed by Furniture Than Killed by a Terrorist." *Washington Post,* November 23, 2015.

Sheehan, James J. *Where Have All the Soldiers Gone? The Transformation of Modern Europe.* New York: Houghton Mifflin, 2008.

Shimko, Keith L. *Images and Arms Control: Perceptions of the Soviet Union in the Reagan Administration.* Ann Arbor: University of Michigan Press, 1991.

Sigal, Leon V. *Disarming Strangers: Nuclear Diplomacy with North Korea.* Princeton, NJ: Princeton University Press, 1998.

Silverstein, Brett. "Enemy Images: The Psychology of U.S. Attitudes and Cognitions Regarding the Soviet Union." *American Psychologist* 44, no. 6 (June 1989): 903–13.

Silverstein, Brett, and Robert R. Holt. "Research on Enemy Images: Present Status and Future Prospects." *Journal of Social Issues* 45, no. 2 (Summer 1989): 159–75.

Skinner, Ellen A. *Perceived Control, Motivation, and Coping.* London: Sage, 1995.

Smith, Merritt Roe, ed. *Military Enterprise and Technological Change: Perspectives on the American Experience.* Cambridge, MA: MIT Press, 1985.

Snegirev, Vladimir, and Valery Samunin. *The Dead End: The Road to Afghanistan.* National Security Archive Electronic Briefing Book 396. 2012. http://nsarchive2.gwu.edu/NSAEBB /NSAEBB396/Full%20Text%20Virus%20A.pdf.

Snyder, Jack. "Imperial Myths and Threat Inflation." In *American Foreign Policy and the Politics of Fear: Threat Inflation Since 9/11*, ed. A. Trevor Thrall and Jane K. Cramer, 40–53. New York: Routledge, 2009.

——. *Myths of Empire: Domestic Politics and International Ambition.* Ithaca, NY: Cornell University Press, 1991.

Snyder, Jack, Robert Y. Shapiro, and Yaeli Bloch-Elkon. "Free Hand Abroad, Divide and Rule at Home." *World Politics* 61, no. 1 (January 2009): 155–87.

Sorenson, Georg. *A Liberal World Order in Crisis: Choosing Between Imposition and Restraint.* Ithaca, NY: Cornell University Press, 2011.

Specter, Leonard S., and Avner Cohen. "Israel's Airstrike on Syria's Reactor: Implications for the Nonproliferation Regime." *Arms Control Today* 38, no. 6 (July/August 2007): 15–21.

Spengler, Oswald. *The Decline of the West.* New York: Knopf, 1926–1928.

Spring, Baker, Mackenzie Eaglen, and James Jay Carafano. "4 Percent of GDP Defense Spending: Sustained Spending, Not Economic Stimulus." Heritage Foundation Web-Memo 2243, January 26, 2009. http://www.heritage.org/research/reports/2009/01/4 -percent-of-gdp-defense-spending-sustained-spending-not-economic-stimulus.

Stein, Arthur A. "When Misperception Matters." *World Politics* 34, no. 4 (July 1982): 505–26.

Stein, Janice Gross. "Building Politics Into Psychology: The Misperception of Threat." *Political Psychology* 9, no. 2 (June 1988): 245–71.

Steinberg, James B., and Philip G. Gordon. "NATO Enlargement: Moving Forward; Expanding the Alliance and Completing Europe's Integration." Brookings Policy Brief Series 90. November 2001.

Stephens, Brett. *America in Retreat: The New Isolationism and the Coming Global Disorder.* New York: Sentinel, 2014.

Storm, Benjamin C., and Tara A. Jobe. "Retrieval-Induced Forgetting Predicts Failure to Recall Negative Autobiographical Memories." *Psychological Science* 23, no. 11 (November 2012): 1356–63.

Strachan, Hew. "The Lost Meaning of Strategy." *Survival* 47, no. 3 (Autumn 2005): 33–54.

Strand, Håvard, and Halvard Buhaug. "Armed Conflict, 1946–2014." In *Peace and Conflict 2016*, ed. David A. Backer et al., 9–24. New York: Routledge, 2016.

Strange, Susan. "The Persistent Myth of Lost Hegemony." *International Organization* 41, no. 4 (Autumn 1987): 551–74.

Straus, Scott. "Wars Do End! Changing Patterns of Political Violence in Sub-Saharan Africa." *African Affairs* 111, no. 443 (March 2012): 179–201.

Stuart, Douglas, and Harvey Starr. "The 'Inherent Bad Faith Model' Reconsidered: Dulles, Kennedy, and Kissinger." *Political Psychology* 3, no. 3/4 (Autumn/Winter 1981): 1–33.

Stulberg, Adam N., and Matthew Fuhrmann, eds. *The Nuclear Renaissance and International Security.* Stanford, CA: Stanford University Press, 2013.

Sullivan, Daniel, Makr J. Landau, and Zachary K. Rothschild. "An Existential Function of Enemyship: Evidence That People Attribute Influence to Personal and Political Enemies to Compensate for Threats to Control." *Journal of Personality and Social Psychology* 98, no. 3 (March 2010): 434–49.

Sung, Ming-Chien, Johnnie Eric Victor Johnson, and Itiel E. Dror. "Complexity as a Guide to Understanding Decision Bias: A Contribution to the Favorite-Longshot Bias Debate." *Journal of Behavioral Decision Making* 22, no. 3 (July 2009): 318–37.

Sunstein, Cass R., and Adrian Vermeule. "Conspiracy Theories: Causes and Cures." *Journal of Political Philosophy* 17, no. 2 (June 2009): 202–27.

Sutton, R. I. "Feelings About a Disneyland Visit: Photographs and Reconstruction of Bygone Emotions." *Journal of Management Inquiry* 1 no. 4 (December 1992): 278–87.

Sylvan, David, and Stephen Majeski. *U.S. Foreign Policy in Perspective: Clients, Enemies, and Empire*. New York: Routledge, 2009.

Talbott, Strobe. *Engaging India: Diplomacy, Democracy, and the Bomb*. Washington: Brookings Institution Press, 2004.

Taleb, Nassim Nicholas. "The 'Long Peace' Is a Statistical Illusion." May 2015. http://www .fooledbyrandomness.com/longpeace.pdf.

Tammen, Ronald L., Jacek Kugler, Douglas Lemke, et al. *Power Transitions: Strategies for the Twenty-First Century*. New York: Chatham House, 2000.

Tannenwald, Nina. *The Nuclear Taboo: The United States and Non-Use of Nuclear Weapons Since 1945*. New York: Cambridge University Press, 2007.

Tao, Xie. "U.S.-China Relations: In the Shadow of Conspiracy Theories." *Diplomat*, February 22, 2016. http://thediplomat.com/2016/02/us-china-relations-in-the-shadow-of-conspiracy -theories/.

Team B. *Intelligence Community Experiment in Competitive Analysis: Soviet Strategic Objectives: An Alternative View*. December 1976.

Tellis, Ashley J. "No Escape: The Enduring Reality of Nuclear Weapons." In *Asia in the Second Nuclear Age*, ed. Ashley J. Tellis et al., 3–34. Washington, DC: National Bureau of Asian Research, 2013.

Thaler, Richard. "Toward a Positive Theory of Consumer Choice." *Journal of Economic Behavior and Organization* 1, no. 1 (March 1980): 39–60.

Thayer, Bradley A. "Humans, Not Angels: Reasons to Doubt the Decline of War Thesis." *International Studies Review* 15, no. 3 (September 2013): 405–11.

Thomas, Helen. "Reagan: Air Strike Against Libya Victory Against Terrorism." *UPI*, April 15, 1966. http://100years.upi.com/sta_1986-04-15.html.

Thompson, John A. "The Exaggeration of American Vulnerability: The Anatomy of a Tradition." *Diplomatic History* 16, no. 1 (Winter 1992): 23–43.

Thompson, Nicholas. *The Hawk and the Dove: Paul Nitze, George Kennan, and the History of the Cold War*. New York: Henry Holt, 2009.

Thompson, William R. "Democracy and Peace: Putting the Cart Before the Horse?" *International Organization* 50, no. 1 (Winter 1996): 141–74.

Thrall, A. Trevor, and Jane K. Cramer, eds. *American Foreign Policy and the Politics of Fear: Threat Inflation Since 9/11*. New York: Routledge, 2009.

Thucydides. *History of the Peloponnesian War*. New York: Penguin, 1972.

Tillerson, Rex W. "Remarks to U.S. Department of State Employees." May 3, 2017. https://www.state.gov/secretary/remarks/2017/05/270620.htm.

Tillman, Barrett. "Fear and Loathing in the Post-Naval Era." *Proceedings* 135, no. 6 (June 2009): 16–21.

Tobey, William R. "A Message from Tripoli: How Libya Came to Give Up Its WMD." *Bulletin of the Atomic Scientists*, December 3, 2014. http://thebulletin.org/message-tripoli-how-libya-gave-its-wmd7834.

Tolstoy, Leo. *What Is Art?* New York: Funk and Wagnalls, 1904.

Tost, Leigh Plunkett, Francesca Gino, and Richard P. Larrick. "Power, Competitiveness, and Advice Taking: Why the Powerful Don't Listen." *Organizational Behavior and Human Decision Making Processes* 117, no. 1 (January 2012): 53–65.

Trautmann, Stefan T., and Gijs van de Kuilen. "Prospect Theory or Construal Level Theory? Diminishing Sensitivity vs. Psychological Distance in Risky Decisions." *Acta Psychologica* 139, no. 1 (January 2012): 254–60.

Trope, Yaacov, and Nira Liberman. "Construal-Level Theory of Psychological Distance." *Psychological Review* 117, no. 2 (April 2010): 440–63.

——. "Temporal Construal." *Psychological Review* 110, no. 3 (July 2003): 403–421.

——. "Temporal Construal and Time-Dependent Changes in Preference." *Journal of Personality and Social Psychology* 79, no. 6 (December 2000): 876–89.

Tversky, Amos, and Daniel Kahneman. "Availability: A Heuristic for Judging Frequency and Probability." *Cognitive Psychology* 5, no. 2 (April 1973): 207–232.

——. "Judgment under Uncertainty: Heuristics and Biases." *Science* 185, no. 4157 (September 27, 1974): 1124–31.

Tucker, Robert W. "America in Decline: The Foreign Policy of 'Maturity.'" *Foreign Affairs* 58, no. 3 (1979): 449–84.

Tyler, Patrick E. "U.S. Strategy Plan Calls for Insuring No Rivals Develop." *New York Times*, March 8, 1992.

Updegrove, Mark K. *Baptism by Fire: Eight Presidents Who Took Office in Times of Crisis.* New York: St. Martin's, 2008.

Uscinski, Joseph E., and Joseph M. Parent. *American Conspiracy Theories.* New York: Oxford University Press, 2014.

Vallone, Robert P., Dale W. Griffin, Sabrina Lin, and Lee Ross. "Overconfident Prediction of Future Actions and Outcomes by Self and Others." *Journal of Personality and Social Psychology* 58, no. 4 (April 1990): 582–92.

Van Creveld, Martin. "The Waning of Major War." In *The Waning of Major War: Theories and Debates*, ed. Raimo Väyrynen, 97–112. New York: Routledge, 2006.

Van Boven, Leaf, Katherine White, and Michael Huber. "Immediacy Bias in Emotion Perception: Current Emotions Seem More Intense Than Previous Emotions." *Journal of Experimental Psychology* 138, no. 3 (August 2009): 368–82.

Van Evera, Stephen. *Causes of War: Power and the Roots of Conflict.* Ithaca, NY: Cornell University Press, 1999.

Van Riper, Paul. "Wake-Up Call." *Guardian*, September 6, 2002.

Väyrynen, Raimo, ed. *The Waning of Major War: Theories and Debates*. New York: Routledge, 2006.

Verba, Sydney. "Simulation, Reality, and Theory in International Relations." *World Politics* 16, no. 3 (April 1964): 490–519.

Vescio, Theresa K., Sarah J. Gervais, Larisa Heiphetz, and Brittany Bloodhart. "The Stereotypic Behaviors of the Powerful and Their Effect on the Relatively Powerless." In *Handbook of Prejudice, Stereotyping, and Discrimination*, ed. Todd D. Nelson, 247–265. New York: Psychology Press, 2009.

Volkan, Vamik D. *The Need to Have Enemies and Allies: From Clinical Practice to International Relationships*. Northvale, NJ: Jason Aronson, 1988.

Wallerstein, Immanuel. "Consequences of U.S. Decline." Web Commentary 364, November 1, 2013. http://iwallerstein.com/consequences-decline/.

——. *The Decline of American Power: The U.S. in a Chaotic World*. New York: New Press, 2003.

——. "The Eagle Has Crash Landed." *Foreign Policy* 131 (July/August 2002): 60–68.

——. "Precipitate Decline: The Advent of Multipolarity." *Harvard International Review* 29, no. 1 (Spring 2007): 50–55.

Walt, Stephen M. *The Origin of Alliances*. Ithaca, NY: Cornell University Press, 1987.

——. "Why Are U.S. Leaders so Obsessed with Credibility?" *Foreign Policy* blog, September 11, 2012, http://walt.foreignpolicy.com/posts/2012/09/11/the_credibility_fetish.

Waltz, Kenneth N. "The Emerging Structure of International Politics." *International Security* 18, no. 2 (Fall 1993): 44–79.

——. "Globalization and Governance." *PS: Political Science and Politics* 32, no. 4 (December 1999): 693–700.

——. "Nuclear Myths and Political Realities." *American Political Science Review* 84, no. 3 (September 1990): 731–45.

——. "The Stability of a Bipolar World." *Daedalus* 93, no. 3 (Summer 1964): 881–909.

——. *Theory of International Politics*. Reading, MA: Addison-Wesley, 1979.

Weisner, Martin M. "Using Construal-Level Theory to Motivate Accounting Research: A Literature Review." *Behavioral Research in Accounting* 27, no. 1 (Spring 2015): 137–80.

Weisz, John R., Fred M. Rothbaum, and Thomas C. Blackburn. "Standing Out and Standing In: The Psychology of Control in America and Japan." *American Psychologist* 39, no. 9 (September 1984): 955–69.

Wells, Samuel F., Jr. "Sounding the Tocsin: NSC 68 and the Soviet Threat." *International Security* 4, no. 2 (Autumn 1979): 116–58.

Wendt, Alexander. *Social Theory of International Relations*. New York: Cambridge University Press, 1999.

——. "The State as Person in International Theory." *Review of International Studies* 30, no. 2 (April 2004): 289–316.

White, Katherine, and Leaf Van Boven. "Immediacy Bias in Social-Emotional Comparisons." *Emotion* 12, no. 4 (August 2012): 737–47.

White, Ralph K. "Empathizing with Rulers of the USSR." *Political Psychology* 4, no. 1 (May 1993): 121–37.

——. *Fearful Warriors: A Psychological Profile of U.S.-Soviet Relations*. New York: Free Press, 1984.

——. "Images in the Context of International Conflict: Soviet Perceptions of the U.S. and the USSR." In *International Behavior: A Social-Psychological Analysis*, ed. Herbert C. Kelman, 236–76. New York: Holt, Rinehart and Winston, 1965.

——. "Motivation Reconsidered: The Concept of Competence." *Psychological Review* 66, no. 5 (September 1959): 297–333.

——. *Nobody Wanted War: Misperception in Vietnam and Other Wars*. Garden City, NY: Doubleday, 1968.

White House. *The National Security Strategy of the United States of America*. Washington DC, March 2006.

——. "Quadrennial Defense Review Report," February 6, 2006. http://archive.defense.gov /pubs/pdfs/QDR20060203.pdf.

Whitson, Jennifer A., and Adam D. Galinsky. "Lacking Control Increases Illusory Pattern Perception." *Science* 322, no. 5898 (October 3, 2008): 115–17.

Wilkinson, David. "Unipolarity Without Hegemony." *International Studies Review* 1, no. 2 (Summer 1999): 141–72.

Williams, Paul D. *War and Conflict in Africa*. Washington: Polity, 2011.

Wilson, Timothy D., Jay Meyers, and Daniel T. Gilbert. "'How Happy Was I, Anyway?' A Retrospective Impact Bias." *Social Cognition* 21, no. 6 (December 2013): 421–46.

Wirls, Daniel. *Irrational Security: The Politics of Defense from Reagan to Obama*. Baltimore, MD: Johns Hopkins University Press, 2010.

Winnefeld, James A. *The Post–Cold War Sizing Debate: Paradigms, Metaphors, and Disconnects*. Santa Monica, CA: RAND, 1992.

Wittner, Lawrence S. *Resisting the Bomb: A History of the World Nuclear Disarmament Movement, 1954–1970*. Palo Alto, CA: Stanford University Press, 1997.

Wohlforth, William C. "The Stability of Unipolar World." *International Security* 24, no. 1 (Summer 1999): 5–41.

——. "Unipolar Stability: The Rules for Power Analysis." *Harvard International Review* 29, no. 1 (Spring 2007): 45–48.

Wolfers, Arnold. *Discord and Collaboration: Essays on International Politics*. Baltimore, MD: Johns Hopkins University Press, 1962.

Womack, Brantly. *Asymmetry and International Relationships*. New York: Cambridge University Press, 2016.

——. "Asymmetry and Systemic Misperception: China, Vietnam, and Cambodia During the 1970s." *Journal of Strategic Studies* 26, no. 2 (June 2003): 92–119.

——. *China and Vietnam: The Politics of Asymmetry*. New York: Cambridge University Press, 2006.

——. "How Size Matters: The United States, China, and Asymmetry." *Journal of Strategic Studies* 24, no. 4 (December 2001): 123–50.

Wyden, Peter. *Bay of Pigs: The Untold Story*. New York: Simon and Schuster, 1979.

Yarger, Harry R. "Toward a Theory of Strategy: Art Lyyke and the U.S. Army War College Strategy Model." In *Theory of War and Strategy*, 4th ed., ed. J. Boone Bartholomees Jr., 44–51. Carlisle, PA: Strategic Studies Institute, 2010.

Yetiv, Steve. *National Security Through a Cockeyed Lens: How Cognitive Bias Impacts U.S. Foreign Policy*. Baltimore, MD: Johns Hopkins University Press, 2013.

Yoshihara, Toshi, and James R. Holmes, eds. *Strategy in the Second Nuclear Age: Power, Ambition, and the Ultimate Weapon*. Washington, DC: Georgetown University Press, 2012.

Zacher, Mark W. "The Territorial Integrity Norm: International Boundaries and the Use of Force." *International Organization* 55, no. 2 (Spring 2001): 215–250.

Zakaria, Fareed. "America is Still Great—But It Needs to Stay Strong." *Washington Post*, May 26, 2016.

——. *The Post-American World*. New York: Norton, 2008.

——. *The Post-American World and the Rise of the Rest*. New York: Penguin, 2009.

Zala, Benjamin. "Polarity Analysis and Collective Perceptions of Power: The Need for a New Approach." *Journal of Global Security Studies* 2, no. 1 (January 2017): 2–17.

Zenko, Micah. *Red Team: How to Succeed by Thinking Like the Enemy*. New York: Basic Books, 2015.

Zenko, Micah, and Michael A. Cohen. "Clear and Present Safety: The United States Is More Secure Than Washington Thinks." *Foreign Affairs* 91, no. 2 (March/April 2012): 79–93.

Zuckerman, Miron, Michael H. Kernis, Salvatore M. Guarnera, et al. "The Ego-Centric Bias: Seeing Oneself as Cause and Target of Others' Behavior." *Journal of Personality* 51, no. 4 (December 1983): 621–30.

# INDEX